MARY BAKER EDDY

MARY BAKER EDDY

Original painting by Emilie Hergenroeder of Baltimore, Maryland, under the direction of Mrs. Eddy. The painting now hangs in the Chestnut Hill Home.

MARY BAKER EDDY

A Life Size Portrait

BY

LYMAN P. POWELL

COPYRIGHT, 1930,

BY THE CHRISTIAN SCIENCE PUBLISHING SOCIETY

All rights reserved—no part of this
book may be reproduced in any form
without permission in writing from
the publisher

The Christian Science Publishing Society
Boston, Massachusetts, U. S. A.

To

My Mother

MARY ANN POWELL

1829–1906

Ye shall know the truth, and the truth shall make
you free.   *John viii : 32*

And we solemnly promise to watch, and pray for
that Mind to be in us which was also in Christ
Jesus; to do unto others as we would have them do
unto us; and to be merciful, just, and pure.
                              Science and Health

I love the prosperity of Zion, be it promoted by
Catholic, by Protestant, or by Christian Science.
. . . I would no more quarrel with a man
because of his religion than I would because of
his art.   *Mary Baker Eddy*

If this work be of men, it will come to nought: But
if it be of God, ye can not overthrow it.
                              Acts v : 38, 39

This biography of Mary Baker Eddy by Dr. Lyman P. Powell has been approved by The Christian Science Board of Directors for sale or use in Christian Science reading rooms. It is a fair and intelligent account of Mrs. Eddy's life and an estimate of her work by an author who is not a Christian Scientist but who, as a minister of another Christian denomination, has observed her career and the development of its results for many years. Such a book by an independent biographer, who has sought information at its natural sources, should be of particular interest to persons who have heard or read accounts of Mrs. Eddy by speakers or writers who were not correctly informed or were actuated by hostility. Dr. Powell's conclusions as well as his narrations are entirely his own.

CONTENTS

ILLUSTRATIONS

MARY BAKER EDDY

PROLOGUE

Nowhere is Thanksgiving Day so meaningful as in New England where the Day originated. To the Rector of St. John's Episcopal Church in Northampton, Massachusetts, Thanksgiving Day, November 29, 1906, proved to be unwontedly significant. Long more or less interested in Christian Science, this interest had a year before been accentuated by the discovery, which many other clergymen were then making, that as a rule conventional Christians who came under the influence of Christian Science were likely to fall away from whatever church to which they might previously have been more or less attached, in order to give full allegiance to the new faith.

In American religious life there was then nothing quite so puzzling as this new phenomenon. Few outside Christian Science knew how to account for it, and not all within, even with the best intentions, appeared able to interpret it with understanding to the average man. The vocabulary of Christian Science sounded strange in his ears. Its teachings required closer consideration than he could give them. The problems it presented were more intellectual than emotional. They had to be thought out, and of course no clergyman could shift his thinking to anybody else.

In many a pulpit, sermons in explanation were preached which did not explain. The pulpit did

1

perhaps the best it could in such a novel situation. But it rarely knew enough, and did not know it did not know. About the only thing concerning which the more thoughtful preachers agreed was that there were certain differences of opinion between Christian Science and other folds in regard to philosophy and theology; and between Christian Science and medicine radical differences in theory and practice which it appeared useless to attempt to reconcile.

The Rector of St. John's preached no specific sermon on Christian Science. When in the pulpit he mentioned it at all, it was usually in casual praise. He had another way — in his opinion more effective — of dealing with a situation for which nothing in his theological training could prepare a minister in that day to deal. Having a church at the center of the biggest woman's college in the world, and a considerable representation of "gown" as well as "town" in his congregation, the Rector of St. John's wrote for his flock alone, a booklet in which he set forth what he believed to be the virtues as well as the defects of a faith which, for practical purposes, had suddenly emerged above the American horizon.

The booklet appeared on November 15, 1906. It began with the comparison, which the author still deems sound, of Christian Scientists with Apostolic Christians:

Some of the purest souls alive today are Christian Scientists. They have done much good. They have helped the sick, reclaimed the prodigal, brought surcease to many a sorrow, tempered men's asperities and given a sense of unity and harmony where before were disunity and discord. To an age grown weary and impatient of dogmatism, ecclesiasticism, and machinery, Christian Scientists have brought something of the warmth and glow, the freshness and the spontaneity, the poise and the sincerity, the gladness and the otherworldliness which suffused the Apostolic age and made it all alive with spiritual power. If Christianity is true, it is joyously, stupendously true. It is so true that all other truths in life seem but partial or secondary by its side.

The early Christians gave proof at every turn that theirs was a faith somewhat like this. They "did eat their meat with gladness and singleness of heart." They lived above life's fret and turmoil. They won and kept the peace which passeth knowledge. They endured whatever came their way, as seeing Him who is invisible. They lived for Jesus Christ, and him alone. Knit together "in one holy bond of truth and peace, of faith and charity," they went out to win the world to Christ. . . .

Christian Scientists have many of the marks of Apostolic days upon them. Some of them are a protest . . . against the worldliness and the ecclesiasticism which afflict the church, and the materialism and meanness which constitute a continuous menace to the world. They furnish men proof positive and peace-bringing, that where there is a will there is a way to live the spirit's life against all odds.

In response to a copy of the booklet sent in courtesy to the Committee on Publication[1] of The First Church of Christ, Scientist, in Boston, a letter of acknowledgment written in a kindly spirit was received in Northampton, on Thanksgiving morning. Its closing paragraph begins: "It is a mystery why you clergymen do not recognize the beauty of Christian Science and recommend it unreservedly to your followers."

Scarcely had the Rector finished his Thanksgiving dinner before he was dictating an eight-page letter in reply so indicative of the author's attitude at the time that it is here quoted freely:

To say that I am interested in your letter is to speak with moderation. I am delighted with it because its friendliness and open-mindedness make it possible for me to hope that you and I may have a freer and a franker talk about the subject . . . than newspaper columns permit.

. . . I do believe that the spokesmen for Christian Science are trying to make their position clear to the great world. . . . I gladly express abhorrence of all that business of a month ago when an aged woman's privacy was so rudely invaded to make newspaper " copy." I . . . yield to no one in my admiration for the singular purity and nobility of many Christian Science characters, and in my sincere gratitude for the great good that has been done. May I go farther and say that every day my conviction deepens that God has called Christian Science to do a work of more significance than can possibly be foreseen?

There are three contributions Christian Science is making to the world . . . :

1. It is turning the thoughts of men back to the power the mind *spiritualized* has over the body. The doctors have neglected this truth to a great extent, the Christian Churches almost altogether. Christian Science is forcing the truth on the minds of men, and in another decade, I believe, thanks largely to Christian Science, every church will emphasize what it now neglects.

2. It is turning men and women into Bible readers and thus bringing them as no other set of people are to the very source of spiritual life. Nothing can be more important than that, and no later than last Sunday I paid glad tribute in my pulpit to Christian Science for this service and called my people to a new and more devout reading of the Bible every day.

3. It is restoring something of Apostolic spontaneity and serenity and devotion to an ideal and of attendance on church services to our time sadly in need of it ; and of this too I spoke last Sunday to my people. It is this especially that makes me feel that God has a good and great work for Christian Science in this land.

Why then do we clergymen, as you inquire, " not recognize the beauty of Christian Science and recommend it unreservedly" to our followers? I will tell you . . . in the same friendliness and frankness which characterize your good letter.

Then follows a detailed statement of the honest differences of opinion, as the Rector understood them, between the orthodox Church and Christian Science in regard to the inner meanings of philosophy, the essentials of theology, and the significance of the sacramental system to which Episcopalians are committed. But points of agreement may, on wiser reflection, claim and reward close examination far more than absorption in dispute over differences. It was for these the Rector looked. He said, "I want to praise. I want to find some common ground on which we both can stand."

As the Rector was then writing much on new developments in religion for the *Review of Reviews*, *Good Housekeeping*, and also various weekly journals, he expressed the hope that it might be made possible for him to interpret Christian Science aright to the general reading public at a time when snap judgments were perhaps too frequent.

No more courteous reply could have been made to this overture than the one received from the Publication Committee on December 5, 1906, and the friendly relationship then begun has proved, at least to the author, advantageous, as through the years he has been making preparations, unconsciously but nevertheless steadily, for the writing of the present book.

That winter the *McClure's* articles on Mrs. Eddy

began to appear. On their face, they seemed to bear evidence of the same will to investigate which characterized the serials running, during the first years of this century, in the magazines, concerning the past of big business and big business men. "Debunking" was the order of the day, and for a time few knew but that it might be their turn next. The Rector's interest in Christian Science, already keen, was further whetted by a publisher's suggestion that he prepare a volume which would answer some of the questions which he had raised in his parish booklet, at a time when the average reader had little choice between books of adulation and of condemnation. He accepted the commission with a strong desire to produce something which would deserve the judgment actually accorded his work, when it finally appeared, by the *Springfield Republican*: "A fair-minded and judicial interpretation of Christian Science by one who is neither its assailant nor its defender."

In the course of his preparation for the writing of the book, he tried to check up by interviews and letters as many of the statements as possible then appearing in the press. On his quest he visited various places. The correspondence which, in some cases, he started, continued after the book was published, and to-day constitutes evidence the more convincing because the letters were sent avowedly to help the author to write with understanding. His correspondents expressed themselves the more spontaneously and freely because never once were they asked to make affidavits.

As a critic has written the author, much of the

testimony of that period was one-sided. Out of the obscurity of small-town life, some of the witnesses — not all — emerged into a nation-wide notoriety, the enjoyment of which they made no effort to conceal. Not in every instance, dryly observes a critic, were "they the kind of sources we would have chosen." Such as seemed accessible were reported to have been interviewed; sometimes also their affidavits were taken.

Just as the author was wondering how he could possibly discover witnesses closer to Mrs. Eddy and more competent to testify, he received on May 4, 1907, a courteous letter from the Committee on Publication in Boston, which opened the way for a discussion of some of the problems involved.

But the summer of 1907 was not a favorable time for the author to collect material. Growth within and public clamor without had thrust so many new and unexpected duties upon all persons in any way engaged in Christian Science work, that granting to such an insistent investigator as the author all the time and help he wished was physically impossible.

Besides, most of the materials now available were yet to be collected; for it was not until the latter part of 1907, that there began the systematic and comprehensive mobilizing of the data, which at first consisted of Mrs. Eddy's letters to church officers. No special need for the materials had been foreseen; or, for that matter, could have been. As always Mrs. Eddy's attention was concentrated on things she counted of more spiritual import than the compilation of information concerning herself. Some of the letters, which perhaps the author might have seen, had come without expectation of their publication; and the mere routine of getting from various quarters permission for their use in a book would have taken time and care not then available to a staff already overworked.[2]

Although the Next Friends suit did not come up in court until August, 1907, the action had months before been brought, and through the entire spring preparation to meet it was taxing every heart and mind in any way concerned. Owing to complete and inevitable failure to understand the conditions surrounding Mrs. Eddy, the author was persistently pressing her people for definite, even documentary, information; to which he added the request that, in company with the venerable Edward Everett Hale, he be allowed at her convenience to pay a call on Mrs. Eddy.

The hesitation and reluctance which the Committee showed to take steps for the granting of a request which seemed to the author altogether reasonable, he did not understand. In his much writing, his habit had always been to go in every instance to the supreme source. Diplomatists and United States Senators, Presidents and Prime Ministers had opened wide their doors to him. In preparing, shortly before, his *Historic Towns of New England*, such men as President Charles William Eliot, Colonel Thomas Wentworth Higginson, Edward Everett Hale, and a score of other eminent New Englanders had personally assisted him. Why Mrs. Eddy's door should be the only one in all New England which would not open to him, puzzled the author.

Now he understands. The circumstances that

year were beyond even Mrs. Eddy's control. Long one of the busiest women in the world, Mrs. Eddy had already been obliged to write her Boston representative, "I shall not be subject to interviews and you must not subject me to them. My time is worth more for good than to risk its *misuse* or to be so used by others." [3]

In due season, the author's book appeared. The preface opened :

Christian Science has long engaged my interest. For years I discouraged none who sought its healing ministry. The undiscriminating censure visited upon it in apparent ignorance or prejudice made no impression on me. The desire Christian Scientists were constantly expressing to be judged by their fruits seemed to me to be both Christian and scientific.

In the copious notes of reference to his sources at the end of the book, the statement was inserted that he had "spared no effort to find all the evidence there is." He took pains also to announce that he would stand ready to revise the book, should new evidence come to light at any time to make revision necessary in the interest of truth.

During the years that followed, his appreciation of Christian Science grew, along with his amazement that no presentation, fully documented and satisfying to critic as to public, was in print touching a woman who had a record to her credit of more extraordinary and benignant things in life than any other woman in the history of the world. He had in fact to wait until 1930 to find that Mrs. Eddy, with characteristic wisdom, had once observed that neither the time nor the person had come to write her life story.

The year 1910 brought to the author's eye many editorial appreciations which were evoked by Mrs. Eddy's passing. As he now looks back across the twenty years which have since intervened, he believes he then took a distinct step forward in understanding her personality and achievements.

Selected the next year by the editors of the Schaff-Herzog Encyclopaedia of Religious Literature to write a judicial estimate, to be published midway between articles of commendation and of criticism of Mrs. Eddy and her faith, his article closed with this paragraph:

The public has no longer any disposition to deny that from the standpoint of achievement Mrs. Eddy stood alone among the women of the world. . . . Mrs. Eddy and her followers have identified themselves as have no others in the world with the religious and the philosophical revolt against materialism.

The Great War broke and furnished the most convincing demonstration in the history of the world of the unspeakable ravages to which wrong thinking may lead. More people than ever began to realize that there is something in Christian Science, as one critic had observed, "wholly gracious and beautiful." Significantly enough he added: "It would be difficult satisfactorily to explain why or how or by what argument that power should be nonexistent in Christians now."

As America in 1917 was on the brink of the Great War, the author again wrote for publication:

In the last ten years Christian Science has certainly encouraged daily Bible reading, until now Christian Scientists are probably the most assiduous Bible readers in the world.

They still avoid antagonisms. They keep singularly serene.
They average high in otherworldliness. It looks as though
. . . they were endeavoring to make the most of the spiritual
reality which those who study far into the movement easily
discover.

While overseas, a little later, to observe the effect
of the war on English and French educational institutions, and during the two or three years that followed speaking in hundreds of places throughout the
land, the author never lost a chance to add new
impressions to the old of Christian Science. Everywhere he found the same devotion to things of the
spirit, the same inconspicuous efficiency, and the
same loyalty to the woman of their love and faith.

Moreover, his community contacts in such places
as Mountain Lakes, New Jersey, where he had a
suburban home, taught him to expect Christian
Scientists to be found on the right side of public questions, from the education of the young to the reclama-
tion of the old. In fact, more than once he had hearty
coöperation from individual Christian Scientists in
what are ordinarily termed ministerial duties, compli-
cated in those days by the social dislocations and the
family smash-ups which the War had brought.

By 1921 when he received an invitation to con-
tribute the article on "Science and Health" to the
Cambridge History of American Literature, he had
become convinced that there was too much constructive achievement to the credit of Mrs. Eddy to
withhold full credit from her longer. "Christian
Science," he therefore wrote, "is really its founder's
creation. Where she got this idea, or where that,
little matters. As a whole the system described in

Science and Health is hers, and nothing that can ever happen will make it less than hers." [4]

Of Christian Scientists his closing words ran thus:

With allowance for those in every religion who do not try to live up to its highest teachings, they measurably avoid friction and irritation and preserve considerable serenity and otherworldliness amid temptations which many of us seem unable to resist. They have to their credit a widely read daily paper which for editorial ability as well as excellent news service ranks among the best journals in the country. Finally, as the years go by, it is thought by many that Christian Scientists seem to be increasingly disposed to emphasize only the outstanding virtues which their book teaches, and in consequence to bring forth " the fruit of the spirit — love, joy, peace, long-suffering, gentleness, goodness, faith, meekness, temperance; against such there is no law." [5]

During the decade which opened with the appearance of the *Cambridge History*, America soared to the pinnacle of material achievement. Power both to earn and to enjoy was increased. The hours of labor were reduced. Comforts multiplied. The so-called hostilities of nature shrank, and her benevolences increased. The standard of physical fitness rose until it became bad form to enjoy ill health, or even to talk of being sick. Speaking of symptoms ceased to be an indoor sport except in institutions tarrying overlong in the past. Death lost much of its terror. Too ostentatious mourning gravitated into the discard. The Christian Science phrase "to pass on" began to dispute popularity with the word "dying," long associated, too long indeed, with the dark and dismal.

Developments during this same decade in the academic world of science took place, which, to say

the least, were hardly anticipated. Millikan began
to strip the "atom" of its coating.[6] Eddington
denied "actuality" apart from consciousness. Hal-
dane made the individual mind a part of that "absolute or unconditioned mind," which was in the
thought of St. Paul when he stated that "in him we
live, and move, and have our being." Kirtley F.
Mather of Harvard observed last April, as reported
in *The Churchman*, in a Boston parish meeting, that
"scientists are more and more coming not only to
acknowledge the existence of spiritual forces, but to
give all phenomena a spiritual interpretation." But
Christian Scientists had long been holding to the
familiar phrase of Mrs. Eddy: "There is no life,
truth, intelligence, nor substance in matter. All is
infinite Mind and its infinite manifestation, for God
is All-in-all."[7]

For better or for worse, religion, as well as science,
began to feel the urge to restate its position. Defining God went on as energetically as ever. If God
has not at last been defined to death in many a
theological camp, most of us may perhaps take to
heart the warning which Goethe gave to Eckermann:

Dear boy, what do we know of the idea of the Divine;
and what can our narrow conceptions presume to tell of the
Supreme Being? If I called him by a hundred names like a
Turk, I should yet fall short and have said nothing in comparison to the boundlessness of his attributes.[8]

Two preachers who grew so discouraged that they
left the ministry this year past would seem to illustrate some adverse consequences of these unsettled
conditions. One is a Presbyterian, two years out of
seminary and still in the middle of his twenties.

The other is an Episcopalian in the maturity of middle life and, till the other day, rector of a conspicuous church in New York City. The reasons for their withdrawal appeared in two popular magazines.[9]

After one year in the ministry, the younger man withdraws because, to cite some of his words :

I am muckle sick of the optimistic slush with which the pastors are lulling their congregations to sleep by congratu- lating them upon their Christian piety and assuring them that God loves them.   I am also sick of all this talk about the hunger of the human heart for "pure religion and undefiled." The attempt to interest men in the church by feeding them chicken dinners belies this theory.   Why can't we say quite frankly that the great majority of moderns care nothing about the church or Him it represents?   Why don't we confess that the statistics showing forty million Christians in this country are a monumental joke?   The religious longing is ineradicably carved upon the human heart, say the philosophers.   Very beautiful, but untrue.   I fear it is a desire for " weenie " roasts and bowling-alleys rather than for religion.

The more mature man has become convinced that the Protestant reformers of the sixteenth century blundered in substituting preaching for worship ; that the recent rapid subsidence of church going leads logically to the closing of the churches ; and that, with little prospect of developing a spiritual tech- nique, which will help the individual every day as well as Sunday to be aware of God, Protestantism will soon be over the abyss.

As between the two diagnoses submitted, the author is unable to accept either. Anxious about many things, he is not anxious about God. Con- scious of human limitations, to the author every new problem is nothing more than a new challenge to wrest a solution out of the unknown; to find in an enlarging understanding of the revelation which Christ Jesus gave of God the solution of all problems, old and new.[10]

But, no matter what the risk in too elaborate defining, each mind must still give its account of God. It must state the reason for the faith within it. The ability to do so always depends on having first-hand faith, on knowing God first-hand. Many of our intellectual interests we may pass on to others. Some we may refer to a "Committee of the Whole." But, in the higher life, each must know God with the heart. If we doubt we have a heart, we have to grow a heart to know God, to know God intimately near as well as infinitely far. The business, therefore, of growing a heart is always pressing. Nobody can grow a heart for anybody else. The only way to prove that we have grown a heart is to submit to the universal test found in Edna St. Vincent Millay's verse:

> The world stands out on either side
> No wider than the heart is wide;
> Above the world is stretched the sky, —
> No higher than the soul is high.
> The heart can push the sea and land
> Farther away on either hand;
> The soul can split the sky in two
> And let the face of God shine through.
> But East and West will pinch the heart
> That cannot keep them pushed apart;
> And he whose soul is flat — the sky
> Will close in on him by and by.[11]

Divisions among Christians have lost God from many a heart. That is why men like Bishops Brent and Manning, Doctors Burris Jenkins and Macfarland (the latter having recently rounded out twenty years of executive direction of the Federal Council of Churches), in season and out, have called Christendom to get together on at least a working basis. That is why as long ago as November 12, 1906, Mrs. Eddy wrote Dr. Hamilton Holt, then Editor of *The Independent*,[12] now President of Rollins College, Florida: "I love the prosperity of Zion, be it promoted by Catholic, by Protestant, or by Christian Science, which anoints with Truth, opening the eyes of the blind and healing the sick. I would no more quarrel with a man because of his religion than I would because of his art."

History has been a succession of revelations of the Highest, flashing forth when the night looked blackest. And so to-day as yesterday:

> I know of lands that are sunk in shame,
> And hearts that faint and tire;
> And I know of men who ask not fame
> Who would give their lives for the fire.
> I know of hearts that despair of help
> And lives that could kindle to flame,
> And I know a Name, a Name, a Name
> Can set these lives on fire.
> Its soul is a brand, its letters flame;
> I know a Name, a Name, a Name
> 'Twill set these lives on fire.[13]

When the resurgence of critical interest in Christian Science came a year ago, the author was invited, at a New York luncheon table, to speak out his opinion of the situation. His reply to the friends who made the request, one of whom had been editor of the Christian Science periodicals and was himself the writer of several books, was an outright declaration that the time had come for the spokesmen of Christian Science effectively and finally to lift discussion out of the lowlands of controversy, to the heights of general understanding. To one he observed :

You ought to write a book based on the hitherto unused materials which your church must have, and for all time lay some of the smaller bothers and misapprehensions which every little while reappear. The climate has changed. The public is weary of controversy. Christian Scientists have done too many fine things to be disturbed so often by vexatious disputation. Bring it to an end the only way you can.

Almost chapter by chapter, the author blocked out the book he thought the times require. As the group broke up, each going his own way, it was assumed that such a book would soon be written by some one belonging to the fold with access to the abundant sources, which have of late been assembled by the authorities of the church. In due season, arrangements were made for a conference between the author and the Board of Directors in Boston, consisting of Mr. Edward A. Merritt, Mr. William R. Rathvon, Mrs. Annie M. Knott, Mr. George Wendell Adams, and Mr. Charles E. Heitman. His vision of the book which he believed should be written could now be thrown on a somewhat larger canvas than was possible at a luncheon table. After several discussions, in which all present shared, agreement seemed to be general that the time at last had come to supplement the writings of the generation past, based on partial knowledge as they had to be, by a life-size portrait of Mrs. Eddy, for which the many new facts available might furnish the material.

Such a book would have to be free from pettiness. Controversy would not be sought. It ought not merely to be based on original sources but also to be written with such simplicity and engaging freshness as would make it readable to all.

While humanizing Mrs. Eddy, this book would naturally not neglect to make much of the extraordinary foresight shown in her constructive work of instituting, organizing, and administering a movement which grew so fast as to attract the world's attention in her lifetime and to hold it since her passing on. Every incident accepted for inclusion would be chosen with relationship to this larger purpose, and nothing intentionally overlooked which would help to give Mrs. Eddy her proper place among world builders.

As the discussions developed, the conclusion slowly emerged that in order to interest and inform the public outside, in addition to those within Christian Science, the book would better be written by one without the fold and yet who had given proof that he possessed a good general understanding both of the movement and of its originator.

By a process of elimination, finally the task fell to this author. The Board generously promised him free access to the rich sources committed to their care, and also to respond to any proper requests for assistance that might be necessary in the execution of the task. No pledge was asked of him, and he gave none.

Before reaching a final decision, he talked over the matter with friends in New York and elsewhere. They agreed with him as to the desirability of such a book, and predicted general interest on the part of the public in it. Dr. Albert Shaw, whose monumental life of Lincoln — now appearing — is a model, tersely advised, "Tell the story as though it never had been told before."

As, at last, the author approached his task, he felt that his background of twenty-five years of deepening appreciation of the significance of Christian Science and of the personality of Mrs. Eddy should be an asset. On the other hand, his conviction seemed warranted that, with access granted to the colossal collection of original materials — the most valuable part of which, for the author's purpose, had been collected in the last few years — the hour had struck for the life-size portrait of Mary Baker Eddy to be made.

On both sides, there was risk. The author might disappoint the Board. Every writer knows that between having a vision and projecting it on paper, a wide gulf yawns. Almost anything can happen to obscure a writer's insight, or to divert him from his course. Many a book has been marred by listening overmuch to counsel in its preparation. Many a book has been dwarfed by refusing counsel altogether. Even after investigation begins, conditions may not prove as favorable as they at first appeared. Sometimes the sources disappoint. They prove less important on close inspection than they promised in the distance, or they turn out so amorphous, so unordered, so impossible to classify, that they are unworkable. But whatever difficulties arise, once an author assumes his task, his is the inescapable responsibility to see it through in his own way.

On the other hand, the Board, through no fault of their own, might disappoint the author seeking all the facts that may be. More than once Mrs. Eddy herself had been misunderstood. Starting out possibly with good intentions members of her own household had, now and then, turned into foes. Furthermore, a part of the failure in those Boston days to grasp her meaning, was due to the novelty of her teaching. She humorously reported that on one occasion asking all those in her audience to stand up who had understood what she said, not one stood up. Since Mrs. Eddy passed on, the directorate, now representing her, have not always found their course clear or their task easy. The responsibility to direct the movement, to care for the flock which Mrs. Eddy mothered so wisely, rests upon their shoulders, and they must take no unnecessary risks.

But, if the task could be performed with the understanding of all concerned, it might be worth doing. The book would then, perhaps, do its bit to instill public confidence in a group which too few outsiders realize train themselves with the same meticulous care to live the higher life as the "track" man trains for his "meet," or the pianist practices for his concert appearances.

Certain conditions, on both sides, would naturally be observed. The author must be left untrammeled in his work. His habits of intellectual creativeness which for years had been developing must be respected. His time must be conserved. In spite of his marked social instincts, he had for a season to deny them indulgence. Financially, he had to be independent. The book was to be his book. If evidently official or inspired, his chief purpose in writing it might be defeated. On these terms the author set about his task; and as he nears its close, he gladly testifies that the faith pledged to him has been kept. He has been permitted to consult everything necessary to the understanding of the subject. Nothing has been withheld to which he sought access. By day as well as night, he has come and gone, as suited his convenience, on these errands of research. Unvarying courtesy has been shown him. There has been no infringement of his personal integrity or of his financial independence. All necessary aids have been at hand.

Being somewhat familiar with some of the greater libraries of the world, from the British Museum to the Library of Congress, the author cannot speak too highly of the originality, resourcefulness, efficiency, and unselfish service rendered by the Christian Science staff. No place does he know where a book of this type could have been done with such ease. In many excellent libraries, an investigator counts it no hardship sometimes to wait long for an important document to be placed before him. In the preparation of this book, the author cannot recall an instance in which what he has required has not been, without delay, forthcoming, so excellently organized is the entire department, so carefully ordered are the rich materials of which they take tender and intelligent care.

Since a biography is rarely written as completely as this from original sources, the reader may care to hear something of them. He will recall — if he has read to this point in the Prologue — that it is almost a quarter of a century since the author began without prevision to collect the materials out of which this book has grown.

Obviously his acquaintance, at first, was confined to those not close to Mrs. Eddy. No others then appeared accessible. As the years elapsed, his acquaintance widened, his correspondence increased with those who could speak with much authority, and the source of the materials grew on which to base the judgment which he was gradually forming. Now, as he nears the completion of a task which he began a quarter of a century ago, he finds that, in all probability, he has known, in one way or another, more of those on both sides qualified to testify concerning Mrs. Eddy than anybody else in the same period. All this time the author has been an ordained Episcopal minister, intensely interested in his Church, and with voice and pen often speaking for it beyond the range of his own parish.

His more immediate approach to the task began by making the personal acquaintance of the Directors, their many helpers, and also others able and ready to assist him. Many who knew Mrs. Eddy in the last years of her life, or their descendants, or even their neighbors, furnished him much information not before available.

The more important places where Mrs. Eddy lived were visited, and of her last home at Chestnut Hill a somewhat careful study was made. The many books she read, and marked, were examined; and the more important of them for his purpose were turned into abstracts for effective use.

Written recollections from almost all who ever

knew her well were supplemented by talks in person
with many of them, some of whom by request came
from afar to see the author.   Judged by the standard which' courts apply to human testimony, these
new witnesses have proved trustworthy.   Intellectually alert, as those associated with Mrs. Eddy had
to be, they are naïvely loyal to her memory.   Yet
without collusion, often indeed never having met or
corresponded, their testimony is substantially free
from contradictions.

The general correspondence of the movement, the
copies of Mrs. Eddy's letters, the letters others wrote
to her, and the multitudinous other materials occupy
a large fireproof vault in the Executive Offices.

Her original letters, amounting to more than eight
thousand, a large proportion of them written with
her own hand and many of special value only recently
added, are mounted in fifty-seven large volumes having a general index, cross references, and a subject
index in concordance style.   Bound in fine leather,
specially imported from England, the volumes are
approximately fifteen inches by twelve inches in size.
They are kept in a moisture-proof vault, specially
fitted for them.   The temperature of the vault is
maintained at from sixty-six degrees to sixty-eight
degrees in summer as well as in winter, and all other
known precautions to safeguard such treasures are
taken.

The preserving of the letters is done by a special
process, in some respects original.   Before its mounting, each letter is placed in a bowl of water and
thoroughly soaked.   Then it is stretched out even
on a zinc board and covered with a coating of paste.

Next it is set in a large sheet of special grade paper cut out to form a frame. Then it is hung up on a line like clothes to dry.

After drying, the letters are put under a heavy press with wax paper between the sheets to keep them from adhering to each other, and large pasteboards beneath them for protection. Then the press is clamped down and they are left there for twenty-four hours. Upon removal silk sheets are placed on either side of the letters, and, to prevent fraying, tissue strips are used to cover the edges where silk and paper meet. Once more they are dampened and pressed until they remain absolutely flat. Afterwards they are assembled in signatures, sewn to make volumes each of about one-hundred pages, and are ready for the binder, who comes to the church offices to do his work.

The leather for the binding is of the best blue-black levant, and the volumes are hand-tooled.

Approaching the volumes in The Mother Church vault, the designation on the back reads as follows:

MARY BAKER EDDY
Letters and Miscellany
Vol. 54
Nos. 7526–7652

MARY BAKER EDDY
Letters and Miscellany
Vol. 55
Nos. 7653–7824

Looking back with reverent appreciation of this rare privilege of studying the life of a notable religious leader, as reflected in this mass of unusual detail over which he has pored both day and night, the author vividly realizes how necessary such sources are in any writing on this theme.

In fact, to attempt to do a biography of Mary

Baker Eddy without steeping the mind in this material would seem as futile as to attempt a biography of
George Washington, without recourse to the Library
of Congress and the fourteen volumes of letters edited
by Ford and containing the recollections of Washington's friends.

In the nineties at Johns Hopkins University, the
author had the good fortune to hear Woodrow Wilson
give the material in lecture form of more than one
book which he was afterward to publish. He recalls
with special vividness his many talks with Woodrow
Wilson about the materials for *Division and Reunion*,
which covers our national history beginning with
Andrew Jackson and ending with the close of the first
century under the Constitution. Woodrow Wilson
still a boy in the South was a loyal Southerner when
the war was on between the States. In the course,
however, of spending his college days in the North
and later, after he took his Ph.D. at Johns Hopkins, of
teaching successively at Bryn Mawr, Wesleyan, and
Princeton, with six weeks of lecturing every winter at
Johns Hopkins, many of his earlier prejudices against
the North died out. Without the loss of his love for
the Southland, he thought and spoke and wrote
increasingly in terms national, once calling his
students to : •

Be strong-backed, brown-handed, upright as your pines ;
By the scale of a hemisphere shape your designs.

Writing his preface after he had finished work on
the manuscript of *Division and Reunion*, Woodrow
Wilson showed that he was keenly sensible of both
the advantages and disadvantages which lay in his

Southern bringing up and his Northern contacts.
In the closing sentence of that preface, after a modest
admission that his work might contain imperfections,
he stoutly laid claim to impartiality; for, he said,
"Impartiality is a matter of the heart, and I know
with what disposition I have written."

LYMAN P. POWELL

1930

CHAPTER ONE

A CHALLENGE

Jesus brought the undistinguished and the handicapped good news. "The blind receive their sight, and the lame walk, the lepers are cleansed, and the deaf hear, the dead are raised up, and the poor have the gospel preached to them."[1]

No news could then have been more welcome to these millions, ever with us, of neglected ones. All the centuries up from the *Egyptian Book of the Dead*, that earliest religious book in history, to Nietzsche, contempt for the average man and fawning deference for the inhumanly unhampered superman have been the rule. Rarely have the sick, the sinful, and the dying heard any good news other than the good tidings which Jesus brought of a Heavenly Father who cares[2] for every one of us, poor as well as rich, young as well as old, who numbers every hair in every head, and lets no sparrow, however tiny, fall unnoticed to the ground.

To the early Christians this radically different understanding of themselves which Jesus brought to them was news too good to keep. They simply had to pass it on. They had no time to stop for argument. To every challenge to engage in disputation they turned a deaf ear. Served with a summons to explain, they quoted the man after his sight had been restored who ended inquiry with the reply, "One thing I know, that, whereas I was blind, now I see."[3]

Christian Science proclaims itself a bearer of the same good news. Christian Scientists could not keep it to themselves if they would and would not if they could; for many of them have experienced in their own persons transformations similar to those of apostolic experience. They have been emancipated from grievous illnesses — not only physical, but also moral and mental. If they were to hold their peace, it seems to them as if "the stones would immediately cry out."[4] That is why their Wednesday evening service is anticipated by them weekly with delight and attended with singular devotion at a time when midweek services in other churches are either struggling for existence or have expired altogether.

There is a challenge here which Christian Science offers to the world, and no longer can it be evaded. In fact, ridicule, flaw picking in this tenet or in that of Christian Science, sometimes tumultuous controversy spiced with outworn gibes, no longer satisfy a reading public every day growing more sophisticated and also better informed.

The sincere testimony offered by thousands and thousands of responsible people the whole world round that they have found joy and peace, healing and a higher aim in life in consequence of their adherence to this faith must now be regarded seriously. Whatever opinion the reader may hold of the theology of Christian Science, the evidence is now overwhelming that for innumerably many, Christian Science works. It meets for them the pragmatic test which Professor William James in 1907 set up that "True ideas are those that we can assimilate, validate, corroborate, and verify."

THE MOTHER CHURCH

It would be a poor compliment, indeed, to the reader if the author did not invite him in this non-controversial book, written by one not a member of the Christian Science Church, to join in a clear-eyed look on at least a few representative testimonies out of the many now available. No other course is open. The evidence is not to be dismissed. It is not negligible. The witnesses are people of social, intellectual, and spiritual significance.

Dr. Laurence McK. Gould, who was second in command to Rear Admiral Byrd in the recent Antarctic Expedition, sent these arresting words:

In the physical world one may endure the hardships of exploration with some confidence that he will receive at least a modicum of approval and appreciation. In the world of things not material this is much less likely to be true. Too often the explorer or pioneer here receives but scant sympathy and seldom lives to see his visions become realities. Probably no person who pioneered or explored beyond the margin of the conventional in this world ever lived to see such abundant and widespread fruitage as did the founder of Christian Science — Mary Baker Eddy. And each day finds this movement just a little bit at least more widespread than it was on the preceding day.

Christian Science is an incontrovertible fact and no one can think to interpret or even understand the trends of modern religious thought without giving serious attention to it. To accurately appraise anything is in part to delimit it and that can scarcely be even attempted in the case of Christian Science. The Christian Science Church with all its affiliated institutions comprehends this movement only in part. The essential philosophy of this faith has found its way into the thought and attitude of many Protestant Churches and there is no measuring its boundaries. This widespread and lasting fruitage is the greatest evidence of the essential soundness of Christian Science teachings.

The next is Philip Kerr, sometime secretary to Lloyd George and now Marquis of Lothian, who has recently written for this book:[5]

Many spiritually minded men and women throughout the ages have found their way to the direct knowledge of God and have taught that knowledge to their fellow men. But Mary Baker Eddy has done something in the field of religion which is unique. Through her study of the Bible and of the words and works of Christ Jesus she has not only given us the full definition of the nature of the living God but she has also analyzed the origin and character of that evil or materialism from which humanity has never yet been able to escape and has shown us how we can destroy it and so prove our birthright as the children of God. Later ages will recognize that the writing of Science and Health, after Mrs. Eddy had demonstrated the truth of the teachings it contains by healing the sick, redeeming the sinner, and raising the dead as no one had done since the days of Jesus, was the turning point in human history. For it has given to mankind in a form which all can understand the Science which will enable it to destroy utterly every phase of evil, sin, sorrow, sickness and death and thereby bring into our experience in all its purity, beauty and loveliness that perfect world which Jesus described as the Kingdom of God. In this age of preoccupation with the cares and pleasures of mortal existence the unique significance of Mrs. Eddy may not be generally discerned. But posterity will recognize her as the greatest woman who ever lived upon this planet.

Next is a word sent in June, 1930, by Viscount Astor, of interest on its own account and also because of the admiration felt for Lady Astor in her own land:

Youth, science, intellectualism, modernism, challenge theology; and theologians are not able to give a satisfying answer to the very reasonable questions the world of to-day insists upon putting. As a result Christianity has lost both adherents and influence.

Compared with this admitted loss the growth and the increasing membership of Christian Science is phenomenal. This is doubly remarkable in a conservative country like Britain with its Established and Free Churches and their great position and tradition. What is the reason for this phenomenon?

Christian Science is logical. Given certain premises which are accepted by all Christians the conclusions of Christian Science are inevitable. The natural scientist, too, who is not an atheist can find in Christian Science a philosophy which fits in with many modern views of the Universe. Lastly, suffering humanity finds in Christian Science a remedy.

Across the years comes drifting the memorable testimony of the Seventh Earl of Dunmore, written in 1907:

I never knew the meaning of real happiness until I became a Christian Scientist. Amusements, relaxations, tastes, and pursuits that seemed to me in the old days the only things that made life worth living, I now know had never the true ring of happiness about them; they afforded me but a spurious kind of satisfaction, which I, in my ignorance of what life really means, mistook for happiness. The world that one day appeared to me so full of what I mistook for happiness and joy, would the very next day appear to me to be gloomy and miserable, full of doubt and discord; whereas to-day there is no shadow of uncertainty over the world as revealed to me in Christian Science, but a lasting sense of peace, sunshine, happiness, and love. Even money troubles can have no power to disturb the equanimity of the Christian Scientist, once he has brought himself to realize that God — and not man — is the source of all supply.

American visitors to Cambridge remember well the distinguished Master of Trinity College, Dr. Montagu Butler. His widow, daughter of the late Sir James Ramsay, is the next witness:

Every day they live, Christian Scientists are indebted to Mrs. Eddy. Through her writings their whole outlook on life and experience of life has been changed. She has enabled them to find convincing proof of the truth of Christianity as taught by Christ Jesus, and has shown them how it may be applied and lived to-day. She has solved enigmas, for an answer to which they had searched in vain in other directions.

Count Helmuth von Moltke, of Berlin, expressed himself as confident that "the Christian Science movement is safely anchored through God's protecting wisdom and love."

Up in Sweden, where Christian Science is growing apace, Count Sigge Cronstedt, of Stockholm, adds his voice:

The more I have the privilege to study Christian Science and to practice what I have learned therefrom, the more I humbly and gratefully acknowledge and appreciate the immense importance of the life work of Mary Baker Eddy.

There is a plentiful supply of impressive confessions from American sources which vie in appreciation with these European ones. As a business man, Mr. J. M. Studebaker, Jr., of the Studebaker Corporation says:

Although I am not as yet a member of the Christian Science Church, I have for many years seen members of my family benefited by the teachings of this wonderful work. I sincerely feel that Mary Baker Eddy, as the discoverer and founder of Christian Science, has given to the world through *Science and Health with Key to the Scriptures* and her other writings, a complete statement of truth which is healing and bringing comfort to every sincere thinker.

For men who "go down to the sea in ships," Commodore John M. Orchard speaks:

Our Master's message, "Go and shew John again those things which ye do hear and see," impels this witness to my grateful appreciation of the work of our revered Leader, Mary Baker Eddy, discoverer and founder of Christian Science and author of its Textbook, *Science and Health with Key to the Scriptures*.

In my own experience, simply through earnest study of the Bible in connection with *Science and Health*, old age glasses were permanently discarded.

At one time the ship under my command was enabled to carry out instructions which necessitated entering a harbor through a channel having outlying rocks and no navigating aids, in spite of dense fog and strong irregular currents.

More than all this is the peace and poise with which Science touches every phase of right endeavor and points it to higher, happier attainment.

Among educators Professor Hermann S. Hering,[6] sometime on the faculty of Johns Hopkins University :

Christian healing is an essential element in Christian living, although not generally so considered. From the inception of Christianity, however, only a few have accepted fully our Master's teachings, caught their spirit, and manifested this Christ-spirit in healing works, notably the early Christians who, during the first three centuries of the Christian era, did such marvelous healing, and led such self-sacrificing and consecrated lives.

Dean William E. Masterson, of the College of Law, University of Idaho, arrests attention with his words :

A thorough and unbiased study of the life of Mrs. Eddy reveals a woman of great personal charm, rare culture and learning, a purity of life and purpose, unsurpassed unselfishness, and the profoundest wisdom and spiritual discernment and understanding. She is, doubtless, the greatest prophet and benefactor that mankind has ever had, with the exception of Christ Jesus. I am convinced that she came according to prophecy and that through her there has been revealed and restored to humanity the comforter which St. John declared would be sent "from the Father." Such a revelation could come only through the noblest and purest type of womanhood. Subsequent to this discovery, which she later named Christian Science, her life was one unselfish and tireless effort to reduce to human comprehension and to establish among men this science as a practical and healing religion. This she did by means of her teaching, her writings, and her church and the manifold channels of its activity. Such was her unswerving devotion to a cause in which her faith remained fixed and unshaken. Only those who have observed the beneficial effects of the application of this science to the lives of others or felt its benign influence in their own lives can properly appreciate Mrs. Eddy and her mission and justly appraise her work in its relation to human welfare.

A former physician, Dr. Walton Hubbard, of Los Angeles, California:

My experience covering a period of nine years in the practice of medicine, followed by the practice of Christian Science, has proved to me that the results following Christian Science treatment are incomparably better than those following the use of material means.

For the stage, Mary Pickford:

We are adjured to count our blessings and I count among my greatest, the clearer spiritual vision that has come to us in the light of Mary Baker Eddy's interpretations of Christ's teachings. Facing a material world and preaching a doctrine of spiritual thought, she stood practically alone and matched her humanity and vision with a high courage that, in itself, should be an inspiration to all of us.

Corinne Griffith:

Mary Baker Eddy is the greatest benefactress the world has ever known, and even to those not interested in Christian Science, the clean-minded, honest influence of her life and works is bound to be felt.

Conrad Nagel:

Mary Baker Eddy has given to the world a religion that is demonstrable and practical, and offers every human being a thorough and complete solution to any and all problems that may present themselves. I have many times discussed Christian Science and Mrs. Eddy with most of the foremost people in the motion picture industry, and find that they all have the greatest admiration for her and for her teachings. I have found that, while not members of any Science Church or even avowed Christian Scientists, the heads of several of the biggest organizations in the motion picture industry have many times turned for help to her teachings.

Religious people outside of Christian Science, and naturally differing widely from those inside, are more and more bestowing upon the good news which Christian Science proclaims appreciative recognition. A few of the more commanding out of a multitude of such tributes are selected for citation here.

In one of the Encyclical letters issued to the Bishops and Clergy of the Anglican Church by the late Archbishop of Canterbury, Dr. Randall Davidson, to begin again overseas, one finds the sentence:

There is much in Christian Science which ought to be found within the Church, where it would be supplemented by truths which in Christian Science are neglected.[7]

The new Archbishop of York, the Most Reverend and Rt. Hon. William Temple, in his book entitled, *Essays in Christian Politics:*

There is no doubt that we have in the church neglected the connection that does exist between faith and health, and it is largely because of that that Christian Science, for example, has been able to gain so many adherents; for the practice of Christian Science has brought incalculable benefit to many people.

One of two London clergymen who have spoken with unusual clearness, the Reverend Edward T. Vernon:

God used Mrs. Eddy for a special revelation, and there is, indeed, no reason why this should not be so. No just person can fail to admire her as a religious leader. She has founded a great church, and, let us say it frankly, brought great blessing on countless lives.

The second, Dr. John Shaw:

I am not a Christian Scientist, but I believe in what I should regard as the essential tenet of their creed, and which I might sum up in the words, " The Lord's hand is not shortened, that it cannot save."

Ireland will be represented by the Reverend Richard W. Seaver of Belfast:

We owe much to Christian Science for emphasizing the fact that " thoughts are things," and insisting upon our power and our duty to manage thought as the root of action.

Returning to the United States, the following admission is made by the new Episcopal Bishop Coadjutor of St. Louis, the Right Reverend William Scarlett:

Christian Science has made the church aware it has overlooked a great power and it has set the church to thinking of healing.

But even more to the point are the words of the Reverend Dr. Elwood Worcester because he is the founder of the Emmanuel Movement, which is largely responsible for the development of the new interest in spiritual healing observable in the Episcopal Church: [8]

The doctrines of Christian Science, for example, have been denounced, ridiculed, exploited times without number, apparently with as much effect as throwing pebbles at the sea checks the rising of the tide. Preachers, physicians, editors of powerful journals, philosophers, humorists, unite in pouring contempt upon this despicable superstition, very much as Juvenal, Tacitus, and Celsus mocked at nascent Christianity, but in spite of them it lives. While most other religious bodies are declining or barely holding their own, it grows by leaps and bounds. All over this country solid and enduring temples are reared by grateful hands and consecrated to the ideal and name of Mrs. Eddy. And this strange phenomenon has occurred in the full light of day, at the end of the nineteenth and at the beginning of the twentieth century, and these extraordinary doctrines have propagated themselves not in obscure corners of the earth, among an illiterate and a fanatical populace, but in the chief centers of American civilization.

Reverend Dr. Charles F. Potter describes Mrs. Eddy as "the most compelling figure in American religious history."

The late President Charles William Eliot, eminent in the field of education, in his customary downright and forthright way once observed that "Christian Science is good Christianity."

President Edward S. Parsons, of Marietta (Ohio) College, gives this explanation of his good opinion:

The Christian Science churches have been crowded because they have been in a real sense the Church of the living God. They have somehow persuaded people that there is a living God, whose strength is in a real way at their command; that not merely the past, but the present and the future, are the field of God's control and action, and that because He is, there can be nothing fundamentally wrong with the world.

Doctors, too, are beginning to show less reluctance in admitting that Christian Science has good unde·niable to its credit:

Dr. William Mayo, of Rochester, Minnesota :

I have sent people to Christian Scientists and they have got relief.

Dr. Copeland Smith, of Chicago, in a radio sermon described Christian Science as :

The opening of a window to the winds of Heaven. It is the mightiest protest yet made by the human spirit against the blatant materialism of the present age.

Dr. Richard C. Cabot, of Boston :

Christian Science has done a great deal of good.

The attitude of the press is no longer so adversely critical as it used to be. Even twenty years ago, Isaac Marcosson could describe Mrs. Eddy as "a striking character, who must be reckoned with in any estimate of the women who have made history."

Thomas L. Masson :

They pay their bills, erect beautiful edifices . . . . heal diseases according to the teaching of Christ, and, owing to the strict discipline of keeping their minds pure, are exceedingly prosperous.

The Editor of the *Daily Journal-Press*, of St. Cloud, Minnesota :

Whatever opinions one may have had regarding the doctrine of this church, it must be admitted that its members are splendid, patriotic, law-respecting people.

Judge William G. Ewing :

Christian Science is the Christian religion pure and simple, a religion of works, a nearer approach to the ministering religion that Jesus taught and practised in the accomplishment of his mission to the world than men have known for seventeen hundred years.

Many of the women who have made places for themselves since the freer entrance of their sex into American public life are giving serious thought to Christian Science.

Mrs. Alvin T. Hert, sometime Vice-Chairman of the National Republican Committee:

The constantly increasing preaching of health by various religions is proof of the truth of what Mary Baker Eddy taught. The lives of Christian Scientists expressing this truth are a benefit to mankind which people generally must acknowledge.

Mrs. Mabel Walker Willebrandt, recently Assistant Attorney General of the United States:

The world is now far enough removed from controversy over Mrs. Eddy as a personality to recognize her wholly spiritual conception of the universe and human personality as a world force making toward the betterment and happiness of individual lives, control over adverse environment, and the purification and elevation of even material and human aims and activities.

The Editor of the *Christian Herald*, Stanley High, who was once a member of the staff of *The Christian Science Monitor*:

From my own observation and my own contact with these friends, I am convinced of the very rich fruitage that Christian Science is bringing about in the lives of many people.

Cecil B. DeMille, of the Metro-Goldwyn-Mayer Studios, Hollywood, California, who is not himself a Christian Scientist:

Mrs. Mary Baker Eddy is one of the great benefactors of mankind. She has given to the world one of the great religions. She has interpreted the life and teachings of Jesus

of Nazareth in a manner to prove a blessing to many hundreds
of thousands of souls. She has carried the light of truth into
many dark places. She has perhaps done more to fulfill the
words of the Great Master, himself, than any individual of
recent centuries.

Mark Twain's final reversal of his previous judgment may come as news to many:

Christian Science is humanity's boon. Mother Eddy deserves a place in the Trinity as much as any member of it.
She has organized and made available a healing principle that
for two thousand years has never been employed except as
the merest kind of guesswork. She is the benefactor of the
age.[9]

Although subject all through its history to ridicule
and criticism so unreasonable as sometimes to cross
the line of persecution, Christian Science has gone
steadily on its way. In fact, opposition at the fiercest
has stimulated its growth. In three years alone, following the hue and cry of 1907, the Christian Science
Churches built and paid for almost doubled. The following dates are stepping-stones in its development:

1875, *Science and Health* was published.
1875–1876, The Christian Scientist Association was organized and services were held under its auspices in Lynn.
1879, church organized in Boston under a charter.
1892, church reorganized under unique statute of Massachusetts and with twelve First Members.
1892, the number of churches and societies was 155.
1907, the number of churches and societies was 646.
1910, the number of churches and societies was 1212.
1930, the number of churches and societies is 2451.*

* (and 39 university organizations)

Those who expected that when Mrs. Eddy passed
on (in 1910) Christian Science would soon begin to

dwindle and in the end disappear will note that, from 1910 to 1930, the increase in the number of churches, societies, and university organizations has averaged between five and six a month, and that for ten years past one new church has been dedicated, and paid for, every week.

To those who ask in good faith, "What are representative Christian Scientists like?" the answer is, "Quite like other people." They smile, but not vacuously. Recruited some may be from the discard and the graveyard as well as from the membership rolls of the churches but they never laugh unnaturally like Lazarus in O'Neill's play. They seek peace with all men, because they start with peace in their own hearts. If they look prosperous that can scarcely be surprising since poverty, like sin and sickness, is to them an illusion and, in accordance with Professor William James' well-known law, they tend to become what they believe they are. Christian Scientists are so busy minding their own business that they do not have, and show no disposition to make, any time to interfere with the business of their neighbors. Taught by their faith that "the powers that be are ordained of God," they of course obey their country's laws. Such bad habits as have not already been crowded out by the adoption of this new interest, the economy of Christian Science is designed to correct.

> Moderate tasks and moderate leisure,
> Quiet living, strict-kept measure, —

it is this which Scientists desire. Never are they noisy or disorderly. They do not fret, nor cry aloud.

Drink they regard as an evil, and fleshly. Tobacco is also taboo. Many of them shun coffee and tea. To Christian Scientists the inner dynamo of the God-life furnishes all the energizing man requires. That without any official compulsion they vote "dry" goes without saying. Contact with the sensational in the newspapers is avoided by the habitual reading of their own dignified daily, which the Rt. Hon. H. A. L. Fisher calls "one of the best-informed journals of our time."

In books ephemeral in content, they take little interest. Their reading taste is kept fine by employment upon a literature of lasting worth. None show more liking for good music than Christian Scientists. They travel, and enjoy it, as do others. For small-town gossip, they substitute an interest in world affairs by which they have become internationally minded and intelligent friends of world peace.[10] While the difference between Christian Scientists and other Christians may appear slight, what difference there is matters. It is often an actual redistribution of the emphasis in human relationships.

Dr. Joseph Wood Krutch [11] observes that, with some of the main trends of scientific thought now headed toward religion and of theological thought toward science, the two may pass each other on the road and not know it. But Christian Scientists believe they have the answer to the riddle. They are openly committed to a mutual and peaceful inter-penetration of religion by science, and science by religion, and they would gladly see all Christians of whatever fold commit themselves to the same.

"The love of Christ in the human heart . . .

creates a new, vast world," says the Reverend John
S. Bunting,[12] "in which the spirit of man may live
and move." Christian Scientists make such constant
daily endeavors to live in that world that many of
them, with St. Paul, might say without exaggeration,
"For me to live is Christ."

All this awareness of God, this demonstration of
the power of God to transform, this devotion to the
Bible, this absorption in the Christ, is the product of
what may perhaps be called a priesthood of democracy, fostered now through almost three generations.
Christian Science makes every man responsible for
his own inner life. Helps he may have, not substitutes. If he is to attain the higher salvation which
expresses itself in perfect health of body and mind,
he must "work out (his) own salvation."[13]

Never can the dubious privilege be his of referring
back to a date, immediate or remote, when he was
converted, and of letting it go at that. He cannot
live on a mere date. The manna on which his inner
life is fed has to be gathered fresh every day. Nor
has he any preacher to whom he can look to keep
up his morale. For there is no place in Christian
Science for any human preacher. "The Bible and
the Christian Science textbook are our only preachers," reports the *Christian Science Quarterly*. The
Readers appointed to read the Bible and the textbook
at the Sunday services hold office as a rule no longer
than three years. No Christian Science Church is
given any chance to grow dependent on the personal
popularity of any man, or any woman. A reminder
to "have no ambition, affection, nor aim apart from
holiness"[14] rings ever through the Christian Science

soul. The springs of its democratic priesthood must be replenished from the everlasting hills.

Nor can the Christian Scientist shoulder off his personal responsibility on to any "group." The obligation Jesus laid on Nicodemus rests likewise on him. "Ye must be born again" is an experience every Christian Scientist must undergo. Everyone must heed this necessity, or forfeit his Christian Science birthright.

Has one a bad temper? He must conquer it. Is his mind unclean? He must clean it out. Is he inordinately ambitious? He is the one to use the curb. Is he avaricious? That is an obnoxious form of selfishness which is taboo. A Christian Scientist supports his church whether or not he can afford to keep a car, to have a radio, or even to go much to the movies.

Without pulpit "begging," without resort to church suppers, without any kind of money-raising by indirection, Christian Science has solved the problem of church support. Its members give to their church for but one reason, gratitude. The loosening of the purse strings has sometimes been called the test of faith most commonly — in college student parlance — "flunked." Christian Scientists when subjected to this test — one of several — rarely fail to pass it. Loyal Scientists give generously to their church because of an almost universal belief that their church has bestowed upon them something beyond money, beyond price. The love of Christ constraineth them.[15]

But the method used in raising the budget by The Mother Church is businesslike. The revenues needed are obtained from a nominal per capita tax of not less than one dollar a year, paid by each member; from the Sunday offerings; from the net profits of The Christian Science Publishing Society; and in part from the profits on the founder's writings which go for special expenses in promoting the Cause of Christian Science. In addition, the Church Directors invite contributions for the support of the remarkable philanthropic institutions [16] in operation under Christian Science auspices and for other benevolent causes such as coöperation in relieving distress of famine, fire, or flood. But in no case is the need felt of any strident call for aid; a simple announcement in its periodicals suffices. The money required comes. Indeed, the amount desired is often oversubscribed.

The grateful show their gratitude in every way they can. Christian Scientists are thankful for the healing which soul and mind and body usually receive. Sharing in the expenses of carrying on its enterprises is to them the most natural thing in the world. The Christian Science priesthood of democracy are glad to accept the full measure of their responsibility, and by their gratitude to let the world perceive that they lay it on themselves.

Simplicity is the outstanding characteristic of the Christian Science organization. The Mother Church (The First Church of Christ, Scientist, in Boston) is the hub. Out from the hub radiate spokes so numerous that the organization may appear complex to some outside who do not understand the centralizing character of the hub.

The organization consists of The Mother Church and its branches — either churches, or societies —

located at all points where enough Christian Scientists have collected to be organizable. A group few in number is formed into a society, and then when its growth warrants, into a church. At colleges and universities the members of the faculty and the students who are Christian Scientists may constitute societies. The rank and file of the membership are protected from all sense of isolation by the dual privilege habitually exercised of membership at the same time in both The Mother Church and the branch church near which they chance to live. To insure this amalgamated dualism, but even more to sustain the vital relationship of branch to vine in full vigor, no branch church or society can be formed until a certain number of the petitioners for the establishment of a local organization have already become members of The Mother Church.

The *Manual* of The Mother Church which contains its By-Laws and related deeds and documents, is both the Constitution and the fundamental law of the denomination. The Directors act within its scope. It sets forth the constituent departments and agencies of The Mother Church, including The Christian Science Publishing Society, and provides briefly for the conduct thereof. Branch churches and societies are formed under the *Manual*, which gives general directions for their government. From first to last, however, each church is a democracy, and makes its own by-laws. Provision for the discipline, if need arises, of a member of The Mother Church, also, is made in the *Manual*.

The founder of Christian Science specifically provided the method to be used for the general supervision of her church, after she should pass on. In accordance with the provisions of the *Manual*, which she prepared, the affairs of The Mother Church are in the hands of The Christian Science Board of Directors. In Mrs. Eddy's lifetime the Directors were nominated by her, elected by the Board, and finally accepted by her; now the Board fills its own vacancies. Besides exercising full administrative responsibility over the congregation of The Mother Church in Boston, comfortably filling an edifice which will seat about five thousand, and over a large local Sunday school, the Board oversees the business of the denomination as a whole, taking final action on all applications for Mother Church membership from the entire field, appointing or electing the officers of The Mother Church and the editors and manager of The Christian Science Publishing Society. They certify the accuracy of the list of those qualified to act as practitioners, published in *The Christian Science Journal*, appoint the lecturers, edit their lectures and supervise their work. In the largest sense theirs is the responsibility to guard the integrity of Christian Science and to take whatever measures they consider best, always in line with Mrs. Eddy's instructions, to make it known to the public. Almost identical in personnel with the Trustees under Mrs. Eddy's will, who pass on all questions relating to the issuance of her writings, the Directors establish the policies and exercise a close supervision over all the other literature of Christian Science published by The Christian Science Publishing Society, including its daily newspaper. William P. McKenzie, Fred M. Lamson, and James E. Patton are now serving as the Trustees of The Christian Science Publishing Society, created by a deed of trust executed by Mrs. Eddy in 1898 to carry on the business of the Publishing Society. It regularly publishes the *Christian Science Quarterly Bible Lessons*, *The Christian Science Journal* (monthly), the *Christian Science Sentinel* (weekly), and *The Christian Science Monitor* (daily), besides several periodicals in other languages.

Every Christian Science Church has a Sunday school which is carefully conducted. The large enrollment which is the rule is to the outsider one of the surprises of Christian Science in recent years. The teaching adheres strictly to the fundamental principles enunciated in the Ten Commandments and the Sermon on the Mount, and does this so intelligently that parents not interested in Christian Science — or for that matter in any religion — send their children as years go by in increasing numbers to Christian Science Sunday schools solely for the effective spiritual training they receive under teachers above the average.

The work of instruction for adults is so regulated as to make it available to all interested. There is a Board of Education which selects, instructs, and certifies authorized teachers, subject to the approval of The Christian Science Board of Directors. Selections from the lists of the qualified are made somewhat on a geographical basis so that in all countries there may be teachers conveniently situated to respond to every call for class instruction in Christian Science. Class teaching is particularly desirable for Christian Scientists who wish to practice healing as a vocation. The relation between teacher and pupil usually becomes close: and is strengthened by the annual association meetings and by the opportunities afforded for special consultations.

The Christian Science staff of lecturers are men and women of culture and distinction. They can hold their own in any company. Dignified, gracious, immaculately dressed, they speak with a serious effectiveness, which is free from all strenuousness and emotion. They do not extemporize. Every lecture, before it is given, has to be approved by the Board of Directors. They interest. They instruct. Year by year their work has grown, until to-day it covers not only the English-speaking world but also the Continents of Europe, Africa, South America, Australia, portions of Japan and China, and many islands of the sea. To keep appointments airplanes are often used by them. During the year past two hundred twenty-eight lectures were given in Great Britain and Ireland to 262,000 people; on the Continent to 75,500 people, eighty-seven lectures of which fifty-eight were in German, five in French, and four in Dutch. In Australia, New Zealand, Tasmania, China, Japan, and the Philippine Islands and Hawaii, sixty-four lectures were delivered to 53,000 people. In the United States, Canada, Mexico, West Indies, Bermuda, and the Canal Zone, 3412 lectures to 2,829,000 people. For the first time, a beginning was made also in South America. A total of eight lectures with an attendance of 1920 were delivered in the larger cities of Argentina, Brazil, Chile, and Uruguay.

In general, attendance on the lectures and enthusi-

asm for them increase as the following typical report
would seem to indicate :

I have just returned from a lecture tour of four months
which has taken me all over England, Scotland, and Ireland,
Paris, Geneva, Zurich, and Berne, Switzerland. . . .

The audiences throughout Great Britain, with possibly
two or three exceptions, have been the largest the Scientists
have ever known. An idea as to the numbers of non-Scientists
attending the lectures can be gained from the following :
in the city of Birmingham we had at the lecture twenty-three
hundred people. Certainly not more than eight or nine
hundred in that audience were students of Christian Science
and the rest were, therefore, inquirers.

The crowds in London were so great and so many people
were unable to gain admission to the lectures that six of the
churches decided to give a joint lecture in the Royal Albert
Hall. I lectured there in 1920 to an audience of six or seven
thousand people which only comfortably filled the great
auditorium. At the recent lecture the place was packed to
the roof with an audience estimated between nine and ten
thousand and a thousand or more were said to have been
turned away. It was a most inspiring experience.

The Committee on Publication has grown from
one, functioning from Boston as a center, till now
every State, every country, where there are Christian
Science organizations has its Committee. Their
responsibility is to give correct information through
the press concerning Christian Science, and also to
correct misapprehensions proceeding from other
authorship appearing in print. It would be impossible to over-estimate the service to Christian
Science rendered by these Committees. Developed
for educational purposes, the Committees on Publication have become the medium of better understanding between the public and Christian Scientists.

Much missionary work is done through literature distribution committees, maintained by the local churches and societies. Copies of periodicals used and new are donated by Christian Scientists and are dispensed in various ways. They penetrate to parts of the world where human missionaries could not travel. Railway stations, fire stations, hotels, theaters, and other public places are equipped with containers kept supplied with literature, which thus falls under the eyes of those interested who might not always care to be interviewed. Quantities of *Christian Science Monitors* are put on board ships for the crews at the large ports.

To overpraise *The Christian Science Monitor* would be difficult. It never exploits crime or scandal. Disaster is only an incident in its reports of the day's news. Unhampered by partisan politics or by fear of financial losses, the *Monitor* acts as the purveyor of world information to its readers with such a fine sense of proportion as to be substantially accurate and informing without becoming dull. Nearly half of its readers live two thousand miles and more from Boston, where the *Monitor* is published. The teeming highways of the world are rapidly becoming the streets where dwell its subscribers as well as the channels of its news.[17]

The establishment of The Christian Science Benevolent Association sanatorium in Chestnut Hill [18] marked a step of policy in advance of larger import than at the time could have been foreseen. Mrs. Mary Beecher Longyear, of Brookline, Massachusetts, generously presented to the church, of which she has long been a member, a tract of twenty acres on beautiful Single Tree Hill; and the Directors, in accepting the gift announced the enterprise in the *Christian Science Sentinel* of October 7, 1916. The characteristically modest notice that funds were needed met with an immediate response from all parts of the world. This enabled the sanatorium to be ready for its first guests on October 1, 1919. Approximately one hundred sixty-five can be cared for besides the necessary attendants or associates, including the staff of Christian Science nurses for whom a training school is maintained. The Assembly Hall, where services are held on Sunday morning and Wednesday evening, seats three hundred people. A temporary haven which offers practical assistance toward the healing of sickness and the removal of distress, it has brought peace in a genuine Christian spirit to thousands of deserving people from all corners of the earth. And this year a similar institution has been established on the Pacific Coast.

The same benevolent purpose of looking after Christian Scientists in need and providing a proper environment for them which led to the establishment of the sanatorium at Chestnut Hill has inspired the Directors of The Mother Church to provide a home for elderly Christian Scientists, whose length of service in the cause, good works, or other special circumstances furnish good reason for giving them a comfortable home. Pleasant View, where Mrs. Eddy lived from 1892 to 1908 at Concord, New Hampshire, was chosen for the site — Mrs. Eddy's home having been torn down years before. Again Christian Scientists were informed through the church's literature about the plan. Again the responses were adequate.

The building, which was ready for use on July 15, 1927, is a beautiful structure of Georgian architecture, containing one hundred forty-four bedrooms, and is now occupied by more than one hundred residents from various places.

Like the sanatorium, the Pleasant View Home has beautiful reception rooms, sun parlors, and assembly hall, a well-equipped library, and besides all this some sixty acres of farm land. Farm buildings also and a commodious dairy have been erected and equipped ; and milk, as well as vegetables and fruit in season, is thus supplied. This Pleasant View Home does a great deal more than simply shelter some aged members of the cause. It supplies them also with discriminating care and comfort, artistic surroundings productive of such a happy spirit that they live together like one big harmonious household. Its table — and the same is true of the sanatorium — would do credit to the best hotel.

With no paid preachers, Christian Science does a successful pastoral work. The Readers preach the only Christian Science sermon heard, when on Sundays they read aloud the Scriptures and their text-book. The lecturers aim to explain the larger meaning of the movement and its message to honest inquirers outside, as well as seekers of a still better understanding within Christian Science. It is the office of the teachers to train the smaller groups. The practitioners treat those sick in mind as well as body. They carry everywhere they go the comfort and the consolation of a faith which makes God real to men, leads many to the way-showing Jesus, and turns them into daily Bible readers.

To many now starting on pilgrimage through this volume, Christian Science may already appear to be — as it actually is — simply a reassertion of Christ's teaching that God is Love and Spirit; and that Love and Spirit are adequate to master sickness, sin, and death. All that Christian Scientists have to do is to live up to the teachings to which they are committed and to be loyal to the founder, a woman who never rose too high in all humility to pray:

> Shepherd, show me how to go
> O'er the hillside steep,
> How to gather, how to sow, —
> How to feed Thy sheep;
> I will listen for Thy voice,
> Lest my footsteps stray;
> I will follow and rejoice
> All the rugged way.[19]

CHAPTER II

A RICH GIRLHOOD

Napoleon had gone at last beyond ambition's lure, and family talk in many a New England home was turning toward the slavery issue just emerging above the horizon, when Mary Morse Baker was born to Mark and Abigail Ambrose Baker on July 16, 1821, at Bow, New Hampshire.[1]

More farm than village, Bow, five miles from Concord, then had its own schools and its meetinghouse. As elsewhere in New England, home was reënforced by school and church, as it rarely is in these days when the community bus carries children from many a mile round to the central school of the township, and the Sunday paper keeps at home most of those whom the automobile does not whisk entirely out of range of worship.

Mary Baker's parentage was New England to the backbone, substantial, intelligent, and very religious. The devout mother [2] was preparing both in mind and soul for the coming of her baby girl, and an understanding neighbor joined her in frequent prayer and Bible reading all through the months before the birth of Mary Morse Baker.[3]

Mark Baker,[4] on his part, led his family in daily devotions and in energetic argument for the Church, then over-inclined to Calvinism. It is, therefore,

55

not surprising that in her mature years Mrs. Eddy should have written :

> From my very childhood I was impelled, by a hunger and thirst after divine things, — a desire for something higher and better than matter, and apart from it, — to seek diligently for the knowledge of God as the one great and ever-present relief from human woe.[5]

It was altogether natural too that in her more intimate talks with friends in later years she should indicate that the goodness and mercy which followed her all the days of her life manifested their presence so early that memory all but failed her when she endeavored to recall their first consoling ministries.[6]

One dedicated, like Mary Baker, from her birth to the religious life, would early learn to pray; and when her mother read to her from the Bible that Daniel prayed three times a day, for spiritual good count she prayed seven times a day, chalking down on the shed wall each prayer in succession, for a while as a settled habit.[7] When as young as Samuel, she, like Joan of Arc, heard voices;[8] and only those will minimize the incident who fail to catch the purport of the reply of Joan to the question put by King Charles, "Oh, your voices, your voices. Why don't the voices come to me? I am king, not you."

Joan: "They do come to you; but you do not hear them. You have not sat in the field in the evening listening for them. When the angelus rings you cross yourself and have done with it; but if you prayed from your heart, and listened to the thrilling of the bells in the air after they stop ringing, you would hear the voices as well as I do."

But Mary Morse Baker was never a theorizer, even

Province of
New-Hampshire,

BENNING WENTWORTH, Esq;

Captain-General and GOVERNOUR in Chief, in and over His MAJESTY'S Province of *New-Hampshire* in NEW-ENGLAND, &c.

To *Joseph Baker Gentleman* — Greeting,

BY Virtue of the Power and Authority, in and by His Majesty's Royal Commission to Me granted, to be Captain-General, &c. over this His Majesty's Province of *New-Hampshire*, aforesaid; I do (by these Presents) reposing especial Trust and Confidence in your Loyalty, Courage and good Conduct, constitute, and appoint You the said *Joseph Baker* to be *Captain*

of the Foot Company in the Foot commanded by Major *by the Name of* _____ *in Coll. Lautburns Seacoast Regiment*

You are therefore carefully and diligently to discharge the Duty of a *Captain* in leading, ordering and exercising said *Company* in Arms both inferiour Officers and Soldiers, and to keep them in good Order and Discipline; hereby commanding them to obey you as their *Captain* and your self to observe and follow such Orders and Instructions, as you shall from Time to Time receive from Me, or the Commander in Chief for the Time being, or other your superiour Officers for His Majesty's Service, according to Military Rules and Discipline, pursuant to the Trust reposed in You.

Given under my Hand and Seal at Arms, at Portsmouth, the Twentieth Day of May in the Twenty-first Year of the Reign of His Majesty King GEORGE the Second, Annoq; Domini, 1758.

B Wentworth

By His EXCELLENCY'S
Command
Theodore Atkinson, Secretary

Copyright 1929 by The Christian Science Publishing Society

GOVERNOR BENNING WENTWORTH APPOINTS JOSEPH BAKER CAPTAIN OF THE FOOT COMPANY OF SUNCOOK, NOW PEMBROKE, NEW HAMPSHIRE

Joseph Baker was Mrs Eddy's great grandfather. He married Hannah Lovewell, daughter of the famous Indian fighter, John Lovewell.

while still in pinafores. She was practical as a little girl, and there is on record an early instance of her putting to quick test the immediate availability of prayer. As her mother was bathing Mary's temples to allay the suffering from a fever, she bade Mary pray. The prayerful obedience was followed by "a soft glow of ineffable joy," and the fever quickly subsided.[9]

From the first little Mary Baker wanted and expected to become "somebody." There is evidence that a sense of mission early lodged in her consciousness. As in the cool of many a summer evening in her latter years, she loved to recall for those whom she knew best treasured incidents of the past, she once half humorously described how her sisters used to take her when a tiny child to school with them, and how they would set her during the luncheon hour on a table and would say, "Mary what are you going to do when you grow up?", to which she would reply, "I will write a book."[10]

Not merely did the little girl with blue eyes and chestnut curls say that she expected some day to write a book, she also began to make ready for the task by reading and by thinking. To her most brilliant brother she said, "I must be wise to do it"; and her pastor, evidently a man of insight, predicted for her "some great future."[11]

Evidence abounds that from the first her mind was quick and active. At a time when social usage encouraged girls to be frail of body, or at any rate to appear to be ready on occasion to faint in full accord with all the proprieties, patterns of "the lass with the delicate air," such an alive and acquisitive mind as

Mary Baker's was apt to overtax the body. Nor was the strain lightened by her habit of taking her books home from school and putting them under the pillow in her little trundle bed.[12]

In later years she often referred to these disturbances of her childhood. Whether they indicated an inherent delicacy or the wideness of margin in vigor between mind and body which made her an easy victim to casual discomforts, it was soon found that the noise and confinement of the country school, which she attended with her sisters, wore on her so seriously that her father promptly heeded the family physician who advised, "Do not doctor your child, she has got too much brains for her body; keep her out of doors, keep her in exercise, and keep her away from school all you can, and do not give her much medicine." [13]

Although as a rule mention of her health was incidental with her, as in a letter written at the age of fourteen to her brother George, always there hovered in the background of her thinking an oppressive sense of the precarious equilibrium of adolescent life which had to wait for larger understanding of ways and means of stabilizing till the coming of such men as G. Stanley Hall and S. Weir Mitchell. In *Doctor and Patient*, published in 1888, Dr. Mitchell, already foremost nerve specialist in the land, wrote that "no one knows women who does not know sick women"; and to the end of his distinguished life, he sometimes seemed anxious lest colleges for women should one day prove over-hazardous to their nerves.[14]

The mind of little Mary actively responded to its first strong stimulus when only nine years old. Her brother Albert was home from Dartmouth — from which he was to graduate in 1834 — on his first vacation. Mary adored Albert. He was her knight without fear, above reproach. Nor was she the only one to find in Albert Baker a youth of unusual promise. A political rival later said of him that "gifted with the highest order of intellectual powers, he trained and schooled them by intense and almost incessant study throughout his short life." [15]

The Dartmouth freshman of twenty and his sister of nine found each other on his first vacation. He knew things and books as yet beyond her reach. Her girlhood ecstasy spared no words to make him understand her joyous pride in him, her purpose to deserve his pride in her. "I must be," she said, "as great a scholar as you or Mr. Franklin Pierce." [16] But there is some reason to believe the brother received as well as bestowed. One of Mrs. Eddy's girlhood friends at least implied in a letter written years later that Albert early shared his sister's feeling about the supremacy of the spiritual. [17]

No wonder then that Albert's good-by to Mary as he turned back to college should take the form of earnest counsel to apply herself to her Lindley Murray Reader, with which she was later to become as familiar as with the Westminster Catechism, which her orthodox father and her godly pastor would make sure she learned. [18]

Before me as I write are the very copies of Lindley Murray's *Introduction to the English Reader* and the *English Reader* itself, which Mary Baker read and marked and inwardly digested at the early age of nine.

While eighteenth century writing is admittedly
inferior to Elizabethan literature, it is at least serious
and substantial, more worth while than much of the
bad art and worse ethics which compel attention
to-day on every news stand, in every railway train.
Even in these high days of up-to-dateness, many a
boy and girl could fare worse than at the hands of
Lindley Murray.

Going with Mary Morse Baker on the journey
she took when she was only nine years old through
Lindley Murray's books one finds much of interest.
These books which were published respectively in
1803 and 1813 at Alexandria, Virginia, open with
"Rules and Observations for Assisting Children to
Read with Propriety." Then follow select sentences,
some of them expressing sentiments as wise as those
of Francis Bacon. Interesting narration, sound
moralizing, vivid description, sustained dialogue,
and "promiscuous" pieces make up the rest.

For those expecting to find little Mary at the age
of nine an infant prodigy moping over the pages of
Spinoza and Leibnitz, it is perhaps worth while to
recall that Emma Willard was only that very year
making her first trip to Europe to get acquainted
with the old world thinkers, and that Mary Lyon's
dream of a real school for girls was not to take form
for some six years yet in Mount Holyoke Seminary,
in turn waiting more than fifty years to become
Mount Holyoke College. Mary might perhaps have
been reading Emerson; but Emerson was still young
and too busy getting married and starting his preaching career at the Second Church in Boston to be
writing anything.[19]

From painting by James F. Gilman.

SUNRISE AT BOW

Down the road, now overgrown, Mary Baker and her sisters trudged to the schoolhouse where she spoke her determination to write a book.

On closer inspection the author notes in these two books of Lindley Murray's, no fewer than forty of the better known writers of the eighteenth century quoted, sometimes at great length. Out of a total of four hundred thirty-eight pages in the two books, Goldsmith has twenty and one-half pages, Addison twenty-one, Pope nine and one-half, Cowper seven, Hume five and one-fourth, Thomson ten and one-half, Cotton eleven and one-half, Milton four and one-half, Samuel Johnson seven and one-half, Young four, Wordsworth three, More three, Lord Chesterfield three, Benjamin Franklin two, Robertson four; with some shorter contributions from Socrates, Horace, Sallust, Cicero, Marcus Aurelius, Plato.[20]

All through the two books the Bible appears in the King James Version or in paraphrase.

In these sophisticated days the choice might fall on more diversified passages from eighteenth century literature than little Mary Baker read; but they would not perhaps be more representative of eighteenth century writing. Most significant is the evidence that she did read and reread them till they were so deeply embedded in her memory that sometimes they reappeared automatically in her own later speech and writing, possibly, as is familiar to all acquainted with modern psychology, unconsciously to point a moral or adorn a tale.[21]

Her marginal markings in the books reveal three of her girlhood tastes in reading:

First, she was always interested in everything about the social niceties. She dwells much on Chesterfield's canons of good breeding. Her pencil often marks such sentences as "Awkwardness can proceed but from two causes; either from not having kept good company, or from not having attended to it." [22] Her love of preciseness in speech, which several near her in later years have emphasized to the author and her many letters before him as he writes confirm, appears in this passage:

To begin a story or narration, when you are not perfect in it, and cannot go through with it, but are forced, possibly, to say in the middle of it, " I have forgotten the rest," is very unpleasant and bungling. One must be extremely exact, clear, and perspicuous, in everything one says; otherwise, instead of entertaining or informing others, one only tires and puzzles them. The voice and manner of speaking, too, are not to be neglected. Some people almost shut their mouths when they speak, and mutter so, that they are not to be understood; others speak so fast, and sputter, that they are equally unintelligible. Some always speak as loud as if they were talking to deaf people; and others so low that one cannot hear them. All these, and many other habits, are awkward and disagreeable, and are to be avoided by attention. You cannot imagine how necessary it is to mind all these things. I have seen many people, with great talents too; and others well received, only from their little talents, and who had no great ones.[23]

Second, a fine balance of interest in the moral and the spiritual at the early age of nine is one of the surprises which her copies of Lindley Murray give us. Already the Bible was the Book of Books to her. It furnished her many a precept on which she relied for self-direction in her personal contacts. The sentences from Proverbs which follow, not merely marked, but also numbered with her pencil, are commended to the consideration of the adolescent of to-day:

He that hath no rule over his own spirit is like a city that is broken down, and without walls.

Happy is the man that findeth wisdom. Length of days is in her right hand; and in her left hand, riches and honor. Her ways are ways of pleasantness, and all her paths are peace.

Faithful are the wounds of a friend; but the kisses of an enemy are deceitful. Open rebuke is better than secret love.

Third, at an age when a girl's interest is usually confined to dolls, little Mary was beginning to take a lively interest in patriotic matters. Lindley Murray goes back to the time in which the Louisiana Purchase was sowing the seeds of discord over slavery. It was a year before Abigail Ambrose Baker was praying for her unborn baby that Maine, neighbor to New Hampshire, was admitted to the union as a "free state" and Missouri also came in, but on terms so questionable that John Quincy Adams read in the historic Compromise of 1820 the "title page to a great tragic volume."

A family of consequence,[24] the Bakers read the papers of the day, particularly the *New Hampshire Patriot and State Gazette* and talked over what they read in the living room.[25] Mary listened in and also joined in. Young as she was, she read the papers both for herself and also to the household. From her little trundle bed at night, as Mark Baker puzzled over the latest news from Washington, Mary would call out, "Father, I know what you are doing: You are reading the newspaper," to which he would reply, "Hush, child, and go to sleep." Then she would say, "I'll read it to you," and though she could not yet pronounce the longer words, she satisfied her father.[26]

These two books of Lindley Murray have much to

say concerning slavery of every sort.   The verses of
Cowper and of Addison on the subject are elaborately
marked by this little girl.   For books published in
Alexandria, Virginia, before the Missouri Compromise, the four articles Lindley Murray quotes on
slavery, significant enough in themselves, become
more so as one reads the following paragraph with
the marginal pencilings of Mark Baker's daughter :

*** It may not be improper to remind the young
reader, that the anguish of the unhappy negroes,
on being separated for ever from their country
and dearest connections, with the dreadful pros-
pects of perpetual slavery, frequently becomes
so exquisite as to produce derangement of mind,
and suicide.**

If already, as she tells us in her writings, Mrs. Eddy
took to verse more readily than to prose and thus laid
herself open to the criticism that her verse was stilted
and bathetic, it may not be amiss to remind ourselves
that the same things are still said of Dryden and of
Pope, whose "couplet," however, was to remain the
model for imitation by succeeding poets until well
along in the nineteenth century.   All through her
life, the strong impression which measured speech
thus early made on the girl's mind endured.   But it
was John Dryden, and not Mrs. Eddy, who wrote
such couplets as :

> Him of the western dome, whose weighty sense
> Flows in fit words and heavenly eloquence.

It was Alexander Pope, and not Mrs. Eddy, to
whom belongs the couplet :

> His soul proud Science never taught to stray
> Far as the solar walk or milky way.

The conclusion to which these small particulars cumulatively point is that Mary Morse Baker was having a normal girlhood. She was the social center in every youthful neighborhood gathering. She loved and quarreled and made up with her sisters and brothers, and with her other boy and girl companions. She read much, and often "took her pen in hand." One of her first incursions into verse was occasioned by the removal of her family from Bow to Sanbornton Bridge. She found parting with her young friend, Andrew Gault,[27] such sweet sorrow that in Popean style she left for him this farewell verse:

> Hard is the task to take a final leave
> Of friends whom we shall see ah! never
> With unaccustomed grief my bosom heaves
> And burns with latent fire forever.
>
> A vernal feeling thrills my very breast
> And scarce the accustomed word is spoken
> We firmer grasp the hand still loath to part
> And wish that grasp might never be broken.
>
> But go — those finer feelings riven
> Which through my bosom shot
> And with the take this flower of Heaven
> The flower forget-me-not.[28]

In letter writing more clearly than in verse making, Mary Baker revealed her girlhood self. The earlier letters, in common with other letters of the time, appear somewhat self-conscious here and there. The spelling at the first is markedly informal, as is evident; so too was the spelling of George Washington until the end.[29] Now and then the characteristic sense of more or less complete isolation apt to be the experience of the sensitive adolescent is revealed along with its conventional concern about her health. But taken in their entirety, the letters which she wrote between her fourteenth and her sixteenth year throw sufficient light on that formative period in her life to convince a keen appraiser like Isaac F. Marcosson that they represent a "find of genuine historic value."[30]

Her first letter extant — the second she says she ever composed — was written September 7, 1835, at Bow to her brother, George Sullivan Baker, whom she loved to call "Sullivan," then living at Wethersfield, Connecticut. It simply expresses the affection of a fourteen-year-old girl for an older brother and her eagerness to have his counsel in all her concerns.

There is one thing if I have not improved it aright I have lerned from expperience to prize more perhaps than ever I did *before* that is *Dear brother* the *friendly advice* and *council* you was ever giving me and the lively interest you ever manifested in my welfare but now when I sit down to my *lonely* meal I have no brother Sullivan to encourage me as formerly — but there is no philosophy in repining I must extend the thought of benevolence farther than selfishness would permit.[31]

The next letter, dated May 2, 1836, from their new home (then Sanbornton Bridge, renamed Tilton in 1869) to the same brother refers to him as "brother S. at Conn." and also makes mention of the more gifted Albert:

My Dear brother
    We have just finished our morning vocations, and I am engaged in the sweet emplyment of writing (or rather talking) to brother S. at Conn, and to comply with good *ton*, I shall first enquire for your health, spirits, and the like of that, hoping time sill continues to glide smoothly as in former years, it continues to do so with us only when we are obligeed

to ride in a *wagon* and then it is rough. . . . I hope after I read the book you sent us, I shal becom some what more civilized in my presant state of ignorance I cannot express the gratitude I feell for the presants you sent us by Mr. C., they meet a weelcom recepttion you may depend, although I should much rather have seen the original. You cannot imagin the disappointment I felt on receiveing your letter that you should not return, but I hope it will not be long before I shal again see you, do not disappoint me but come and see us if you cannot stay. We received a letter from Albert not long seince, he informed us he had written to you but had received no answer. Mother wishes to be remembered to you with all the kindness of parental love, but none more sincerely than your Sister

Mary.[32]

Another letter which was written to "Sullivan," December 20, 1836, is alive with happy references to those she loves. The election of Franklin Pierce to the United States Senate calls forth proud comment on the prospect of even closer relations between Albert and the future President. After a reference to the illness of her "Uncle Baker," she runs on about affairs in this fashion:

We attended a party of young Ladies at Miss Hayes last evening she was truly sorry our Brother from Conn. was not there, but she is soon to be married and then the dilemma will close as it is your fortune to have some opposeing obstacle to extricate you. Oh brother I wish I could see you, and I hdly think Abby and I would be as sleepy as we wer the last night you spent with us; but could amuse ourselvs (if not you) by telling you things that would excite laughter if nothing more, but when are we to realize this this happiness? I am impatient to learn soon verry soon I hope: but if we are not to see you soon, to hear of your health and prosperity is a pleasure that none but those to whom we are most nearly can experience. But I must obey Mothers motto to be spry —

and hasten to a close with executing her commissions to give her love to Sulivan — hoping you will receive the same from us all not forgetting to tender it to Mr. Cutchins.

Write soon Dear brother and excuse the *unpardonable sin* of our writing so often but do retaliate if you have any resentment in writing to us. Pardon all mistakes for I am in hast and accept the well wishes of yours truly

Mary M. Baker.[33]

Spring was in the air when April 17, 1837, Mary, now near sixteen, writes "Sullivan" a long letter, more illustrative than ever of her widening interests and her growing sense of humor. She says:

It is a little funny, I will give you an abridged sketch of a gentleman recently from Boston, now reading medicine with a doctor of this town, a *perfect complet gentleman I met him a number of times at parties last* winter he inviteed me to go to the shakers [34] with him but my superiors thought it would be a profanation of the sabbathe; and I accordingly did not go. But I have since then attended a wedding with a Mr. Bartlett he was goomsman and I bridsmaid; we had a fine time I assure you.

Referring to her sister Martha's illness she adds — as though foreseeing later years, "I should think her in a confirmed consumption *if I would admit the idea*, but it may not be so, at least I hope not."

To "Sullivan" the news may not be altogether welcome that "Father has been speculating of late, . . . he has swaped your favourite horse with Mr. Rogers. And he thinks it a fine trade."

The writing master is urging the Baker girls to join his village class, writes Mary, "but Martha is not able and I have not wherewith." And she closes her long letter thus:

Write soon dear Brother and give me all the good advice you

can for yours is the genuine growth of experience don't forget
but remember the solicitation of your affectionate

Mary [35]

The letter which she wrote home when she was
paying her first real visit to another town, Haverhill,
evidently belongs to her sixteenth year. She was
then, as a friend in later years recalled, frail and
fair with "brilliant blue eyes, cheerful, hopeful, and
enthusiastic," [36] as this letter's account of the many
impressions made on her will show:

My dear Brother:
Since I left you I have made it a religious duty to obey
you in *all things*. And today, according to promise, write
you the order of exercises since Wednsday — I reached here
about 6 o'clock P.M. was the only passenger inside, and such a
sky-rocket adventure I never had; some times I really thought
I was at least *midway* between heaven and earth, till the
driver's shrill whistle, or a more tolerable road would restore
my senses; Mr. Hale is the very most polite good natured
driver in the *whole world* (As *I have seen it all*) and was very
kind to me on your account I suppose — You cannot know
how *lame* and unwell I felt *yesterday;* Augusta would sleep
with me the first night, and kept me awake so long after we
retired, I did not rest much, if any, that night. Yesterday
in the afternoon, we both took off our dresses and went *to
bed* — I rested some, and to-day am as well as usual — have
not been any where. Augusta and *all* want me to stay here until
commencement And then attend with them, but there is
so much to excite me here, and such a teazing etiquette in
this vill. it is not best for my health And I go to L. to-night
— *God bless you*

Mary [37]

G. Stanley Hall's words,

"that bright girls of good environment of eighteen or
nineteen, or even seventeen, have already reached the above-
mentioned peculiar stage of first maturity, when they see the

world at first hand, when the senses are at their very best,
their susceptibilities and their insights the keenest, tension
at its highest, plasticity and all-sided interests most developed,"

would appear from the letters [38] to be presented next
an almost photographic likeness of Mary Baker at
that age.

Her interest in books is now spreading and deepening. She writes her friend, Augusta Holmes: [39]

My dear Augusta, Have you Surwalt's gramar? If so,
would you do me the favour to loan it to me for a short time?
I am told it is easier than Levizac's — at least if it is not I
shall have the *horrors* worse than last evening — *after you left*
are you well, and did you return safely? but answering echo
must reply to this. Much love to Abi- As ever your aff

Mary

P.S. In looking over some books yesterday I spied an *essay*
I think must be *yours* will forward it the first opportunity.

Even in inviting Augusta to a "party" Mary's
eagerness for books vies with her enthusiasm for the
party. In a postscript longer than the invitation
she writes: "You will please to bring along with you
that favourite book of mine, — entitled, *Forget me
not*, I have not had an opportunity to send to Concord for one yet."

A few weeks later Mary Baker is reading Byron's
Corsair and *Manfred;* but not as yet, she says, *The
Prisoner of Chillon*. Incidentally she wonders if her
friend ever sees (Godey's) *Lady's Book*, forerunner of
The Ladies' Home Journal, and sharing with *Graham's
Magazine* the interest of young women of about that
day.[40]

Illness almost drops out of this buoyant correspondence with Augusta. Even the occasional

"molting" spells by which girls up to the nineteenth century often sought to win attention are dismissed with the remark, "I am low spirited occasionally, as you know I am subject to such 'fits'!"

At a Methodist revival, which lasted five long weeks at Sanbornton Bridge, while Mary Baker was interested, she evidently had her doubts in some instances as to whether conversion had gone beyond the talking stage, shown by "the *marvelous* James Smith! Your *crazy correspondent* was correct, so far as pretensions warrant; he professes to have religion, and so far succeeded in *exhausting* that interesting and exalted subject, I grew weary and retired."

She hastens to describe the meetings themselves as "very interesting." Entertaining friends and relatives — the Bakers had many — who drove in from miles around to attend the daily services, involved Mary and her family in much "extra labor." She hopes Augusta will forgive her for neglecting to write oftener, and would have her know that almost all her

acquaintances are now rejoicing in the hope set before them of higher aims and nobler joys. The sceptic's scoff, and the ribaldry of the multitude is scarcely left among us. I will mention some of your particular acquaintances who have experienced a change indeed since you were here *Esqr. Cate & wife*, Mr. Curry, wife, and *two daughters* Mr. Wingate. *N. Atkinson.* J. Tilton Mr. BARTLETT, Mr. Carr & wife My sister, Mrs. Tilton; with a hundred of others, I cannot mention, and with whom I am unacquainted. Would that you were here to witness with me this changed scene! tho I *fear* for *some*, I rejoice with *many*, whom I doubt not possess the " pearl " which is priceless And do you not also rejoice with me if it were but for *one* sinner that hath repented? Doubtless as you feared, there are some who have deceived *themselves* by " zeal without knowledge " — But methinks we have less to fear from fanaticism, than from stoicism; when a question is to be decided that involves our weal, or woe, for *time* and *eternity*.[41]

Everything of concern to Augusta is of concern to Mary. She ardently hopes:

that the friendship which has existed between us, is founded upon a basis too solid to be shaken by trifles. How many friendships (so called, but sadly miscalled) have such a foundation that a mere word is sufficient to dissolve them forever. But I *hope* such will not be the case with us. If we each possess a forgiving spirit, much pain may be spared us.

Almost a century later, reading Mrs. Eddy's own copy of Hugh Black's *Friendship*, published in 1898, the author is not surprised to find her little blue pencil underlining the words: "friendship in its essence is spiritual. It is the free, spontaneous outflow of the heart, and is a gift from the great Giver."

When Augusta's father died Mary wrote April 9, 1840:

It must be a great affliction to be deprived of the watchful care and guardianship of a kind and tender father. But Augusta, there is one who has promised to be a "father to the fatherless," and if we go to him, we shall indeed find consolation. Have you not been enabled in this time of sorrow and distress to cast all your care upon Him who careth for us? I believe you once told me that you had a hope in Christ. If so you will not need to turn to the world for comfort, and for balm for your wounded heart, for in Christ "all fulness dwells."

Already her love of nature leads her in visiting Boston to single out Mount Auburn and Cushing's garden as "delightful places." "Nahant is also a beautiful place . . . refreshingly cool, and the prospect is certainly delightful." Augusta's description of Haverhill is, Mary writes, "indeed interesting to me, for I well remember your love for what was wild or picturesque in nature."

Late in February as the sap begins to flow, Mary facetiously promises to "magnetize a letter with '*sap sugar*' and send you." [42] Bits of human, harmless gossip impart homely touches here and there to the correspondence. Mary wrote:

I rec'd letters a few weeks since from Miss Balch & Greenough. Miss G— was then at Salisbury on a visit to an aunt. She thinks of going to Ipswich this summer to school. Miss Balch expects to go somewhere, had not decided where. I rec'd a letter from Miss Burnham in Jan. & am expecting another daily. She was then attending school at R — Miss L. Howard wrote me last week. She has been attending a singing-school & dancing-school. She wrote that Miss Sheed is engaged, and that Caroline Dean received letters from George A. Merrill, who, by the way, is now at Boston. Miss Sutherland's father has been very sick. I have heard that Miss Delano is preparing in all possible haste to be married next autumn. I cannot vouch for the truth of it, for I believe but few reports that I hear " now a-days," I think if every one would be cautious in reporting flying stories, a great deal less of falsehood would be spoken. I have not heard from Elisabeth Noyes for a long time. I have expected a letter for more than a week. I cannot write more now, for I must write a letter to our daughter Betsy this P.M. I rec'd one from her week before last. Her school has closed. Please to write soon, if you can take the trouble. I have written in great haste.

The one subject of which happy girls are sure to talk is not absent from these letters. Mary teases Augusta about "*Enoch.*" "Mr. Noyes," she admits, had called on her, but simply "to be polite." Augusta Holmes will care to hear that "Mr. Lawrence is inquiring where 'Miss Holmes' is now," and Mr. L.

had made "an incoherent speech about 'Diana.'"
She would have Augusta "say something *nice*" to
"Mr. Dickey" in her name. She admits she would
be willing to share with her friend the high responsibility of "making *cold* hearted *man* raise his standard
of female excelence, still higher." But "as to my
being married, I don't begin to think much of that
'decisive step,' neither do I intend to be 'married' at
present. I am sure, I feel as though I should like
my liberty a while longer."

But it was to be only a little while. Mary Morse
Baker was now in her early twenties. George
Washington Glover was heading her way.

CHAPTER III

FINDING HERSELF

The Christmas spirit was already in the air when Mary Baker was given in marriage to George Washington Glover on Tuesday, December 10, 1843. The wedding guests, from Concord and Boston, as well as from Sanbornton Bridge and from the surrounding country, came in sleighs to the little farmhouse, a mile and a half from the town. All the other Baker children were there, Samuel, George, Abigail, and Martha, except Albert, whose lovable character and whose brief career of rich promise had kept the family grief green for two years.

Samuel brought with him from Boston his new wife, previously a missionary to the Indians. From Concord came Martha with her husband, Luther C. Pillsbury. Abigail, more sure of herself than ever because six years before she had made the best marriage in the Baker family, brought her husband, Alexander H. Tilton. The father's and the mother's cup of joy was now full with the sight of the family they had founded starting well in life.

Mary Baker looked her best. Past twenty-two, she was drawing near to wifehood.[1] George Glover was no stranger. Collaterally related and once of Concord, he had learned the building trade in Boston with Samuel Baker, and for four years had been making for himself a place in Charleston,[2] South

Carolina.   On a former visit to Boston he had run up
to Tilton with his friend, Samuel, and had left his
heart with Mary Baker, who was eleven years his
junior.   An impetuous wooer,[3] scant delay intervened
till the day when the long loved pastor of the Baker
family, Corban Curtice, made the two one.[4]

The wedding night was spent at Concord, and the
next day the bride and groom drove up to Bow for a
fitting farewell to the birthplace of the bride.[5]   Then
Mr. and Mrs. George W. Glover set sail from Boston
for their new home in the South.   There were no
domestic storms to mar the honeymoon, but the ship
did run into heavy weather, and on Christmas Day
the gale was so severe that even the captain became
alarmed.

Mrs. Eddy in her later years related to Miss
Shannon, Mr. McKenzie, and Mr. Tomlinson this
almost tragic experience.   She told them how after
she and her new husband knelt in their cabin and
prayed to God to save them, in a short time the wind
subsided and she, as always in a crisis, gave God
the credit.   The captain also was so impressed with
the sudden cessation of the storm that he called it
"a miracle."[6]

Young Mrs. Glover was not the first bride — nor
yet the last — to find a sea voyage little conducive
to the happiness of the honeymoon.   A penciled
note in Mrs. Eddy's handwriting on the margin of
her old scrapbook records that she "was hopelessly
seasick."   The letter of counsel which her mother
had given them to ponder when halfway on their
voyage, she was scarcely in a mood to read with the
storm adding its aggravation to her discomfort.   But

of her husband she writes, "When I grew better" I "saw the tears wet on his cheek," as he read what her mother had given him under seal to be opened "when we were midway on our journey South."

Normal mothers are torn between tears and smiles when they see a daughter whom they love passing into the most complex experience which ever comes to a woman. But they rarely show the tender forethought of Mrs. Glover's mother in counseling the man to whom she gives her daughter to take heed of Mrs. Sigourney's verse, popular in those days on both sides of the Atlantic; and we of these more prosaic times may perhaps overlook the sentimentality of a less sophisticated age.

Deal gently, thou, when, far away,
'Mid stranger scenes her feet shall rove,
Nor let thy tender cares decay —
The soul of woman lives on love;
And should'st thou, wondering, mark a tear
Unconscious from her eyelid break,
Be pitiful, and soothe the fear
That man's strong heart can ne'er partake.

A mother yields her gem to thee,
On the true breast to sparkle rare —
She places 'neath thy household tree
The idol of her fondest care;
And by trust to be forgiven,
When judgment wakes in terror wild,
By all thy treasured hopes of heaven,
Deal gently with my darling child.

Then, as now, the approach from the sea to Charleston was attractive. Josiah Quincy of Boston who made the same trip not long before left record in his diary:

This Town makes a beautiful appearance as you come up to it, and in many respects a magnificent one. I can only say in general that in grandeur, splendor of buildings, decorations, equipages, numbers, commerce, shipping and indeed everything, it far surpasses all I ever saw, or ever expect to see in America.[7]

And the Philadelphian, Owen Wister, in his *Lady Baltimore* called Charleston "the most appealing, the most lovely, the most wistful town in America."

Not even in Boston, or in Philadelphia, was the pursuit of culture for its own sake keener than in Charleston, when Mrs. Glover arrived. Had she stayed long enough, Mrs. Glover might have been admitted to *The Southern Review*, then the leading literary journal of the South. Or she might have made the acquaintance of Edward Malbone whose minatures on ivory were already taking high place in the world of art.[8] She might even, had she remained long enough, have been invited to attend one of the concerts of the St. Cecilia Society, the most exclusive social club in all the land. Save for the fact that John C. Calhoun was in that same year to leave for Washington to become Secretary of State to President Tyler, she might, after establishing herself securely in Charleston society, have contemplated the possibility at least of measuring swords over the question of slavery with the man then dominating South Carolina.

Mary Baker Glover chose to turn as usual toward the moral, and this meant the particular issue to which her attention was most sharply called by her transfer to Southern soil. Already in her Tilton life, she had observed the slavery question dividing families.

Her father was a Northern Democrat who, like Franklin Pierce, was in favor of letting slavery alone. Still mindful of her early training in the Lindley Murray [9] *Reader* — the influences of which in her life have often been overlooked — Mary Baker Glover took a stand stoutly against slavery. As practiced in Charleston it only deepened her conviction that slavery was too wrong for talking to make it right. The simplicity of the negroes appealed to her, and their religious earnestness touched her heart. It is on record that she once drove up to a little chapel where negroes were at worship and listened to them express "their trust in God and Jesus Christ their only Saviour from slavery." [10]

There may be room for differences of opinion concerning some other of Mrs. Eddy's views; but nobody who knows whereof he speaks can question that from childhood till the day she looked out for the last time from her Chestnut Hill window this woman believed with all her heart and soul that "All God's Chillun's Got Wings."

Never in her long life was Mary Baker Eddy content to stop with anything so unaggressive as mere opinions. Her opinions soon climbed up into convictions. Quick to catch the point, she never remained long the noncommittal spectator cautiously and objectively weighing evidence. She soon became the passionate and prophetic proponent of profound conviction. No grays crept into the warp and woof of her mentality. The scarlet thread of spiritual conviction ran conspicuously and unweariedly through all the thinking of the fourscore years and ten of her extraordinary life.

But there were circumstances during those first weeks in Charleston by which the young bride from the North was somewhat handicapped. Her husband for a newcomer was a man of some consequence; for in barely four years he had built up a business already past the stage of promise, and "possessed real estate of considerable value."[11] Among these assets, however, were a few slaves, readily accepted in payment of debts at a time when slaves passed as current coin.

His wife would have had her husband free his slaves at once but he had lived in Charleston long enough to be well aware of the difficulties in the way. Not only was there local condemnation with which to reckon; there was also a State law, passed in 1820, before Mrs. Glover's birth, which forbade the formal freeing of slaves except by special act of Legislature. Though the ardent young wife could not but admit that her husband had no power in the circumstances to do her will, one thing at least to her seemed possible and that she did in spite of all the admonitions of expediency. Under a pen name she pointed out the inherent wrongness of slavery in a local paper which drew from its rival a query, not at all courteous, as to the identity of "that damned Yankee"[12] who had come to Charleston to rob people of their property. Thus early giving evidence in the South, as had been her habit in the North, of living up to her convictions, she clinched the point as soon as the passing of her husband gave her the sole power so to do by letting her slaves "go free without any formal act of emancipation."[13]

February 1844 found her accompanying him on a

business trip to Wilmington, North Carolina, where an epidemic of yellow fever was then in full swing. And George Glover was soon laid low by it. His brother Masons — for he ranked high in Masonry — attended his sick bed, where Mrs. Glover also would have been, but that both the doctor and the Masons forbade her, realizing that she was soon to become a mother.

But what she could not do with loving hands she tried to do with prayer; and to such purpose that it drew from the doctor the remark that George Glover would have died earlier but for his praying wife.

The dying man's last words were a pathetic plea to his brother Masons to see his wife safe to her home in the North.[14] Faithful to their trust, they laid their brother's form to rest with the full Masonic ritual in the cemetery of St. James' Episcopal Church at Wilmington. During the weeks that followed they gave the grieving widow tender care while, with their counsel, she salvaged what she could of her husband's estate, informally allowed the slaves, now hers alone, to go free, and under Masonic escort made the journey to New York where her brother, George, was waiting to greet her.[15]

In August Mrs. Glover was once more under the Baker roof. For her, romance was at an end. No care her childhood home could give was compensation for the piteous completeness of her loss. The tender grace of a day that was dead would never come back to her. In a nature so vital as Mrs. Glover's, love would awake again. This was as inevitable as it was desirable. The life urge was not buried. The life urge cannot be. It knows no grave.   But the men who came into her life in after years never evoked what she gave George Glover during those six months of happy expectation that their marriage would run the usual appointed course, with children playing round, with home ties growing stronger, and sweet responsibilities heavier.

Motherhood was near.   Her whole being was making ready for it.   As the autumn opened she said good-by to that high spot which Charleston represented, in the verse :

> For trials past I would not grieve,
>   But count my mercies o'er ;
> And teach the heart Thou has bereaved,
>   Thy goodness to adore,
> Thou gavest me friends, in my distress,
>   Like manna from above ;
> Thy mercy ever I'll confess,
>   And own a Father's love.[16]

Born September 12, 1844, her son was named George Washington Glover, II, for his father. Childbirth all but plucked life from her body.   For a time her family gravely doubted whether she would survive.   Not even her stout-hearted father thought she would ever regain strength enough to nurse her child and bring him up.   In his own arms Mark Baker carried little George to a nursing mother at a neighbor's home, where shortly before one of twins, newly born, had died, and Mrs. Glover's baby was therefore welcome.[17]

Recovery from this, her first and only childbirth, was long delayed, and during this period Mary Baker Glover herself needed as tender care as any baby.   Mahala Sanborn, the blacksmith's daughter, became her faithful nurse. Even so, Mark Baker, whose heart was as big and active as his mind, used for hours at a time to hold his nerve-racked daughter in his arms and rock her gently to and fro, enforcing silence in the house; and with rare forethought taking the precaution to deaden the clatter made by passers-by, he strewed the road outside with straw and tanbark.[18] If in her girlhood there had been clashes of will between the strong-minded father and the even stronger-minded daughter, now in her extremity there was nothing left but the devotion of an anxious father and the confident dependence of a frail daughter on a father's strength.

The story of those years of widowhood can be quickly told. Mrs. Glover, try as she would, and did, found herself not vigorous enough to care for the little boy she had brought into the world and always dearly loved.[19] He was left too much for his best interest to the company of his good nurse and her indulgent associates. Attractive and precocious, in the circumstances his spoiling was inevitable.

Changes, too, were making in the Baker home. Mark Baker, growing every year more prosperous, now built a comfortable house in Tilton and moved his family to town.[20] George Baker married and departed for Baltimore to start a branch of the successful mills owned by Abigail's husband in Tilton. About the time Mrs. Glover might have given the measure of care which one so frail would naturally bestow on the child she loved, her mother, whom they all adored, fell ill and after six months passed away. Mrs. Glover sat down the morning after, November 22, 1849, and wrote to her brother George:

My Dear Bro':

This morning looks on us bereft of a Mother! Yes, that angel on earth is now in Heaven! I have prayed for support to write this letter, but I find it impossible to tell you particulars at this time. She failed rapidly from the time you saw her, but her last struggles were most severe; her physician spoke of it as owing to so strong a constitution. Oh! George, what is left of earth to *me!* But oh, my Mother! She has *suffered long with me;* let me then be willing she should now *rejoice,* and I bear on till I follow her. I cannot write more. My grief overpowers me. Write to me.

Your affec' Sister,
(Signed) Mary.

Died last night at half-past seven o'clock; will be buried next Saturday. I wish you could be here.[21]

The coming into the home next year of a stepmother left the young mother in an awkward predicament. There was no room any longer in her own mother's house for the frail young widow. When a stepmother comes, even one as kindly as was Elizabeth Patterson Duncan, there is rarely room in any home for such a charge. The situation was not to be evaded. Something had to be done about it. Mrs. Glover had no private means. She had flung away her only potential assets when in Charleston at the call of conscience she had freed her slaves. She was not well enough to earn a living for herself. She did the best she could. She wrote for the weekly papers; but this, as usual, brought a precarious income. She tried teaching, but teaching proved to be a makeshift — a poor one at that.

Her sister, Abigail, expressed a willingness to receive Mrs. Glover into the comfortable Tilton home; but as she had a somewhat younger boy of her own there seemed no room even in that ample house for little George, who had in consequence to go with Mahala Sanborn, by this time Mrs. Russell Cheney, to live in Groton, forty miles away.

Mrs. Glover had no alternative. If her life with her generous, but dominating, sister did not prove satisfactory to either, perhaps it could not be. The situation was impossible. No family roof is wide enough to cover long an adult dependent of different habits and ideals. Mrs. Glover, still frail in body, often confined to her bed, was, however, mentally independent and spiritually resourceful. Beholden, of necessity, for bed and board to Abigail, who was herself under much nerve strain, due to hernia,[22] Mrs. Glover saw no reason for subservience also to her sister's intellect. There had never been a time — no matter how young she was — when she had not done her own thinking. She knew no reason why, amid the new conditions, she should not continue to think for herself.

In the nation, the irrepressible conflict was steadily moving on to its climax. Down in Washington, Henry Clay was now espousing the adoption of the Compromise of 1850 to avert open war. Daniel Webster who was born and spent his earlier life in Boscawen, twelve miles from Tilton, threw in his lot with Clay, and made his Seventh of March Speech not without the forlorn hope of inducing the South to help him to the nomination for the Presidency.

Many a substantial home became a hotbed of discussion. The Tiltons one day turned a community reception, given in their home, into a political discussion. Graceful and attractive in spite of her delicate health, Mrs. Glover assisted Mrs. Tilton in receiving. But she kept out of the discussion until one of the guests openly insisted on hearing what she thought concerning slavery. She replied, with her Charleston days in mind, that the South as well as the North suffered rather than benefited from the continuance of slavery and its spread to other States; that the election of Franklin Pierce would involve the whole country in fiercer and more menacing disputes; and that victory for him would therefore be good neither for the North nor for the South.

With the Tiltons and the Bakers siding with the Northern Democrats, and in a community so divided that some of its members as late as 1865 illuminated their homes when news came of Lincoln's assassination, Mrs. Glover's words created consternation. Mrs. Tilton is reported to have said in protest, "Mary, do you dare to say that in my house?"

"I dare to speak what I believe in any house," [23] was the decisive reply she received, uttered with dignity.

Mrs. Tilton, with that strange disposition observable in some families to force on blood relations the adoption of group opinions, a policy which in friendship's circles is tabooed by conventional courtesy, would have constrained her sister to think as well as live like her. But during the three years that followed, Mrs. Glover held her own in all their repetitious discussions, even though that course could scarcely have promoted household harmony. Mrs. Tilton's persistence, however, lasted to the end; for when she reached threescore years and ten she wrote her sister, by that time famous, a letter so little to her credit as

to be hardly fair to quote, to which Mrs. Eddy
replied :

How my heart goes out to you in sorrow that you are not
filling the last pages of your life with better thoughts, motives,
and aims. May our dear Father forgive you and fill you
with the sweet peace that I find in His love.

Through the long nine years that followed the
experience of childbirth, Mrs. Glover suffered from ill
health, which persisted almost unbroken until she
was in middle life. The symptoms were different
from the earlier adolescent disturbances. All
through her correspondence until well on into the
sixties mention of these symptoms now and then
recurs as a matter of course. The nervous agitation
which her father had quieted by taking her into his
arms, her sister endeavored to allay by putting up a
swing in her bedroom, forerunner of the chair swing
in which in later years at Pleasant View she liked to
sit on summer evenings, rocking back and forth,
while passing in review for the entertainment of her
house friends various episodes of her earlier days.

Seldom after George was born can she be said to
have rested well. She suffered from pangs of indigestion traceable to the stomach, as well as to the
intestinal tract. Incidentally it may be mentioned
that graham bread, rye pudding, and fruit were in
those days staple foods in her diet.[24] But it was the
persistent pain she habitually located in her spine
which indicated that something may have gone wrong
when George was born.

In spite of all her physical distress, however, Mrs.
Glover often participated in church and lodge and
other social life. She prayed in public. At the lodge

she was the star speaker. She obviously had rare social charm. Of a certain John M. Burt she had occasion to write [25] as though the coupling of his name and hers in village gossip had gone too far to please her. James Smith [26] seemed disposed to seek her heart through the pious pathway of the consolations of religion. But, persistent and pervasive as he was, she never took him seriously.

John H. Bartlett, however, made more headway in his suit. In her letters years before to Augusta Holmes, she had habitually underscored his name. In opening his campaign, March 21, 1846, for her heart, he presented her with the conventional auto-graph album of that day, fondly indicating in the opening pages his hope that she will remember him "when friends near and dear are far away." [27] Some sort of understanding between them for a time ex-isted, with reservations on her part. She was not the woman to make a marriage that would leave out of the home she craved the boy for whom the Tilton house was never big enough. Winsome as young Bartlett was, she never could be sure that he could furnish the conditions necessary for the proper bringing up of her young son. For that matter, he had doubts himself; for in his acceptance of what looked like a dismissal, he indicated that he agreed with her as to his financial outlook, and he called heaven to witness that he would insist on nothing that did not appeal to her feelings and in addition promise family support.

Some of the reasons why Mrs. Glover, June 21, 1853, married Daniel Patterson are not difficult to give.

EARLIEST KNOWN PICTURE OF MRS. EDDY

This picture was photographed from a daguerreotype, made in
Mrs. Eddy's young womanhood.

The Cheneys were, not long afterward, to take young George far away with them. Meanwhile, Mrs. Glover, as she found living through those days of humiliating dependence on her strong-minded elder sister increasingly irksome, was trying to find a way to keep her young son at least within hailing distance. Abigail was so immersed in her unceasing efforts to bring up her boy, Albert, to be a "gentleman" that she felt she had no right to let him play daily with his somewhat rougher and more boisterous cousin. There was something to be said on both sides. There always is. But it is scarcely open to discussion that real home life was not to be expected in an atmosphere too often charged with controversy and perhaps acrimony.

That herein lay an impelling motive for Mrs. Glover's second marriage is, also, indicated by the removal of Dr. and Mrs. Patterson, after their first three years of married life in Franklin, during which her invalidism continued, to North Groton in order to be near her son.

The very happiness, in fact, of Mrs. Glover's brief wifehood, so swiftly ended, had made her eager, as is usual with normal people, for a closer comradeship and a more intimate understanding than she was now experiencing in these years of isolation. Her letter about this time to Martha D. Rand (later wife of her brother George) speaks for itself :

Now dearest Mathy, I am alone to-day. The family are all at church, and solitude, and silence, reign supreme, meek dwellers in the old chateau. Two things well calculated to influence memory to bring up the light of other days, when "*we two* have met" — Alas! for the bye-gones in memory, would that I possessed the power of Magic, to command the delicate spirits of fancy to reproduce the dear reality, that would bring you to my side, — where in one fond embrace of affection I could clasp thee to my lone heart, so weary of solitude I have half determined this very moment to throw aside my pen and wait to *weep*.[28]

Apparently Dr. Patterson was well equipped to comply with some of the conditions required to satisfy the lonely widow. He was big, handsome, healthy — such a Beau Brummel as was never seen before in Tilton. Confidence in himself was another asset which would appeal to Mrs. Glover's need for a strong arm on which to lean. Incidentally, too, he was a relative of Mark Baker's second wife. His wooing proceeded apace. He soon convinced her that no honor in his estimation could possibly equal the right he craved to help her in the care of George. To Mrs. Glover he became the one person in the world who seemed to understand her invalidism and to be qualified to make her well, if he might have the chance which marriage would afford to keep her under close professional as well as loving observation.[29] On his side, he evidently believed that if she could once be taken out of the depressing conditions in which she was living she could certainly be restored to health and happiness.

He confided to Mrs. Tilton his conviction that Mrs. Glover's suffering was due as much to separation from her boy as to any possible organic or functional disorder. Mrs. Tilton, therefore, had the right to feel that she was acting in her sister's interest as well as in her own in encouraging a marriage which would take out of her home an invalid not of

her immediate family.[30]   Mrs. Glover's father was not
so easily convinced.   He endeavored to impress on
Patterson, whom he did not wholly trust, the gravity
of the double responsibility which he would be
assuming, for a wife who was a sick woman and a
stepson, self-willed like all the Bakers, and in addition already showing at the age of nine, the unhappy
results that usually follow being "handed about"
from babyhood.

In this marriage Mrs. Glover's heart did not go
freely with her hand.   But at last, almost desperate,
her personal tragedy deepening, she accepted the
bewhiskered, broad-clothed, silk-hatted suitor in
kid gloves.   Looking back in October, 1891, across
the years to this decision which she made in 1853,
and its disappointing consequences, she wrote, "My
dominant thought in marrying again was to get back
my child, but after our marriage his stepfather was
not willing he should have a home with me."[31]

The years she spent as wife to Dr. Patterson
proved as drab as any years could be for a woman
always virile in mind, no matter how her body failed
her.   In the three years passed at Franklin the income of the itinerant dentist was disappointing.   The
two lived in a little house, kept a cow, and a horse
which, however, Dr. Patterson needed most of the
time for his tooth-pulling peregrinations.   Neither
her mind nor her body found health in this second
marriage.   For several years her sole attendant was a
girl incapacitated by her blindness and, like herself,
unwanted in the average home.   Often depressed as
well as ill, sometimes, as this companion — dear to
her through many years — wrote in 1911, Mrs. Pat-

terson would grow violently impatient under the
goad of nervous irritation with the blind girl's uncertain movements, but "immediately came and put her
arms around my neck and said that she was sorry." [32]

She yearned more than ever for her boy; and it
was this, on her part, that took them in 1855 to live
in North Groton.[33] Now her liege lord, obliged to
add the running of a sawmill[34] to his dental work in
order to make both ends meet, showed himself more
reluctant than before to take in little George, who
finally, therefore, at the age of twelve, said farewell
in 1856 to his mother and went off to Minnesota with
the Cheneys. At seventeen, when the Civil War
broke out, he joined the army and went South to
fight for the freedom which his mother had for years
been preaching both with voice and pen.

A wife's ill health and a husband's broken promises
due to his conspicuous inability to make a living, to
pay even fifty cents on the dollar of the obligation
he had expressly assumed to make a home for a stepson as well as for an ailing wife, were not contributory
to that happiness in marriage which is dependent on
generous reciprocity. The neighbors began to talk
about the inharmony in the Patterson home, and the
"blind girl," looking back long afterwards, admitted
sadly that "they often quarreled." [35]

One of the many children who loved Mrs. Patterson through all these years wrote in 1916, when she
was then an aged woman:

My blind sister Myra Smith (Myra Smith Wilson) worked
for Mrs. Patterson, consequently I was at the house two or
three times each week She was ill nearly all the time and
would lie in bed, with a book for her constant companion but

when I came up to the bedside she would lay aside her book and pat me on the head and say "Oh you dear little girl. You are worth your weight in gold. I wish you were mine."

Every pleasant day my sister would wrap Mrs. Patterson up and draw her out on the piazza and when she was too tired to stay longer out of doors would draw her into the house & she would retire and rest.

When she was ready for breakfast she would ring the bell and my sister would cook a rye pudding to be eaten as a cereal. When she ate pie it had to be made with a cream crust as she could eat no fatty substance. One of the greatest pleasures of the children was to carry in the earliest berries and wild flowers to the "poor sick lady" but they did not call when Dr. Patterson was at home for we were all afraid of him.[36]

Dr. Patterson soon tired of the inconveniences to which a husband with a wife of "nerves" must, at least, try to grow accustomed. Nor could she on her side continue in heart to "honor" one who kept his promises no longer than it was convenient. There were scenes. The husband's absences from home grew more frequent and lengthy than his scant business required.

Things went from bad to worse. The mortgage on the Groton house came due, and the holder resorted both to law and to his fists to collect his money. Mrs. Tilton was importuned to come to her sister's rescue. The foreclosure which followed sank Mrs. Patterson into the deepest depths of humiliation. As her sister drove her down the mountain side while the hard-hearted holder of the mortgage had the church bell tolled in ironic glee, Mrs. Patterson broke into tears, and the "blind girl" who stumbled after on foot wept bitterly in sympathy for the woman whom she truly loved.[37]

There followed a superficial resumption of home ties. The doctor made some effort to keep the home together. The unhappy couple boarded with a Mr. and Mrs. John Herbert at Rumney Station. Mrs. Patterson turned all but hopeless, and Dr. Patterson took her to a little house in Rumney Village. Then, early in the Civil War, he went off to Washington, commissioned by the Governor of New Hampshire to collect a fund for distribution among Union sympathizers in the South. He left his wife without money, and also without food. Before he started South, Mrs. Patterson wrote him:

I have had one good ride with D. Lang and Barnes. He took us over to Franklin and I went to see E. J. Cate, stopped about one hour. I paid, 50 cts — and I cant go again for lack of money. I felt better for the ride; 'twas yesterday and the air did so brace me, and O, 'twas so delightful to see so much of beauty on this earth. . . . I have not had any Graham bread since you were here, if you come by railroad I think you better bring some wheat.[38]

With customary carelessness, straying in March, 1862, too near the Confederate lines, Dr. Patterson was captured and sent to Libby Prison, from which, on April second, he wrote his wife the following letter in which he expresses the lively hope that God will find her food and shelter and seems also to hope that some way may be found to salvage for him the inconsequential boots and traveling bag he had left behind in Washington and to commandeer the interest of their Congressman in effecting his release:

Dear Wife

You will be amazed to learn that I am in prison in the confederate States prison, but it is so, I was taken one week

ago today. Give yourself no uneasiness about me. I have
found very gentlemanly officers and friendly gentlemen as
fellow prisoners, But God alone can tell what will become of
my poor sick wife with none near to care for her "but God
who tempers the wind to the shorn lamb" will care for you, I
have no care except for you — I left my travelling bag and a
new pair of boots at 381 Pensylvania Avenue Washington at
Mrs. C. W. Heydon's — perhaps you had better write to our
representative in congress T. M. Edwards M.C. and ask him
to see that I am exchanged if there is any exchange of citizens
— I became somewhat acquainted with him while in W. if
you write to me direct by way of Fortress Munroe and put
on a confederate state stamp which I will enclose if I can find
one, and also a United States one, I would send you some
money if I thought it safe, and I would write more but fear
if too long it will not pass, it will have to be sent unsealed as
yours must also, write short and plain or it will be burned
perhaps instead of forwarded — My anxiety for you is intense
but be of as good cheer as possible and trust in God

Your Affectionate Husband
D. Patterson.[39]

To occupy her mind there was news coming almost
every day from the battlefields, and Mrs. Patterson
rose to her intellectual best in interpreting to the
Kidders and other friends the deeper meaning of the
war. Then too, spiritualism, mesmerism, and other
psychical phenomena were on the air and in town talk
as much as radio to-day. Mesmer had died, but
mesmerists were everywhere in evidence. A certain
Charles Poyen had been talking in places where
Mrs. Patterson later was to live, of the "Power of
Mind over Matter," and had made ready for the
publication in 1837 of his book on *The Progress of
Animal Magnetism in New England*. What Braid
had done in England to make mesmerism popular,

Grimes was doing in New England, and Dods and
Stone, Andrew Jackson Davis, and Warren F. Evans
were to follow him.[40]

How much more widespread was the interest in
these related subjects than is now commonly believed
may be inferred from the fact that the Boston Medical Library to-day contains ninety-three books dealing with animal magnetism, and the Boston Public
Library has over one hundred, of which seventy-seven
bear a date previous to 1870. Of magnetizers or
mesmerists there were almost three hundred listed
in Boston, and in every New England town lectures
and séances were the "movies" of that day. Not a
few were reading *The Magnet* and *The Mesmeric
Magazine* — for mesmerism had even its own magazines.

But Mrs. Patterson was too broken in body, too
wounded in spirit, too troubled in mind to find such
interests more than superficial and temporary. A
lonely, forsaken woman often too weak to stand on
her feet, confined day after day to her bed, already
long suffering from the spinal trouble which made her
a "helpless cripple," [41] needing even fifty cents to get
an outing and wheat with which to make the bread on
which to keep alive at all, Mary Glover Patterson,
in the nature of the case, was not likely to be as much
occupied as some of her neighbors with mesmerists
or sitting in as often at séances.

More likely she was praying with the Psalmist:
"Out of the deep have I called unto thee, O Lord;
Lord, hear my voice." She, who in childhood at
her mother's knee, had listened with joy to the Bible
stories about the healing of the sick, was now prom-

ising God — as thinking backwards at Pleasant View she once remarked — that if He would raise her up to health she would give her life to the help of the sick.[42]

Of her mother, Reverend Richard S. Rust wrote that, to her entire family, Abigail Ambrose Baker was "a living illustration of Christian faith."[43] Mrs. Eddy also recalled to a friend that once when a heated discussion with her father about everlasting punishment brought on her a fever, it was her mother's comforting exhortation to "lean upon divine Love"[44] that drove down her temperature. Always in her brilliant daughter's thought, Mrs. Mark Baker was associated with God and health, with love and goodness; and when in 1849 the mother passed away, Mrs. Glover, following her habitual impulse to express in verse[45] her deeper feeling, wrote:

> Supporting faith be mine below,
> Life's parting words to greet;
> Thy mantling virtues o'er me throw,
> Till child and mother meet.[46]

Still earlier in her teens, she sent word to a friend bereaved of a dear father: "There is one who has promised to be 'a father to the fatherless.'"[47]

At the time her brother George was seeking Martha Rand in marriage, his widowed sister wrote:

Let us ever remember, there is One "who careth for us" — too wise to err, too *good* to be unkind. On Him may you rely, and find a Father and a friend. Yes, dear Mathy, this is my only consolation, *unworthy* as *I* am — and tis the greatest I can recommend to those I love.[48]

Later, on the eve of her marriage to Dr. Patterson, she made it clear that what Mrs. Tilton, outclassing the new husband in power to bend others to her will, had failed utterly to do, he need not so much as try to do; for hers was a "fixed feeling that to yield my *religion* to yours I *could not*." [49]

Throughout this period she was, says Mrs. Turner, "a very spiritual woman." [50] In the Congregational Church at North Groton Mrs. Patterson frequently responded to the call to offer prayer in public, and her prayers were long remembered as uplifting and helpful. All through her life there surged such a tide as never seemed to ebb of consciousness of God, a sense of absolute dependence on Him. Her most recent critic of distinction admits that:

> Prayer, meditation, eager and puzzled interrogation of the Bible, had claimed from childhood much of her energy, so that those who met her in later times were conscious of a certain quiet exaltation, such as may come to a woman nursing a secret spiritual advantage. [51]

In spite of her ill health, of which the sign manual was an evident nervousness of manner which caused some to regard her as "peculiar," [52] Mrs. Patterson, as she came toward forty, was a very attractive woman. [53] She had a grace of manner the more appealing, because of her habitual neatness and exquisite taste in choosing and in wearing clothes. A frailness unmistakable and apparel indicative of poverty were much in evidence, when Mrs. Patterson came to P. P. Quimby's office in the International Hotel at Portland, in October, 1862. The young George Quimby — he told the author so himself in 1907 — helped her up the stairs. "She was too feeble," wrote her sister-in-law, Mrs. Mary A. Baker, who went with her, "to go unattended."

P. P. Quimby was Mrs. Patterson's last hope.

She had heard of him a year before, for stories were in wide circulation of his magic cures. People reported that he used no medicine and was particularly helpful in afflictions of long standing. Her husband was so impressed that on October 14, 1861, he wrote Quimby:

My wife has been an invalid for a number of years; is not able to sit up but a little, and we wish to have the benefit of your wonderful power in her case. If you are soon coming to Concord I shall carry her up to you, and if you are not coming there we may try to carry her to Portland if you remain there.[54]

The next May, when her husband was in Libby Prison, Mrs. Patterson herself wrote Quimby:

I have entire confidence in your philosophy as read in the circular sent my husband Dr. Patterson. *Can* you, *will* you visit me at once? [55]

She then thought that all the ways to Portland were closed to her. Mrs. Tilton believed Quimby to be a quack and the reports of his cures greatly exaggerated. She would not lift a finger to help Mrs. Patterson get to Portland. Mrs. Tilton did, however, agree to finance her sister if she would consent to go to Dr. Vail's Hydropathic Institute at Hill, New Hampshire, and there take the water cure. In no position to make terms, obliged to accept the best that she could get, and therefore scarcely in a mood to receive help from any water cure, Mrs. Patterson arrived at Hill as summer dawned in 1862. She found few of the patients were settling down to profit by Dr. Vail's care. Reports of Quimby's wonderful cures at Portland, coming day after day, sowed the seeds of unrest and of longing in the minds of the unfortunates at Hill. Now and then a patient would slip off to Portland to see Quimby. When one of them, Julius Dresser,[56] returned visibly improved, Mrs. Patterson became sure her very life depended on seeing Quimby. A letter she wrote to him in August, 1862, runs:

Dear Sir: I am constrained to write you, feeling as I do the great mistake I made in not trying to reach you when I had more strength. I have been at this Water Cure between 2 and 3 months, and when I came could walk ½ a mile, now I can sit up but a few minutes at one time. Suppose I have faith sufficient to start for you, do you think I can reach you without sinking from the effects of the journey? I am so excitable[57] I think I could keep alive till I reached you but then would there be foundation sufficient for you to restore me — is the question. I should rather die with my friends at S. Bridge, hence I shall go to you to *live* or to them to *die* very soon. Please answer this *yourself*.[58]

The more her physical ailments challenged her resolution, the more determined Mrs. Patterson was to have her way. The little sums of money which Mrs. Tilton kindly sent her now and then for "extras" she hoarded until she had enough to pay her fare to Portland.[59] She came expecting much — altogether overmuch — and in consequence she responded quickly to the treatment she received. As with kindly eyes and sympathetic heart, Quimby looked into that wan, worn face, his friendly understanding went out to her in a consuming desire to do all he could for her. His diagnosis in itself increased her faith. He told her that she was "held in bondage by the opinion of her family and physicians," and "her animal spirit was reflecting its grief upon her body and calling it spinal disease."[60] His assurance that she would soon be well was accompanied by his usual manipulation of the head to generate the flow of healthy electricity, on which he laid great stress.[61]

Encouragement to expect recovery Quimby furnished with persuasive forcefulness. With her flaming faith the patient helped herself while she thought she was only helping Quimby to help her. The change was instantaneous. Her pain and weakness disappeared. A sense of comfort and well-being stepped into their place.[62] Within a week she says that without help she climbed the one hundred eighty-two steps to the dome of the City Hall.[63] And in this whole experience she furnished, though she was not to realize it until 1866, a new illustration of the words Jesus spoke to the woman healed after twelve years' illness, "Thy faith hath made thee whole."

At last the prayers of years seemed to be answered. Though her healing was not permanent and she soon suffered a relapse,[64] she told others of the change that had come over her; and to Quimby, almost two years later, she wrote: "I have often repeated the first instance of my salvation to wondering hearers, and if when we are converted we should strengthen our brethren how ought I not to preach."[65]

Out of the thirty-four hundred cases[66] which Quimby treated in those last two years at Portland only one at once felt any obligation to pass on the healing gospel. Mrs. Patterson did not delay. She was not content merely to be healed. She would know how the healing was effected. With becoming modesty and characteristic deference she wrote the *Portland Courier* that "At present I am too much in error to elucidate the truth." [67] She would know all before she ventured to apply any. That was Mrs. Patterson's way. That was why at last she traveled far in heavenly healing.

During those autumn weeks of 1862 she haunted Quimby's office. She asked him questions. She read all the notes accessible to those in whom Quimby showed some interest. She studied his method. He was impressed by her, as by no other patient. More than once, he buoyantly remarked "She is a devilish bright woman." [68] As weeks went by, Mrs. Patterson grew greater in his estimation, which once led him to remark to another patient: "This is a very wonderful woman and in comparison I am the man, but Mary is the Christ." [69]

After her three weeks in Portland with her daily talks with Quimby, she went back to her sister's home. Mrs. Tilton was so impressed by the change in Mrs. Patterson that she took her son Albert to Portland and put him under Quimby's treatment for alcoholism; but to no purpose. The boy knew not how to make himself the vehicle of the curative forces which his aunt's faith alone had so promptly brought to her, and which she then in turn too generously ascribed to Quimby. But even that benefit was only temporary. When she turned back to Tilton, Mrs. Patterson soon grew ill again. She reported to Quimby that the spinal trouble had returned, and with it the chronic indigestion. [70] But faith like hers was not readily put down. In the spirit in which the Fourth Gospel describes Christ as "the true Light, which lighteth every man that cometh into the world," [71] she once inquired in print, "Is not this the

Christ which is in him?" When in January, 1866, Quimby passed away, she paid this tribute to his memory:

> Rest should reward him who hath made us whole,
> Seeking, though tremblers, where his footsteps trod.[72]

What Quimby by his own method did for many, none would undervalue. Generous as usual, Mrs. Patterson overrated his method and underrated the efficacy of her own abounding faith. Not only did he, with his vitality, encourage her to expect much but he also confirmed and deepened her conviction — already larger far than his, had she only known it — which she had had since 1844, that God in Christ has a message for the body as well as for the soul, and that Jesus knew whereof he spake when he once observed, "If ye have faith as a grain of mustard seed . . . nothing shall be impossible unto you." [73]

But Mrs. Patterson meant much to Quimby — more perhaps than he or anybody then could be expected to realize. Close contact of two such vivid personalities was bound to be significant to both. She was always about. This, George Quimby, in his early manhood, resented. He was too young to understand; to have as yet, perspective. To him his father was a finished product. George was jealous for his father's reputation, and fearful lest the most arresting personality he had ever met might endanger it. That was the boy of it. To himself, of course, no man is ever finished.[74]

Seventeen years later, the interest which she was the first generously to show in Quimby, others one by one began to show. No evidence is more illustrative of her magnanimity than her appeal, soon after Quimby's death, to Julius Dresser — with Quimby much the last few years of Quimby's life — to "step forward into the place he had vacated. . . . You are more capable of occupying his place than any other I know." Nor could any answer be more illuminating than Julius Dresser's of March 2, 1866:

As to turning Dr. myself, & undertaking to fill Dr. Q's place, and carry on his work, it is not to be thought of for a minute. Can an infant do a strong man's work? Nor would I if I could. Dr. Q gave himself away to his patients. To be sure he did a great work, but what will it avail in fifty years from now, if his theory does not come out, & if he & his ideas pass among the things that were, to be forgotten? He did work some change in the minds of the people, which will grow with the developement & progress of the world. He helped to make them progress. They will progress faster for his having lived & done his work. So with Jesus. He had an effect which was lasting & still exists. But his great aim was a failure. He did not succeed, nor has Dr. Q. succeeded in establishing the science he aimed to do. . . . No I wouldn't cure if I could, not to make a practice of it, as Dr. Q. did.[75]

In the period which followed it was Mrs. Patterson who kept green the memory of the unusual man, and but for her supreme success Quimby would, as Dresser in 1866 predicted, long since have joined the forgotten failures of the world.

Mrs. Patterson went away from Quimby with the same faith in God she had when she came to him, and which she was in a few years to make so effective in the healing of the sick that in retrospect Quimby became to her scarcely more than an interesting episode.

Certain phrases which developed in their frequent conversations were to stick in her vocabulary for a while. Of them in February, 1899, she wrote:

Quotations have been published, purporting to be Dr. Quimby's own words, which were written while I was his patient in Portland and holding long conversations with him on my views of mental therapeutics. Some words in these quotations certainly read like words that I said to him, and which I, at his request, had added to his copy when I corrected it. In his conversations with me and in his scribblings, the word science was not used at all, till one day I declared to him that back of his magnetic treatment and manipulation of patients, there was a science, and it was the science of mind, which had nothing to do with matter, electricity, or physics. After this I noticed he used that word, as well as other terms which I employed that seemed at first new to him. He even acknowledged this himself, and startled me by saying what I cannot forget — it was this: " I see now what you mean, and I see that I am John, and that you are Jesus." [76]

Quimby never rose to the spiritual heights scaled by Mrs. Eddy. However, with her habit of impressing upon other minds what was dominant in her own, she gave Quimby credit in full measure,[77] running over, for all she thought at the time he did for her, but which it is now plain was the product of her own faith. But, as her understanding grew with ripening experience, she was soon filling old words and phrases with new meaning, then coining her own unquestioned terms to elucidate her system, and at last in obedience to the same persistent urge, writing the book.

She discovered Christian Science in a larger sense than ever Columbus discovered America. Hers was no peep at a new world and then a scuttling back to the old. Hers was that real discovery which consists of finding an age-old truth, settling in it, sharing it with others, and making the most of it for the redemption of the world from sickness, sin, and death.

This was essentially the discovery which Shakespeare made in drama when reading Plutarch, Holinshed, Sir Thomas More, and even Fox's *Book of Martyrs*, he sent characters singing down the ages who otherwise would long since have faded out of memory.

· This was the discovery in government which the Fathers of the Constitution made, in 1787, when they gave us what Gladstone mistakenly called "the greatest work ever struck off at any one time by the mind and purpose of man"; of which James Bryce was then to say "there is little in that Constitution that is absolutely new, there is much that is old as Magna Charta"; and of which no less an authority than Sir Henry Sumner Maine with veracious accuracy ultimately said: "The Constitution of the United States of America is much the most important political instrument of modern times."

What did Mrs. Eddy owe to those who went before her?

The name at last she gave her church, Christian Science?[78] As early as 1866 Abraham Coles used the name in verse, and earlier, in 1846, an English clergyman in a lecture published in 1847. The Episcopal Bishop of Wisconsin, Dr. William Adams, had also, in 1850, published his addresses on Moral Philosophy under the caption, "Elements of Christian Science." But his book was not yet to come her way, and when it came, through the gift of a student, the book bore no relationship to Mrs.

Eddy's faith. Two years before, a friend of Dr. Oliver Wendell Holmes, Mrs. Sarah Josepha Hale, followed her somewhat familiar, "Mary had a little lamb," [79] with a more ambitious poem in which the line occurs :

'Tis Christian Science makes our day.

But there is no evidence that the poem affected Mrs. Eddy. Nor would the phrase Christian Science be now significant if it had had only such casual launching.

Did Mrs. Eddy get the title of her book from Quimby who once spoke of the "science of health"? [80] Again, the evidence is lacking that Quimby's phrase ever made on anyone a lasting impression. Of the thirty-four hundred whom Quimby treated thirty-three hundred ninety-nine went their way like the nine out of the ten cured of leprosy in the New Testament. In 1902 Mrs. Eddy wrote that the title came to her in the silence of the night, and not till six months later did a friend find "science and health" in John Wyclif's version of the New Testament, and bring it to her notice. [81]

God as love, spirit, truth, and life is found in one version or another of the Bible, and they are terms used in many a theology long before the day of Quimby and his more famous patient. [82]

As for the nothingness and erroneousness of matter, this is an idea almost as old as human thinking. Before ever Gautama took his seat beneath the Bo-tree, India was accepting it as a general concept. As early as four hundred thirty B.C. Democritus of Abdera remarked, "Man lives plunged in a world of illusion and of deceptive forms which the vulgar take for reality." Plato esteemed matter nothing, and mind everything.[83] Being without well-being is naught, "John the Scot" was teaching France in the ninth century.

In the years when Spinoza was resolving to remain a materialist "until the last king had been strangled with the entrails of priestcraft,"[84] he was heading towards Mrs. Eddy's "Infinite Mind" with his talk of "Universal Substance." Berkeley came to the conclusion that apart from some mind to perceive it, matter would be nonexistent. Jonathan Edwards, rated by A. M. Fairbairn as "the highest speculative genius of the eighteenth century," could say that the "Material Universe exists only in the Mind."[85]

"The laws of nature" were to Kant "creations of our own understanding, acting upon the data of the senses." "Man has no body," wrote William Blake, "distinct from his soul." Lotze avowed "that matter is nothing but an appearance for our perception." Like the morning stars, the Transcendentalists all sang together of "the supremacy of mind over matter"; and Emerson required no urging to report that :

> Out of thought's interior sphere
> These wonders rose in upper air.

But before her views could run into a complete system Mrs. Patterson was again in need of help. In the early spring of 1864, she paid another visit to Quimby. As late as 1904, Mrs. Eddy was able to recall a conversation with a fellow patient in 1864, in which she expressed her judgment that "Dr. Quimby is the most progressive magnetic doctor I

MARY BAKER EDDY

From a tintype thought to belong to the period, 1864–67.
Waiting to be photographed, Mrs. Eddy quieted a crying child
and then their picture was taken together.

ever knew, and back of it all there is a science that some day will be discovered." [86]

On this visit Mrs. Patterson was keener than ever to exhaust the possibilities in Quimby's teaching. No other patient ever took such pains to understand him. This was the more necessary because, as Horatio W. Dresser says, "he could not express his thoughts accurately. One searches his manuscripts in vain for a clear explanation of his method of silent cure." She talked things over afternoons with Quimby and sat up "late at night" writing down "what she had learned during the day." [87] All the time, at first unconsciously, she was reading into Quimby's teaching what had been growing in her own consciousness amid vicissitude and change, in loneliness and destitution. Beginning in those early days when she was no older than thirteen and yet used to "converse on deep subjects" [88] with her pastor, no one can go intelligently with her all those years from 1844 to 1866 without hearing now and then a lonely and heroic soul singing to herself:

> *I shall arrive!* What time, what circuit first,
> I ask not; but unless God send his hail
> Or blinding fireballs, sleet or stifling snow,
> In some time, His good time, *I shall arrive;*
> He guides me and the bird. In His good time. [89]

Eager to practice what she had learned and was spiritualizing for herself, in the spring of 1864 she went to Warren, Maine, to try to complete the restoration, begun in Portland weeks before, of Miss Jarvis's health. Later in the year found her stopping at Albion, Maine, with Mrs. Sarah G. Crosby, who in 1907 recalled to the author that on that visit

Mrs. Patterson seemed as "*one* fired with the pre-science of a great mission." Even in 1909,[90] as she was near her passing, Mrs. Crosby tenderly observed:

Many months Mary Patterson was a beloved guest in my home, — for I had a most unselfish love for her and deep sympathy with her, when in her poverty she came to me, — no money, scarcely comfortable clothing, — most unhappy in her domestic relations. Her only assets being her indomitable *will* and active brain.[91]

This, then, was Mrs. Eddy at the age of forty-three, her health improved but not yet all it should be ; somewhat better friended than before, but still hard pressed to make a living ; overrating in a grateful woman's way what she owed to Quimby, and looking vainly for a man to carry on his work, — and, when none appeared, carrying on herself till the hour struck when she could write with truth : "in the year 1866, I discovered the Christ Science."[92]

CHAPTER IV

BUILDING THE BOOK

Twice between 1866 and 1875, the period when the book was building, Mrs. Eddy lived with Mr. and Mrs. George D. Clark on Summer Street, in Lynn. The names of the group of persons gathered round Mrs. Eddy in the Clark home as the time drew near for publication and even the places where they sat at table are known, thanks to a diagram [1] prepared by George E. Clark, the son.

Mrs. Eddy

14

Mrs. Raymond 13	1 Hiram Crafts
Minot Raymond 12	2 Mrs. Crafts
George Clark 11	3 Mrs. Brene Paine Clark
John Bogart 10	4 Charles Porter
Nathaniel Brookhouse 9	5 Mrs. Porter
John S. Keyes 8	6 Wm. Wadlin

7
Joshua Sheldon

If there were not, in that friendly circle, any fisher folk, as among the twelve who surrounded Jesus, emphatically there were nineteenth century equivalents — workers in the Lynn shoe factories, salesmen in shoe stores, a painter, and a teamster.

Mrs. Eddy sat at the head of the table. Wherever Mrs. Eddy sat, at any time, was the head of the table. The years which followed were abundantly to justify the soundness of judgment of Asa G. Eddy expressed in a letter written on August 5, 1880, that, as a matter of course, in any project success was certain only when Mrs. Eddy led the way.[2]

Records reveal to us how Mrs. Eddy looked in the days when her book was going through its final stage of preparation for the printer. Though entering the fifties, she still retained the complexion of her girl-hood, the color coming and going in her fair cheeks, and her hair falling in a shower of brown curls around her face. Her blue eyes, as she talked, shone more brilliantly than ever. Says Mr. Clark:

> She usually wore black, but occasionally a violet or pale rose color, and I remember well a dove-colored dress trimmed with black velvet that she wore in the summer. She was a little above medium height, slender and graceful. Usually she was reserved, though her expression was never forbidding. But when she talked, and she talked very well and convinc-ingly, she would make a sweeping outward gesture with her right hand as though giving her thought from her very heart.[3]

Argument was frequent at that dinner table. Wherever fourteen New Englanders are met together serious discussion, and often actual debate, is likely to spring up. Young Clark, soon to go to sea and already feeling his importance, became at times apprehensive lest the pitch of intensity to which discussion was carried should lead to dissension. But courtesy invariably tempered feeling, and saved the day, much of the credit for which belonged to Mrs. Eddy. One of her friends thus drew her picture from memory in later years, "I can seem to see her now as she sat before us with that heavenly spiritual expression which lighted her whole countenance as

MRS. EDDY AS SHE LOOKED AT LYNN AND STOUGHTON
ABOUT 1867

she expounded the truth . . . her conversation was always an inspiration and instructive." [4]

Naturally enough, the talk sometimes turned to Quimby. At the Wheelers his name was often on her tongue.[5] During her stay with the Crafts family, in the winter of 1866–67, Quimbyism was not infrequently her theme. Notes in Mrs. Eddy's handwriting, which Hiram S. Crafts preserved, still exist, however, as proof that Mrs. Eddy was already thinking independently of Quimby, and identifying "'the whole idea man' with the perfect man of God's creating." [6]

At the Wentworths she took advantage of the opportunity to add an introduction to *Questions and Answers;* and as her two years with them drew to a close, her incessant talk concerning mind and matter bored some of the intellectually incurious members of the family.[7]

By 1871, she was leaving Quimby far behind, and no one was more aware of it than Mrs. Eddy herself. She was coming to realize the full import of his admission to her in 1864 that she had discovered something different from anything he ever taught, which now no open-minded investigator can doubt who has access to these comprehensively informing sources the author has studied and also to the author's extensive personal correspondence, supplementing his face to face talking with Quimby's son. During this same year, in writing to her friend, Miss Sarah Bagley, Mrs. Eddy's reference to some unknown person whom she described as "that *half*[8] scientist, a former patient of Dr. Quimby"[9] indicates this clearer understanding of herself. If further testimony were needed her severest critic of a generation ago conceded that "she had improved upon the original Quimby method and left it behind her"; [10] while one of her most recent critics [11] affirms that: "In those eight years Quimby had ceased to be an entity" in her life.

In this connection her own observation late in life is worth consideration that for "a time (after 1866) she was somewhat hampered by the theories of Quimby." [12] Of aid, also, in plotting correctly the upward curve of her development is this other later statement:

What I wrote on Christian Science some twenty-five years ago I do not consider a precedent for a present student of this Science. The best mathematician has not attained the full understanding of the principle thereof, in his earliest studies or discoveries. Hence, it were wise to accept only my teachings that I know to be correct and adapted to the present demand. [13]

The table talk at the Clarks was often of her fall in Lynn. It was one of the most significant experiences in Mrs. Eddy's significant career. Its consequences in dealing with the years that followed no one will minimize who cares to understand her extraordinary career. Starting from Swampscott anticipating a happy evening at a temperance meeting in Lynn, on Thursday, February 1, 1866, Mrs. Patterson had a hard fall on the ice, of which this account appeared the next Saturday in the Lynn *Reporter:*

Mrs. Mary Patterson of Swampscott fell upon the ice near the corner of Market and Oxford streets on Thursday evening and was severely injured. She was taken up in an insensible condition and carried into the residence of S. M. Bubier, Esq., near by, where she was kindly cared for during the night. Dr. Cushing, who was called, found her injuries to be internal and of a severe nature, inducing spasms and

intense suffering.   She was removed to her home in Swampscott yesterday afternoon, though in a very critical condition.[14]

Forty years later, Dr. Cushing, near fourscore years,
recalled that he found Mrs. Patterson very nervous,
partially unconscious, semi-hysterical[15]; symptoms
not unusual in cases of profound shock.   The next
morning he gave her one-eighth of a grain of mor-
phia as a sedative.   Her response to this small dose
was such as to indicate that she was not in the
least accustomed to the drug; for she was so late
in awaking from the profound sleep into which she
fell that the doctor feared he had given her a larger
dose than he had the night before intended.   Incidentally, once when talking to the author he observed, "Probably one-sixteenth of a grain would
have put her sound asleep."[16]

It was in the summer of 1907 that the author had
a long talk as well as correspondence with Dr. Cushing, who was spending his last years in Springfield,
near the author's Northampton home.   Across the
twoscore years he recalled with pride the days when
he was a popular doctor and a man of social consequence in Lynn.   His eyes brightened in describing
the "spanking" team which he often drove on sunny
afternoons along the Lynn speedway.   He observed
that one day he had prescribed for as many as fifty-
nine patients.[17]

About the value of attenuated doses both of arnica
and "Belladonna to the two hundredth attenuation,"
he spoke with not a little gusto.   Having spent a
summer not many years before with Osler, the world-
eminent diagnostician, later Sir William, of Oxford,[18]
and helped him daily in the preparation of his still

world-used book on *The Practice of Medicine*, and
having also heard at length his well known opinions
about homeopathy, the author was not impressed
with Dr. Cushing's missionary zeal for "attenuation" to the two hundredth degree of such drugs as
arnica and belladonna.

Although of less importance than the spiritual consequences of the fall in Lynn, the former physical
symptoms soon returned. Within two weeks Mrs.
Patterson was writing Julius Dresser for mental aid
to forestall a possible return of "the terrible spinal
affection from which I have suffered so long and
hopelessly." [19]

On June thirtieth, the Mayor of Lynn presented
to the city government a communication from Mrs.
Patterson:

in which she states that owing to the unsafe condition of
that portion of Market Street at the junction of Oxford Street,
on the first day of February last she slipped and fell, causing
serious personal injuries, from which she has little prospect
of recovering, and asking for pecuniary recompense for the
injuries received.[20]

But the fall did bring its spiritual revelation. She
never in the years that followed doubted that it led
her farther on the way to God. The Sunday following the fall, still prostrate in her Swampscott home
from the accident, as she was reading the Bible narra-
tive of how Jesus healed the palsied man, she experienced one of those rare visitations reserved for the
religious discoverers of the race and thus describes it:
"The lost chord of Truth (healing, as of old) I caught
consciously from the Divine Harmony. . . . It was
to me a revelation of Truth." [21]

Her consciousness of God's power to heal, which had been ever growing brighter with the years, and had been enhanced by the idealizing faith which for a while she honestly believed that Quimby also had, was now at its full. She was sure, as the Rt. Hon. H. A. L. Fisher writes, that "a spiritual life transcending the human formed the ultimate basis of reality." [22] No matter what might happen to her in the years ahead, never again would she doubt the literal truth of the New Testament promise, "My grace is sufficient for thee."

Not that she understood it all at once. She was, in fact, to spend her life in plumbing its depths upon depths. In the calm of eventide in her swinging chair at Pleasant View, musing over this experience, she confided to a friend [23] that she had come to the realization that:

She had been thinking about God, and it dawned upon her that it was the attitude of mind which she was in that made it possible for the divine power to heal her, that in some unknown way she had attained unto that consciousness of the divine Presence which heals the sick even as the natural musician without scientific knowledge touches the harmonic chords. [24]

Like Jacob at Peniel, with many a weary mile yet to trudge before his journey's end, Mrs. Eddy always afterwards felt that she could say, "I have seen God face to face, and my life is preserved." [25]

The way now began to clear for that complete concentration on her life work which was essential if the goal she set before her was ever to be reached. In 1862, poor and sick as she was, from her husband's brother [26] she borrowed thirty dollars, with which to try to bring about the release of her blundering

husband from prison.   In 1864, an effort was made,
in all good faith, to reëstablish a home in Lynn.
But in his consort's dreams the husband sought and
took no lot or part; for in the summer of 1866 he
eloped with the wife of another man; [27] was divorced
in 1873 for unfaithfulness; and in 1896 died at Saco,
Maine,[28] in the poorhouse.   But, long before this, he
took on himself the full responsibility for the failure
of his marriage, when to a friend he described Mrs.
Patterson as "a pure, estimable and Christian
woman," and added "that if he had done as he
ought he might have had a pleasant and happy home
as one could wish for."[29]

Already Mrs. Eddy was well along with the building of her book.   But there was other building to be
finished before the book could be completed.   At
this time, Mrs. Eddy was a disadvantaged woman.
Between her fall in 1866 and the appearance of her
book in 1875, more than once she lacked both friends
and "where to lay her head."   Her father had died
in 1865.   Not merely was her boy, now a grown man,
gone to war, but there were years when she knew not
so much as his whereabouts.   Mrs. Tilton's doors at
last swung open very grudgingly.   Ellen Pillsbury,
her own niece, had attended to that.   Healed by
Mrs. Eddy of a serious illness, Ellen went with her
aunt to complete her recuperation at Taunton, where,
like a typical Baker, she reacted against the plain-
ness of the Crafts home and returned to Tilton with
such sorry tales as ever after made the older aunt shut
Mrs. Eddy out of her heart.[30]

There were times when Mrs. Eddy had to fight for
her personal independence.   Now and then every

man's hand seemed to be against her. In 1890, she told her good friend, Miss Shannon, that for a time, while living in Lynn, she was annoyed almost beyond endurance.[31] No wonder that in a day when the law was often a woman's only protection from imposition, Mrs. Eddy sometimes felt the need of legal aid.

The situation grew acute. She was rarely free from grave anxiety. She became sensitive even to the thoughts which she believed were directed at her, and she wrote one to whom she had given confidence and who was failing her,[32] "won't you exercise *reason* and let me live or will you *kill me?* Your mind is just what has brought on my relapse and I shall never *recover* if you do not govern yourself and TURN YOUR THOUGHTS wholly away from me . . . won't you *quit thinking* of me."

She needed at her right hand some one who would ask nothing except the chance to help her carry out her larger purpose. And the man was there. Asa Gilbert Eddy was kindly, modest, unassuming, patient, sensible, methodical, reliable, no trouble-maker, and "careless in nothing but his own comfort."[33] To some originality and considerable ability, he added a true man's instinct to defer to superior wisdom and to work with others. Into the expanding life of this unusual woman Asa Gilbert Eddy came unobtrusively. But here is her own story, written January 12, 1877, to a friend:[34]

Last Spring Dr. Eddy came to me a hopeless invalid. I saw him then for the first time, and but twice. When his health was so improved he next came to join my class (his residence was South Boston). In four weeks after he came to study he was in practice doing well, worked up an excellent reputation for healing and at length won my affections on the ground alone of his great goodness and strength of character.

On New Year's Day, 1877, they were married, and a satisfying home was now hers which all her life she had been craving and sometimes seemed destined never to possess. Writes one who knew them well,[35] "This home in Lynn was very simple in all its arrangements, but immaculately neat."

On the death of her husband, June 3, 1882, she wrote to this same friend from the Vermont hills, whither she had gone in her bereavement:[36]

I can't yet feel much interest in anything of earth. I shall try and eventually succeed in rising from the gloom of my irreparable loss but it must take *time*. *Long* after I shall smile and appear happy shall I have to struggle alone with my great grief that none shall know if I can hide it. I think of you at the fort and always as little, or rather great heroes and pray that my coming shall be a joy and not a sorrow to you I know you will hail it but O! I hope I shall be more useful to you all than a *mourner* is apt to be. I shall never forget dear, dear Gilbert his memory is dearer every day but not so sad I think as when I left home. It is beautiful here the hills vales and lakes are lovely but this was his native state and *he is not here.*

More and more the truth pressed home that she could never hope to build her book until she had first acquired an income on which to live; a sum at least above the margin of actual want. To this grilling task she set her hand while her spirit ranged the skies. Who shall say that it may not have been with these hard days in mind that she wrote in 1893:

O, make me glad for every scalding tear,
   For hope deferred, ingratitude, disdain!
Wait, and love more for ev'ry hate, and fear
   No ill, — since God is good, and loss is gain.[37]

Written in 1867

Book   By Mary Baker G. Eddy

The presence of her first Student, Hiram S. Craft

Matthew

Argument against the spiritual phenomena

" in favor of the spiritual sense only of the scriptures.

The principle going before the shadows —

A call for matter to feed on, and the reply of Truth.

Guide in a chemical.

Truth calling upon error, and the fear of of error causing it to lose sight of Truth

An enquiry of error why Truth doth lift the tradition of the elders, in that it takes no matter form in healing the sick. Wisdom answers, why do ye transgress the commandments of God by your traditions.

Men should honor the Father, which is your principle. The error which curseth this Wisdom let him die the death of error.

But whosoever says, I have given the gift of healing, dishonoureth his Father, Wisdom.

Ye hypocrites, which draweth near to Wisdom with the lips, while the heart is far from it; i. the understanding is not in Truth while they claim to know it.

Such as teach for their doctrine the belief of men, need not claim to worship Wisdom, for Truth says it is in vain.

It is not that which produces only a sensation, which defiles a man or idea, but when the reason accepts it as a belief, then it cometh out of the mouth, and is that which defileth.

Truth, or its disciples, said to wisdom

NOTES OF INSTRUCTION IN MRS. EDDY'S
HIRAM

HANDWRITING GIVEN TO HER FIRST STUDENT,
S. CRAFTS

If she was to write, she had to have a roof over her head, and food to eat. The Phillipses gave her shelter for a while, and in the Clark home there was good food, and happy company. Then, too, she earned a little by her healing work. Her first student was Hiram S. Crafts, whom she taught from the Bible and her manuscripts.[38] The pages of her notebook, which he retained, the first two of which are now before the author, are expositions of the first Gospel which are full of her reliance on God, and descriptions of the harmony and healing which she said outright would naturally result from such a faith. He paid her while they were fellow boarders at the Clarks; and, when he set up for himself as a practitioner, she went to live with him and Mrs. Crafts, first in East Stoughton, then in Taunton. At the Wentworths, where she stayed two years, in exchange for her "keep" she explained to Mrs. Wentworth her new method of healing and also allowed her to copy *Questions and Answers* together with her comments. But the time came when that was not regarded as compensation enough; and at last she was obliged to move on.[39] During one of the years of that long period while her book was building, she tells us that she moved eight times.

Never in the years from 1866 to 1875 was she happier than while with the Ellises,[40] spending many an evening with the family. Kindly Mrs. Webster at Amesbury, who was interested in spiritualism[41] was hospitable to Mrs. Glover until her son-in-law came from New York and made conditions so impossible for Mrs. Glover that she moved to Miss Bagley's.

But always this woman of the book kept at her

task.   Nothing else — not even a living — seemed so
important to her.   Some of her students paid her
one hundred dollars for ten lessons, and promised
her a commission of ten per cent on their future
earnings.[42]   This arrangement appeared necessary at
the start; but it later proved to be unwise and was
discontinued.   Mrs. Eddy looked upon a contract as
a contract even with her earlier students; as is
evident from a letter which she wrote one of them
July 28, 1869:

I learn from your own signature that you have retained a
copy of those MSS.   This was a fraud for which I must hold
you or any other person responsible who should commit such
an act.   Now if you wish for a private settlement I will spare
your feelings and charge you fifty dollars only for the copy;
but if you do not wish to settle in this manner I shall certainly
take measures to protect myself against such damage.[43]

Once in those early days when other helpers failed,
Mrs. Eddy felt driven to invoke legal aid to protect
her teaching in the well known Arens' Case, and with
success.   Without her consent some suits were brought
against students.[44]   Richard Kennedy, her business
partner from 1870 to 1872, however, told the author
in 1907 that after their partnership was dissolved and
her income was decreased she felt the pinch, and did
the best she could.[45]

But her habitual policy is clearly stated in the
Church Manual:[46]

A member of The Mother Church shall not, under pardon-
able circumstances, sue his patient for recovery of payment for
said member's practice, on penalty of discipline and liability
to have his name removed from membership.   Also he shall
reasonably reduce his price in chronic cases of recovery, and
in cases where he has not effected a cure.   A Christian Scien-

tist is a humanitarian; he is benevolent, forgiving, long-suffering, and seeks to overcome evil with good.

Poor as she was in those days, not letting her left hand know what her right hand generously gave, she often helped substantially both the worthy and also the less worthy. Mrs. Annie Macmillan Knott recalls the authentic case of a woman who for two years was taught by Mrs. Eddy without charge. S. P. Bancroft[47] paid his three hundred dollars, which Mrs. Eddy promised to refund if he found he could not "demonstrate" what she taught him. And when James C. Howard was unable to meet his obligation, he received from his generous teacher a receipt in full, along with a check with which to buy an overcoat which he conspicuously needed.[48]

At last, after much experimenting, she came to the conclusion, confirmed by general experience, that people habitually value only that for which they pay. Just why she raised her price to three hundred dollars and later reduced her lessons from twelve to seven may never be known in full. There is reason to believe it was a wise decision, and that it was not made at the expense of her high standard. In a letter which she sent to Mrs. Clara E. Choate she declared, "I shall teach them as soon as they will study. The taxes, coal and repairs on building, and *book* have drained. But not for that would I teach this Science." [49]

Years later she wrote:

When God impelled me to set a price on my instruction in Christian Science Mind-healing, I could think of no financial equivalent for an impartation of a knowledge of that divine power which heals; but I was led to name three hundred dollars as the price for each pupil in one course of lessons at my College, — a startling sum for tuition lasting barely three weeks. This amount greatly troubled me. I shrank from asking it, but was finally led, by a strange providence, to accept this fee.[50]

To the impartial observer, nothing more surely indicates the prevision and administrative wisdom of the founder than the financing of the Christian Science movement. The present situation in some parts of Christendom is intolerable. The shabby money-raising devices to which some churches resort which hark back to the time of Jesus when a settled income was not necessary, and when the poorest peasant in the region around Galilee, might, like the Pilgrim Fathers, "suck of the abundance of the seas, and of treasures hid in the sand," are out of place, archaic, adventitious, and distinctly hurtful to the larger cause. This is no plea to turn the minister into a man of wealth, but to save him from deteriorating into what a young man, who recently left the ministry at the end of his first year, describes as "the proverbial, down-at-the-heels, dispirited, sad-eyed parson."

Mrs. Eddy's views were products of a personal experience which had cost her much travail. Her belief never wavered that the truth she taught was for the rich, as well as for the poor. "Seek ye first the kingdom of God, and his righteousness; and all these things shall be added unto you,"[51] was the basis of her economic counseling. She said, "Soul has infinite resources with which to bless mankind.[52] . . ." "We are all capable of more than we do."[53] To one of her students, having "quite a financial struggle,"

Mrs. Eddy cheeringly observed: "Keep on in the work of Science and you will always be glad that you did. Know that you are fed and clothed by Spirit, and you will be fed and clothed and to the world it will be a miracle." [54]

In those dark days when, with the odds against her, she learned to make a living, she demonstrated that those who, in singleness of mind, seek the kingdom receive all the human things of which they have real need. The mind that is set on higher things draws to it the lower if only — like the sheaves in Joseph's dream — to do homage to the higher. That is why Christian Scientists look prosperous and are often prosperous. They seek the kingdom of God, and other things are usually added to them. God keeps His promises.

Mrs. Eddy had to protect her spiritual morale as well as win her economic independence. Sensitiveness over the attitude of public opinion toward the domestic differences with Dr. Patterson led her, unfriended and distressed as she sometimes was in her Lynn days, to turn back to the name Glover. The aloofness and censoriousness of her relatives cut her to the heart. The one sweet note of her earlier home was struck by her sympathetic stepmother who wrote her on a pale little postcard: [55]

My own Dear Daughter

It is a long time since I have heard one word from you. Hope you are well and enjoying the light of God's countenance and surrounded with kind friends, a good Minister, and good society. I know you must miss your own dear relatives and former friends. . . . My love to yourself and all who are kind to you.

E. P. B.

How to sheathe her sensitiveness from exposure to
the world's venom and indifference took her many a
year to learn. But she learned. Richard Kennedy[56]
once said : " It was an unfortunate fact that Mrs.
Eddy with her small income was obliged to live with
people very often at this time in her life who were
without education and cultivation."

A woman sharing the same house with her when
Mrs. Eddy was busiest on her book, described her
to Miss Emma C. Shipman[57] as " The purest minded
woman I ever knew." But she added that she
thought Mrs. Eddy a " crank." Asked to explain
what she meant by " crank" the aged woman
answered : " Mrs. Eddy wished the house kept so
still, "— a condition essential to intellectual creativeness which every educated household, where books
are written, accepts without calling names.

But whether people understood her or not, Mrs.
Eddy lived with them. " It was never her custom
to keep apart from the family. She invariably
mingled with them and through them kept in touch
with the world." Even in what in 1869 she called her
" time of severest trial," she wrote :

My Father chastens in love, and I know if my physical
frame endures I shall rejoice here for every tear I have shed,
and ere long enter the lighted sanctuary, and cast off my
crown won from the cross at the foot of the throne, whither
have gone through great tribulation such as have washed their
souls in the blood of the Lamb which is the spirituality of
truth bleeding from the wounds of error.[58]

There were, however, some to give her loving
sympathy. That summer of 1866, which she spent
with the Phillipses at Lynn, Grandmother " Mary"

A GENEROUS TEACHER

and Mary Baker Glover — many years her junior — were so completely one in mind and heart that one time when "Uncle Thomas" came home and found them side by side on the sofa talking of the higher things of life, he remarked to his wife, "Hannah, do you see our two saints? There they sit together, the two Marys." [59]

Though personally and industriously building up a growing business, George Oliver was known, when Mrs. Eddy was at his house, deliberately and repeatedly to overstay his luncheon hour. Returning to his office, he never offered an excuse. One day, however, he did casually observe: "I would rather hear (her) [60] talk than make a big deal in business."

Hiram S. Crafts, that first student in whose home she lived for some months, paid the last tribute to his teacher on December 20, 1901, in a renewed confession of loyalty to her teachings which covered all his later years. [61]

The Wentworths were a large household. During the two years from 1868 to 1870, when Mrs. Eddy lived in their home, now and again her relationship with some members of the family became somewhat strained — a not unusual experience. But what one of the sons, Charles O. Wentworth, remembered in 1909, when trivialities were fading out of mind, was that her "gentle, unassuming nature made her a peacemaker." [62] This confirmed his mother's judgment expressed in 1869 that "If ever there was a saint on earth it is Mrs. Glover." [63]

She had constant need of a full suit of armor for her natural sensitiveness. No sooner was she fairly launched upon her teaching enterprise than some of

her first students — usually crude, frequently un-
teachable, and sometimes merely mercenary — began
to make trouble for her. When to his amazement
George Tuttle, home from a sea cruise to Calcutta,
seemed easily to cure his first patient, he fell into a
panic and nothing could induce him to try to repeat
his experience. His brother-in-law, Charles S. Stanley, gave such free vent to his argumentative spirit
in class that Mrs. Eddy in the interest of her other
students, had to dismiss him to make him realize
that he was not the only student in the class.

A certain young bank clerk, Wallace Wright, would
not — or perhaps in his crassness could not — for
the life of him see how mesmerism and Mind Science
differed. With retaliatory zeal he hurried into print
to attack a teacher whom he did not understand ;
whereupon five of her larger-visioned students came
to her defense. In consequence, young Wright disappeared from public view and also from history after
making the somewhat premature announcement, on
February 24, 1872, "that Mrs. Glover and her Science
were practically dead and buried." [64]

Of all those earlier students Richard Kennedy gave
most promise. From 1870 to 1872, he was in partnership with Mrs. Eddy. Under her inspiring touch
he was from the first a growing success as a healer,
which at last left her free entirely to teach. At the
end of two years, Mrs. Eddy had six thousand dollars
in the bank.[65] But young Richard found the business
obtainable by rubbing heads so satisfactory that he
felt no desire to study under Mrs. Eddy what she
taught. Why bother about theory, so long as he
could make a good income from his practice. The

more he used those expert hands of his, the more he closed his agile mind until, by mutual consent, on May 11, 1872, the partnership was dissolved.[66]

Daniel H. Spofford brought into Mrs. Eddy's life a more mature and less ebullient personality. He won much success at first in healing, and was also more or less helpful for a time in the management of her growing interests. As the months slipped by, however, his interest in her teaching did not keep pace with her enlarging plan. As she turned more to Asa Gilbert Eddy, she depended less on Spofford. Personal difficulties arose, and Spofford went the way of others.[67]

In 1881 eight of her students — none of them at all concerned about what she considered the real issue — openly rebelled and put her leadership to a severe test. As usual, Mrs. Eddy made appeal to rise above the pettiness of personalities. Getting no response, she read the eight out of connection with the Cause,[68] rallied to her side the better disposed members, and as the event proved gave a conclusive demonstration that she ruled, no matter what might happen, in the little world around her. After that it was clear that she would be able to cope with any crisis which might arise.

The spring before the book appeared in 1875, Mrs. Eddy was living in a boarding house at Number 9, Broad Street, Lynn. Still pursued by controversy and overtaken by much contumely, she yearned even more intensely for the quiet which a home of her own would probably provide. Leaning one day from her window, she observed a sign "For Sale," fastened on the two-story frame house. with attic, at Number 8,

across the street. She resolved that this should be
her haven and on March 31, 1875, she bought the
place for five thousand six hundred and fifty dollars.

But her income was not yet adequate to maintain
so large a house. She was obliged to lease all but the
front parlor on the first floor, and on the third floor
the tiny upper bedroom under the sloping roof, in
which during the months that followed, she completed
the preparation of her book.

Number 8 was not a mansion. It, however, put a
roof over her head. Fancy perhaps might see in its
modest bow windows and little balconies tokens of the
comforts and the beauty to be hers. The enforced
wandering, which for years had handicapped and
humiliated her, she now believed was near an end.
Status, at last, she had — the security furnished by
the owning of property. It was little enough, but that
little was sweet to one who had known less. Number
8 might possibly, she dared to hope, one day bring
her the condition "when an ounce of sentiment may
save a ton of sorrow." [69]

At any rate a student of those days reports that
he "never knew her so continuously happy as in that
summer at Number 8." Sibyl Wilbur, too, says:

the little place grew most attractive. The affectionate
zeal of her students, many of whom she had healed from
serious complaints or diseases and some of whom she had reclaimed from intemperate lives, made her gardens bloom,
kept her grass-plot like velvet, and relieved the austerity of
her parlor with decoration. Mrs. Glover's balconies were
filled with calla lilies of which she was particularly fond, and
when she stood among them tending and caring for them with
the sunlight sifting through the leaves of the elm, making
splashes of green and gold upon her cool white gown, she made
a picture of composure and purity.[70]

Not only in numbers, but also in love and loyalty, her students seemed to multiply. No service, at that time, appeared too great for them to render. Often they anticipated her unexpressed wish; and with them she shared her confidences and also took them to her heart. Some she addressed by endearing names. To many she opened a new heaven and a new earth. Letters written by students in their old age are on record in which words fail them to describe all that she had meant to them in the elysian days they spent with her.

To ensure her independence against all accident Mrs. Eddy needed not merely to triumph over the sordid and the commonplace with whom she overlong had been obliged to associate, but also to be drawn increasingly within range of the circles in Boston and in Concord devoted to those higher ideals and cultural interests congenial to her.

Certain phrases used by Emerson are faintly reminiscent of *Science and Health*. Those were the days when he was telling lecture audiences: "Mind is supreme, eternal, and one. . . . The universe is the result of mind." But we have Mrs. Eddy's own word dictated to a secretary that she never read Emerson till after her book was published.[71] Between Emerson and Mrs. Eddy there was a great gulf fixed. He was all for thought, and she for demonstration. He never fired her imagination, or awakened her enthusiasm. The Reverend Thomas Van Ness says:

I asked Mrs. Eddy one afternoon, when we were talking on the subject of her plans, whether she cared much for the teachings of Emerson. . . . Her reply was vague. The subject did not interest her and we soon drifted away from it, or rather, she did.[72]

But to Whittier Mrs. Eddy turned instinctively. He was more approachable and more responsive. Eight of his poems, in which she took a great personal interest, were put into the *Christian Science Hymnal*,[73] and to the end it was a joy to her to hear people sing:

> The healing of his seamless dress
> Is by our beds of pain;
> We touch him in life's throng and press,
> And we are whole again.

On one occasion when Sarah Bagley took Mrs. Eddy to call on Whittier, they found him "sitting before a fire in a grate (in July) coughing incessantly with hectic flush on his cheeks and scarce able to speak above a whisper." As she talked and showed a sympathetic interest over his indisposition, he brightened up and appeared to be much better. Of her visit Mrs. Eddy writes, "When I rose to go he came to me with both hands extended and said 'I thank thee Mary for thy call, it has done me much good, come again.' " Afterwards he pronounced her "a gifted woman."[74]

For all his kindly reserve, Bronson Alcott had a sympathetic nature which appealed to Mrs. Eddy. Concerning slavery, their opinions were identical. After her book appeared and the storm of criticism broke, he introduced himself to her with this salutation, "I have come to comfort you."[75] For that reason, she sent him on January 14, 1876, a copy of the book, which he acknowledged in the pleasure-giving words:

The sacred truths which you announce sustained by facts of the Immortal Life, give to your work the seal of inspiration — reaffirm in modern phrase, the Christian revelations. In

NUMBER 8, BROAD STREET, LYNN

Asa Gilbert Eddy seated at an upper window of the little house.

times like ours so sunk in sensualism, I hail with joy any voice speaking an assured word for God and Immortality. And my joy is heightened the more when I find the blessed words are of woman's divinings.[76]

Twice he visited her in her own house at Lynn. He showed an interest in the class work, and indicated clearly that he had abundant reason for his confidence in her and in her followers.[77]

Again, on June 5, 1878, in company with the Reverend J. L. Dudley, Mr. Alcott was a welcome guest at a Christian Scientist Association meeting. Should the question ever arise as to whether Mrs. Eddy borrowed from Alcott, the author would refer inquirers to the Minutes of the meeting, now in the Files of The Mother Church, and reading thus:

After listening to questions & answers between teacher & class, Mr. Alcott presented his argument of the working of mind from Spirit down to atom & "vice versa." It was interesting to notice how near some points in the argument approached to the true argument in Science.[78]

At the Emersons and elsewhere in Concord in those days, there was much talk of Mrs. Eddy; and Mrs. Emerson, whose time usually was altogether occupied in balancing with her practical sense the unpracticalness of her husband, expressed a wish to meet her. Mr. Alcott often spoke to his daughter, Louisa M. Alcott, of "Little Women" fame, to Frank Sanborn and various Concord Brahmins of his new friend; and among them so little opposition developed to her teachings that he evidently believed there could be little of it also among people worth while anywhere.[79]

As the years passed Mrs. Eddy won a place in

Boston life, and met many Boston people. But by that time she was so engrossed in writing, in teaching, in building up her book and her church, and in multitudinous details of administration, that she had little time to spare for those occasions which have always given dignity and distinction to Boston society, and still give it a unique place among the cities of the land.

All those years when she was building up her health, her income, her equilibrium, she was qualifying more and more for building up her book. Her very hardships lent substance to her writing. She was coming up through much tribulation. As the Scriptures put it, "The earth helped the woman." Speculation about what might have been may be interesting, but it is scarcely worth the time and trouble. Yet had not Mrs. Eddy been so absorbed in building up her book from 1866 to 1875, when life was seldom kind to her, she probably would never have become infused with the heavenly courage to go on and on more soundly building up her health, her income, her equilibrium.

The work on the book, exhausting as it sometimes must have been, was her anchorage to reality when a lesser soul would have drifted to oblivion. Did she, like St. Paul, have to become all things to all men that she might save some? It was the honest toil she gave the book which taught her tact and courage. Was it necessary to pay attention to the spiritualistic rhapsodies of Mrs. Webster[80] in order to keep a roof over her head? She could bring herself to do it for the sake of the precious hours it would give her every day to write. Did she have to sit in at a game of cards to keep on good terms with acquaintances, when she so begrudged every minute stolen from her writing that to some she now and then appeared distracted, even cross? There was sure to be some hour of the day when, huddled in her shawl, with the house rocking in the wintry wind, she could be at her book. Were there times when, with children mimicking her, with adults insulting her and even threatening her with harm, her pride was wounded sore, and her heart was broken, by the cruel trivialities inflicted upon a woman striving to establish her spiritual security? Her book brought some relief from pain, and assistance to forget. Who shall say that it was not this absorption in the book which gave her power to rise above cold,[81] above hunger, above all the thousand stings of petty persecution to regions where nothing counts but Spirit, regions which sustain in the supreme conviction that nothing exists but Spirit?

For years Mrs. Eddy was working on her book. As her students more and more desired to see her teachings put in writing, she first fed them the familiar *Questions and Answers*, to which she was soon adding an Introduction — almost immediately to find its way into the text itself. By the summer of 1869 another booklet was ready — forerunning *Science and Health* — which later received the title *The Science of Man*, but at first evidently was called *Science of Soul*.

On June 7, 1869, from East Stoughton (now Avon) she wrote a Tilton friend of her earlier days:

I have just sent a work to the press for publication entitled — *Science of Soul* — I mean you shall read it sometime. I have written this and notes to the entire book of Genesis within the last year and this, besides laboring for clothes and other expenses with teaching I am worn almost out, have lost my love of life completely and want to go where the weary have a rest and the heavy laden lay down their burdens.[82]

The postscript to this letter further indicates that she was hard pressed at the time for money:

I am anxious to know why Dr. P. (Patterson) does not send me my annual remittance.

In February, 1872, she began to write what in her little notebook — in the author's hand — she calls "The Science of Life." A little later she was putting out "Soul's Inquiries of Man," on which there are more touches than ever of Mrs. Eddy's individuality. While traces of her state of mind in the fast receding Portland days may here have lingered on, they steadily grew fainter until, at the very latest in 1875, she gave her students printed instructions they could not misunderstand to omit "manipulation"; after which Quimby's name was very rarely mentioned by her.[83]

Perhaps, therefore, the author of this book was justified when he wrote, in 1921, for the *Cambridge History of American Literature* that "As a whole the system described in *Science and Health* is hers, and nothing that can ever happen will make it less than hers."[84] As though to confirm the author's judgment, which had for years been growing, the *New York Times*' review in 1922 of *The Quimby Manuscripts*, which appeared in 1921, adds:

It is a gigantic task which the editor of *The Quimby Manuscripts* has undertaken when he offers this loosely arranged mass of writings and reflections as not only containing the beginning of spiritual healing but also the origin of Chris-

tian Science. . . . Science and Health, whatever views may
be held concerning it by individuals, has served to build up a
mighty organization which could hardly have been reared on
the uncertain foundations of the Quimby manuscripts.

Under the tiny skylight which, even in that cool
summer,[85] focused the hot rays of the sun uncomfort-

Boston, _Oct, 30_ 1875

M* _Edward Hutchins & Geo. M. Barry._

To W. F. Brown & Co., Dr.

Job, Card, and Book Printers,

W. F. BROWN.
G. M. A. TWITCHELL.

No. 50 Bromfield Street.

ably on the head of Mrs. Glover, writing her first book
at a time in life when many a writer has said farewell
to his creative power, Mrs. Glover, in 1875, put
the last touch on the first edition of _Science and
Health_. To find a publisher was no easy task. She

had long been trying. Nothing could be impossible to one who, more than a half-century before had prattled in the schoolroom "I will write a book," and had never quite lost sight of her high purpose.[86]

Mrs. Glover had already taken young George Clark [87] with her to Boston in search of a publisher, with no more to show him than the prospectus which she carried with her. Seeing no profits in an enterprise which might even to-day appear an unpromising business risk the publisher expressed the usual regrets. To publish the book would cost more than fifteen hundred dollars. Two of Mrs. Glover's friends advanced the required amount, and the first edition of one thousand copies of *Science and Health* appeared on October 30, 1875. The bill for its production, which came the next day from the printers, W. F. Brown & Company, of No. 50 Bromfield Street, Boston, mounted to $2285.35, of which Mrs. Glover paid seven hundred dollars.[88]

The book now lies before the author, in its pale green cover and in a style of type usual at that time. As a piece of bookmaking it is somewhat like *The Bible Looking Glass*, *Fanny Fern*, *Nurse and Spy*, and also other books then popular. In appearance, it is no better and no worse. No sooner was it off the press than Mrs. Glover was visualizing, in a letter written to a student,[89] a new edition, which she hopes will be an improvement on the first:

There are grammatical errors in Erata and some in the book doubtless that I have not touched . . . and if you see them and are sure of what is right in the case correct them but *not* otherwise dont meddle with the punctuation but mark any doubtful cases so you can point them out to me. Our next printer should have a proof reader who is *responsible* for this.[90]

If this first edition bears some marks of a first book, Mrs. Glover at once began to remove them and continued to improve the successive editions till at last *Science and Health* became, next to the Bible, the "best seller" among serious books.

Like the Bible, *Science and Health* was published — as Mrs. Glover says in her first preface — "to do good to the upright in heart, and to bless them that curse us, and bear to the sorrowing and the sick consolation and healing." The style is well adapted to the end in view. Without sacrificing dignity, the language is often conversational. Developing out of her rich experience among plain people, the *Science and Health* of 1875, like the King James Version of the Bible, is easily "understanded of the people." Help does come to those who would be "upright in heart" when they read, "Every pang of repentance, every suffering for sin, (accompanied with reformatory efforts) and every good deed, atones for sin." [91] There is blessing for those whom the world would curse in such a glowing sentence as, "Love must triumph over hate." [92] Rightly understood, there is ample comfort for all who sorrow and who suffer in the seven words, "Mind, and not matter, embraces all suffering." [93]

Never was Mrs. Eddy satisfied with anything she wrote. The publication of each edition of *Science and Health* was simply a new challenge to make the next edition better. Between the table of contents of that first edition of 1875 and the latest of 1910,[94] there is not merely a wide difference but also a complete reordering. The first reads:

Natural Science, Imposition and Demonstration, Spirit

and Matter, Creation, Prayer and Atonement, Marriage, Physiology, and Healing the Sick.

The latest edition runs as follows :

Prayer, Atonement and Eucharist, Marriage, Christian Science versus Spiritualism, Animal Magnetism Unmasked; Science, Theology, Medicine; Physiology, Footsteps of Truth, Creation, Science of Being, Some Objections Answered, Christian Science Practice, Teaching Christian Science, Recapitulation, Genesis, The Apocalypse, Glossary, and Fruitage.

All the way through the thirty-five years which elapsed between the first edition and the last, she was consumed with a desire to make her book more accurately express her meaning, more perfectly disclose the revelation she never doubted God had given her. Never could she be too busy — and no busier woman ever lived — to find time every day to work upon the book. The story in detail of her revisions would make a volume in itself. Before the author, as he writes, are the very copies in which her own corrections and additions are penciled on many a page in almost bewildering abundance.

Even in 1907, when she was eighty-six years old and the attacks upon her, culminating in the " Next Friends" suit, were suggesting to her and to her friends that :

When sorrows come, they come not single spies,
But in battalions,

she was revising, and revising. Her pencilings crowd the margins, interline the text crosswise, and all but wear the flyleaves threadbare. Every problem then confronting her church, and as time was to prove almost every problem that could come, is reflected in her pencilings.

There were times, as in this 1907 period, when the copy which she then used of *Science and Health* evidently served somewhat as a diary in which she wrote down her inmost feeling. Did persecution strike her a new blow? She pencils the appropriate sentence, "It is our ignorance of God, the divine Principle, which produces apparent discord." [95]

Was there misunderstanding of her use of the quotation:

> I, I, I, I itself, I
> The inside and outside, the what and the why,
> The when and the where, the low and the high,
> All I, I, I, I itself, I?

She substitutes for it in pencil:

> O! Thou hast heard my prayer;
> And I am blest!
> This is Thy high behest: —
> Thou here, and *everywhere*. [96]

Were the "Next Friends" [97] pressing over much? In a burst of righteous wrath, supremely justified, she cuts out from page four hundred thirty of the 1907 edition, the expression, ordinarily colorless, "next friends."

At midnight of September 25, 1907, she was reading about death on page one hundred sixty-four, when, as though anew to defy death, this woman, in her eighty-seventh year, changed the subjunctive to the indicative mood and declared that death "*does* not in the least disprove Christian Science." And then recalling St. Paul, she joyously exclaimed, " 'Death is swallowed up in victory.' "

It was not long before Mrs. Eddy entered into those business arrangements which were to continue

for many a year with John Wilson,[98] head of the
Cambridge University Press, the artistic craftsman-
ship of whose books has in all the years been matched
by their intrinsic worth. With the entire firm her
relations remained until the end both friendly and
agreeable. Indeed, the story of the successive editions of *Science and Health* can be traced in detail
from the letters and the memoranda of such representatives of the University Press as John Wilson,
William Dana Orcutt, and William B. Reid.[99] They
are used here the more lavishly because they dismiss
much idle speculation — including Mark Twain's —
about the originality and the orderly development of
Mrs. Eddy's thinking, as revealed from year to year
in *Science and Health*.

From the first, Mrs. Eddy made on these substantial men a profound impression, which they saw
no reason to change in a business and personal relationship lasting through an entire generation. To
them she seemed a high-bred gentlewoman, to the
manor born, sure of herself and her ideas, yet considerate and courteous to all. Upon every detail
they indicate Mary Baker Eddy lavished care constant and untiring. She moved in a large orbit.
She saw things whole. She saw things in their true
harmony. To all, she was an object lesson, not
merely in her penetrating insight but also in her habit
of doing more than her share of the hard work necessary for its practical expression.[100]

From the head of the firm down to the youngest
office boy, she knew them all. Her frequent visits
were awaited with pleasurable anticipation. She
earned the respect they freely gave her; and increas-

ingly their personal affection. As late as February 11, 1897, John Wilson, head of the firm, after many years of business intercourse with Mrs. Eddy spoke of her "gentleness and sweetness." [101]

When she inquired where she could obtain the services of a trained editor, the Reverend James Henry Wiggin, staff reader for the University Press, was "detailed to the work (punctuation, capitalization and general smoothing out as to construction of sentences); and, as he did this on his own time, the payment for these services was made by Mrs. Eddy. . . . This was well known to those in our office," says Mr. Reid, "as well as in our proof reading department, and caused many a smile among us when we read, from time to time, the repeated assertion that Mr. Wiggin had written the book, and it tickled him, more than perhaps anyone else to read that he was the *author* (instead of corrector)." In later years, Mr. Wiggin once remarked to Mr. Wilson: "Wouldn't it have been fine if I had?" [102]

Now and then some writer, unacquainted with such convincing documentary evidence as this in the files of The Mother Church, circulates again the overestimates of the very helpful service which Mr. Wiggin rendered Mrs. Eddy. It may, therefore, be worth while to quote another representative of the University Press, a man of no less standing than William Dana Orcutt, friend of William James and Roosevelt, Bernard Shaw and Sir Sidney Lee, who testifies:

Mr. Wiggin was still proof reader when I entered the Press, and he always expressed great pride to have been associated with Mrs. Eddy in the revision of this famous book.

I often heard the matter referred to, both by him and by John Wilson, but there never was the slightest intimation that Mr. Wiggin's services passed beyond those of an experienced editor. I have no doubt that many of his suggestions, in his editorial capacity, were of value and possibly accepted by the author — in fact, unless they had been, he would not have exercised his proper function; but had he contributed to the new edition what some have claimed, he would certainly have taken credit for it in his conversations with me.[103]

There is finally another witness whose testimony may be of greater value because she always held her highly esteemed editorial assistant "in loving, grateful memory."[104] That is why these few extracts from Mrs. Eddy's letters to Mr. Wiggin[105] may seem timely:

July 30, 1885: Never *change* my meaning, only *bring it out*.

June 14, 1886: They (your corrections) are all right in grammar and I understood you should do no more for the proofs than to attend to that.

July, 1886: Please send both copy and proof to me and have no alterations made after I return the proof to press.

June 14, 1890: I shall request Mr. Wilson to send the proofs to you and then you to me and I to him.

Years later (in *The Christian Science Sentinel* of December 1, 1906) recalling again Mr. Wiggin's editorial service, Mrs. Eddy said, "In almost every case where Mr. Wiggin added words, I have erased them in my revisions."[106]

CHAPTER V

FOUNDER

In 1882, Mrs. Eddy went to live in Boston. The golden age had already dawned on the "Athens of America."[1] The comforts of every day existence were now matching the charm ineffable which was gathering round the city. More and more, rich memories were accumulating as conditions changed. Dignified amenities were becoming social customs which Bostonians observed, and practiced, without boasting. To the political equality first flowering out in the Town Meeting was now added a certain "quality," still suggested in the humorous verse of Samuel C. Bushnell:

> Cabots speak only to Lowells
> And the Lowells speak only to God.

Though years had passed since grand dames milked their cows on the public street and a little boy, named Ralph Waldo Emerson, was doing his bit to add to the meager family income by minding his mother's cow on the Common, Boston had retained its earlier simplicity, and had also added to it a quality of thinking and of writing which then made the city the undisputed literary center of the land.

By this time Boston had produced such a crop of native writers as no other city in the New World ever dreamed could anywhere be raised this side of the Atlantic. It was neither conceit nor affectation that occasioned the casual inquiry, when friends met in Cambridge, Concord, or on Park Street: "How is your new book coming on?"

And already from states south and west, where Holmes, Emerson, and Alcott had been lecturing, as far even as the Mississippi Valley, pilgrims with eyes wide open for "whole shelves of their library walking about in coats and gowns," were reverently wending their several ways to Boston. Some were still talking of Brook Farm with its coterie of cultural celebrities. As in his last years Hezekiah Butterworth showed the author over the site of that social experiment, he told him how Margaret Fuller came here to gaze at the stars and to her disgust discovered that she had to "milk a kicking cow."

In 1882, Longfellow was just passing on, but Holmes and Whittier were not yet "nearing the snow line"; and, in addition Lowell, Emerson, Aldrich, Whipple, Agassiz, Francis Parkman, and Charles Eliot Norton might be found, almost any Saturday morning, looking over the new books at the Old Corner Book Store, and at least once a month meeting for luncheon and high talk at the Saturday Club.

Marion Crawford was serving his literary apprenticeship before going to Italy. Roosevelt was graduating from Harvard, where William James was then getting his start as a brilliant teacher. Henry James had already published his brief critical study of Hawthorne, shot through with penetrating criticism and over-punctuated with irritating condescension. Thus early, premonitory symptoms were showing of his exclusive interest later in things English; and it was about this time that Julia Ward Howe, on one

MRS. EDDY IN THE EARLY DAYS AT BOSTON

This picture was made at the request of Mrs. Eddy and still
hangs on the wall of her Chestnut Hill home.

occasion feeling that he "professed" too much, sharply remarked to him : "Don't lie to me, Henry."

The *Globe* was prospering under General Charles H. Taylor. The *Herald, Post,* and *Traveler,* too, were flourishing. With Louis Elson and Henry Austin Clapp on the *Advertiser,* music and the stage were adequately reported and interpreted. *The Evening Transcript* was almost a family oracle, and in its field *The Atlantic* had come to a preëminence which none disputed.

The cornerstone of the new Public Library on Copley Square was laid in 1888. Those were the days when Major Henry L. Higginson was founding the Boston Symphony Orchestra, and the audiences were all appreciation as William Gericke interpreted the great masters. Though Boston's literary lights had not been hasty to shine on aspiring art, the School of Drawing and Painting under the leadership of Otto Grundmann, who was called in 1877 to be its director, was growing apace ; and William Morris Hunt was introducing Boston connoisseurs to the Barbizon school.

Past Hawthorne Hall, where in the eighties Mrs. Eddy won her first reputation as a preacher, Charles Sumner had strolled with his friend, Thackeray ; and James T. Fields had taken Dickens for the daily constitutional needed to keep him "fit" for his evening "appearance." The author, still a Fellow at the University of Pennsylvania, recalls walking in the nineties here with youthful pride between James Whitcomb Riley and the aged Edward Everett Hale, down whose bearded cheek a tear trickled as, retelling a story related to him in his boyhood by an aged veteran of the American Revolution, Dr. Hale would have his young friend know, "That was just three days before the British hanged my great-uncle, Nathan Hale."

In those years Boston had arresting preachers. The Reverends Joseph Cook and Adoniram Judson Gordon were in fighting trim; and Phillips Brooks, rated by Edwin D. Mead[2] as "the greatest preacher in the world," was at his best.

Mrs. Eddy was outgrowing Lynn. Then — as now — Lynn had people of importance. But small town curiosity cabined her spirit and cramped her individuality. Backdoor gossip always annoyed this woman of the stars. Through her long life, wherever she might be, Mrs. Eddy was "news"; her every accidental utterance town talk or "copy" for the papers. Eavesdroppers usually kept within earshot, keen to twist any casual word to her discredit. Sometimes she broke under the strain of keeping constantly on guard. Not even Red Rock,[3] with its outlook seaward, invariably brought the quiet and the isolation which her soul craved.

Long in need of someone more congenial than Barry, Spofford, Kennedy, and Arens,[4] in 1877, while still living in Lynn, she married Asa Gilbert Eddy. No easy rôle awaited him. His unassuming manner some mistook for weakness. His business, as he was well aware before his marriage, was to be helpmate to a wife indissolubly wedded to a public purpose already well defined. Amid these difficult conditions, he did himself credit. Wise in counsel, increasingly he won the recognition to which his sound judgment entitled him. A man of solid parts, he wore well.

To her service he brought tact conjoined to tried efficiency at a time when his wife was harassed by the pretentiousness, the irresponsibility, the inefficiency, and the general inconsequence of those around her.

Miss Julia S. Bartlett's estimate of Asa Gilbert Eddy is reliable. Grateful for the healing which he brought her, she was also often in and out of the Lynn house. As a friend and student, who often saw him, she writes:

They kept no servant at that time, but Dr. Eddy did much to help in every way for the Cause that would otherwise take her time, and attended to business outside. He was always the kind husband and friend and ready helper in all things.[5]

Though his capacity for initiative was not extraordinary, he employed it when he could, and Mr. Frye, on June 27, 1895, wrote that Mr. Eddy was "the first organizer of a Christian Science Sunday School . . . also the first individual who put onto a sign the words Christian Scientist." [6]

In a letter dated June 27, 1882, to Colonel E. J. Smith, Mrs. Eddy said her husband had "the sweetest disposition" [7] she had ever known. To Judge Hanna she wrote, March 25, 1896, that he was "in a humorous way gentle but firm," [8] and two years later in another heartfelt letter to him she added: "You have said *all* When you touched on the tenderest chord of my human heart in your allusion to my late husband." [9]

During their first months in Boston Mr. and Mrs. Eddy stayed with the Choates at 551 Shawmut Avenue. In her recollections, Mrs. Choate describes him as incessantly busy with the publishers, arranging for the Christian Science services, the multiplying lectures, and also the Association meetings. Mrs. Choate characterizes him "a very gentle man, but firm & quiet."[10]

The man's unapologetic understanding of his position, his frank admission that his wife was the prime mover and he the helper, combined with freedom from all signs of false modesty and self-depreciation, are indicated in the following summation of the common enterprise in which they were all engaged: "Mrs. Eddy is the rightful head and we have never yet succeeded unless she filled that place and we abided by her direction."[11] Again:

We have just been listening to the reading and explanation of the Scriptures by Mrs. Eddy as is our wont to do on the Sabbath and from which we are refreshed; though the hour seems dark and the exertion of the wicked great, yet in mercy and goodness will we abide.[12]

If to some Mrs. Eddy's final tribute to her husband, "'Mark the perfect *man*,'"[13] seems overstrained, perhaps even they will admit that any man who adapts himself perfectly to the situation in which life places him and gets the best results attainable in the circumstances is no failure.[14] In a period when many others were making life almost unbearable for this woman with a vision, Asa Gilbert Eddy moved with discretion among the contradictory forces that crisscrossed her plans, acting with decision when there was need of action, and bringing to a woman often hard pressed the peace and understanding of which she often stood in need. When after their five years together, he passed on, by those who knew him best he was accredited the place Lowell allows to the modestly efficient:

That loved heaven's silence more than fame.

The Church Christ Jesus founded began, we are told, with a membership of no more than twelve. Only eight rallied to Mrs. Eddy's standard when, in the summer of 1875, she held her first church services in accordance with her revelation of 1866.

The program made provision for Sunday services in a hired hall, with Mrs. Eddy as preacher and director, on a budget of ten dollars a week, pledged by the charter members as follows:

Elizabeth M. Newhall	$1.50
Dan'l H. Spofford	$2.00
George H. Allen	$2.00
Dorcas B. Rawson	$1.00
Asa T. N. MacDonald	.50
George W. Barry	2.00
S. P. Bancroft	.50
Miranda R. Rice	.50 [15]

On July 4, 1876, Mrs. Eddy organized the larger Christian Scientist Association, and three years later, August 23, 1879, came the legal incorporation under the title "Church of Christ, Scientist," with a mandatory provision that the church be established in Boston.

While Mrs. Eddy gave the credit for the official organization of the Sunday School to her husband, she declared that Warren Choate, the pet of the household, was the little child who led to the genesis of the idea in her mind.[16]

As the year 1883 drew to a close, the Sunday services were held in Hawthorne Hall, at No. 2 Park Street, which, with its seating capacity of two hundred and thirty-two, seemed too big at first for that group of twenty-six. After two brief years the services had, in fact, to be moved to Chickering Hall, which was larger still.   Mrs. Eddy was at last "arriving," and Boston was furnishing the platform from which her message was to cross the continent.   Men and women still recall those Sundays in Hawthorne Hall.   While the attendants were, in general, of a higher type perhaps than those at Lynn, not all, however, who came to Hawthorne Hall remained to pray.

At these meetings Mrs. Eddy always appeared well dressed.   She knew by instinct how to dress becomingly.   Like many another wife who is a good manager, she could make a good impression on a small outlay.   She wore her clothes well.   She bore herself with an air of distinction, which made everything she wore count for more than it cost.   In the hour set aside for questions from the audience rather impertinent inquiries were sometimes made.   One Sunday she was asked : [17]

"Do you think it Christian to wear purple velvet and diamonds?"   I'll never forget the sweet expression on her face while answering.   She said as near as I can remember, "There are ladies here I presume with much more expensive dresses on, as this is velveteen, thirty-six inches wide, and only one dollar per yard.   The cross and ring were given me by those who had been healed in Christian Science with the request that I wear them."

Those Sunday services in Hawthorne Hall soon began to attract public attention.   In their planning and conduct Mrs. Eddy devoted that tireless attention to detail which to-day gives Christian Science services an appeal different from others.   She began, and closed, on time.   Usually she opened with a

familiar hymn like "Nearer My God to Thee."
Then there was silent prayer ending with the Lord's
Prayer. Another hymn was sung, and next the ser-
mon was delivered.

Mrs. Eddy compelled interest in herself and her
subject from the start. Sometimes even when
scheduled, she would not begin because when the time
came she did not feel the inspirational surcharge on
which she counted to command her audience. She had
pulpit personality. Her dainty and engaging figure,
eyes "large, deep and soulful," waving brown hair,[18]
her hands half outstretched in irresistible appeal, all
aided her voice, which none ever forgot who heard it
from the pulpit or the platform, to carry home her
message. With or without notes, she spoke rapidly,
and that Iowa woman, who found in Mrs. Eddy's
sermon "never a trivial thought," was not alone in
her findings. No matter what her text, her sermons
all revolved around the central thought that God is
Spirit, God is All-in-all, matter is insubstantial, and
sin, sickness, and death can be vanquished by Spirit.
But no one can to-day read back across her printed
sermons without seeing the Way-shower in them all.

As to the content of her preaching, listeners might
differ. But in the eighties — like John Wesley —
she was still desiring "to have a league, offensive and
defensive, with every soldier of Christ." Once she
preached for six months in a Baptist Church,[19] without
compromising her own message. That her attitude
toward others of all types should be well understood
and proper precedent be set her followers, she placed
among the By-Laws of The Mother Church the specific admonition: "A member of this church shall not

publish, nor cause to be published, an article that is uncharitable or impertinent toward religion, medicine, the courts, or the laws of our land." [20]

As truly as William James, Mrs. Eddy was fitted to teach and her talents were already trained to a fine point by long practice when she arrived in Boston. Miss C. Lulu Blackman, who came in 1885 all the way from Nebraska, to join Mrs. Eddy's autumn class, wrote : [21]

When she entered the Class-room, I saw her for the first time. Intuitively, the members of the class rose at her entrance, and remained standing until she was seated. She made her way to a slightly raised platform, turned and faced us. She wore an imported black satin dress heavily beaded with tiny black jet beads, black satin slippers, beaded, and had on her rarely beautiful diamonds. These she spoke of in one of the later sessions. She stood before us, seemingly slight, graceful of carriage and exquisitely beautiful even to critical eyes. Then, still standing, she faced her class as one who knew herself to be a teacher by divine right. She was every inch the Teacher. She turned to the student at the end of the first row of seats and took direct mental cognizance of this one, plainly knocked at the door of this individual consciousness. It was as if a question had been asked and answered and a benediction given. Then her eyes rested on the next in order and the same recognition was made. This continued until each member of the class had received the same mental cognizance. No audible word voiced the purely mental contact. Experience has been the lightning flash, that has revealed to me something of the mass mentality she confronted.

The session began with so impressive a repetition of the Lord's Prayer that one student reported : [22]

It was not as though she had gone to the Father in prayer, but rather as though, because she was with the Father, she prayed. . . . After this audible repetition of the Lord's prayer, Mrs. Eddy took her seat and the students resumed theirs. As she began to speak, many of the students opened notebooks, and began to write. Instantly and peremptorily she said, " Put up your notebooks." I had written but one sentence and no other was ever added. There were others who refused to consider the command as final and, almost at once, covertly began again to make notes. With eagle eyes she detected the overt act, and again, repeated the words, " Put up your notebooks." All complied, some willingly and some with silent but resentful protest ; then she resumed her teaching. A little later, one student began again surreptitiously to make notations. Stopping her discourse, Mrs. Eddy for the third time repeated the words emphatically and clearly and never again was there an effort on the part of any to write down a thought or word that came from this great Teacher. She, at no time, made any explanation of this arbitrary requirement, but all my days I have blessed her for this ruling, because it compelled us to let the form go so that limited finite statements of Truth might not circumscribe the pinions of her thought. Her impartations transcended the medium of words. Words served only to convey her revelations. She gave both the letter and the spirit, but she took away the letter, lest any should substitute it for the wine of the Spirit.

In such teaching no incidental interruption was tolerated. Even that bane of every classroom, noisy coughing, once received this firm rebuke from her : "Anyone with the least understanding of God does not cough." [23] Even to-day physical distractions like coughing and sneezing, so much a matter of course in other assemblies, are heard less often in Christian Science meetings.

Questions, however personal, Mrs. Eddy welcomed, and answered them without evasion. She encouraged comments out of a conviction that they might open the door to truth which otherwise, perhaps, would not come through at all. When some over-

zealous students in the class of 1889 volunteered the
statement that they had tried in vain to bring back
some who had strayed away and were no longer loyal
to their teacher, Mrs. Eddy advised:

"Do not try any more. The love that is going out to the
world through Christian Science is the greatest power there is
and the only thing that will change that thought" — adding,
"I have often felt these hard unloving thoughts of others
come about me like dark clouds, and seem to surround me,
but they never touched me, and why? Because my thoughts
were going out to them all the time in love and with a desire
to help them." [24]

It was perhaps in her presentation of God, as
"incorporeal, divine, supreme, infinite Mind, Spirit,
Soul, Principle, Life, Truth, Love," [25] that Mrs. Eddy
towered in her teaching. Sometimes, when she
opened her soul concerning prayer, her students were
swept up to a perception of the way to become a
"new creature in Christ Jesus." Referring last
winter to the chapter on Prayer in the Christian
Science textbook Dr. William L. Stidger is reported
by the press to have said from a Boston pulpit, "I
wish for my own life, and my own home that I might
have in it the beauty and power and the spirit of
prayer that is in that chapter."

In every class there were Marthas cumbered with
much care and serving, and not infrequently weighted
down with the imponderable burden of fear. Some
were small of mind, some small of soul. Mrs. Eddy
understood all. Of all she sought to make something.
She gave to all solicitude. But she kept her mental
balance. First things were put first in all her teaching; and, say what one will about her terminology,

error never deceived her into regarding it as other than the nothingness which she proclaimed it to be.

"What would you do," she once inquired, "if you knew that some one was trying to kill you through mental arguments?" With me this question created a great sense of fear and I believe it was the same with other members of the class. After waiting a few moments for an answer Mrs. Eddy said, "Cast it in the waste basket." This light remark concerning the error, and her realization of the powerlessness and nothingness of the highest form of error, destroyed my sense of fear and left with me a great sense of peace and fearlessness of the claim of error to harm.[26]

She had a way of bringing students down out of the clouds of vain aspiring and idle sentimentalizing. Says Mrs. Foye:[27]

One day a friend of mine, who was also a student of Mrs. Eddy's, called to see her on business. As she was about to leave, Mrs. Eddy invited her to stay for lunch, and just then the housekeeper came in, and, hearing my friend declining, said to her, "You had better take off your wraps and stay, I've just made a strawberry shortcake that will melt in your mouth." Whereupon Mrs. Eddy said, "There's a scientist that isn't soaring o'er the church steeples."

Bliss Knapp recalls that on another occasion, to a too dreamy student, she observed, "Come down. Your head is way up there in the stars, while the enemy is filling your body with bullets."[28]

Back of all the give and take of class contacts, back of every word she spoke and also of every gleam in her eyes, glowed a faith in her message, which she never failed to impress upon her students nor allowed them to supplant by any other interest. The correctness of her thinking might be challenged, never her sincerity. She was true to her conviction when she

pronounced Jesus in nothing "more divine than in
his faith in the immortality of his words." [29]

But it was not interest in sheer metaphysics which
brought those crowds of students to Mrs. Eddy's
classroom. It was eagerness to learn her method of
healing. To theorizing about healing she habitually
brought the sharp test of practice. The swift
growth of Christian Science in Boston during the
eighties was due to its effective healing. Critics
might explain it as they would. There were by that
time enough well people in evidence who once were
sick, to bring of their own accord the sick of body and
of soul in ever growing numbers to Christian Scientists
for treatment and then, automatically, to enlarge the
group of prospective healers trained in Mrs. Eddy's
classes.

Her understanding of the great need of the sick
and sorrowing for healing is shown in a letter she
wrote to Calvin C. Hill at the time he was leaving
business in order to devote himself wholly to the
practice of Christian Science:

> There are the sick the halt the blind to be healed. Is not
> this enough to be able to accomplish? Were I to name that
> which is most needed to be done of all else on earth — I
> should say heal the sick, cleanse the spotted despoiled mortal;
> and then you are being made whole and happy, and this is
> thine. "Well done good and faithful" enter thou into all
> worldly worth and the joy of thy Lord, the recompense of
> rightness.

By 1883 not merely were Mr. and Mrs. Dresser in
California hurrying East to have a hand in mental
healing, which they were hearing that Mrs. Eddy was
conducting with success, but pulpits also were un-

limbering their big guns on something few as yet
understood. Yet before the tumult and the shouting
ceased, Mrs. Eddy was writing tenderly of her girlhood pastor, Dr. Bouton of Concord: "The religion that he taught and lived, I love and honor.
It was the vestibule of Christian Science."

No Boston preacher was more outspoken in censure
than the Reverend Dr. L. T. Townsend. Nevertheless in the book which he wrote in 1887, to express his
mature judgment, he freely admitted "that this
woman . . . is successful in healing disease." Looking back to-day upon those same years one critic says,
"There is a central core which is true."[30]

All the while hundreds, whose health had been
improved by Mrs. Eddy's prayers, when subjected
to cross-examination were quoting, to describe their
experience, the man whose sight Jesus restored,
"Whether he be a sinner or no, I know not: one
thing I know, that, whereas I was blind, now I see."[31]

Out of many cases, a few of the more significant,
because of the high reputation of the parties concerned, will now be cited to serve as types of healing
in the period we are considering. Miss Julia S.
Bartlett, later one of the early church officers, had for
seven years been bedridden. Physicians who had
done their utmost for her, would hold out no hope of
recovery. In April, 1880, Miss Bartlett turned as a
last resort to Mrs. Eddy. Under Asa Gilbert Eddy's
care, "I began," says Miss Bartlett, "to improve
immediately. I felt like one let out of prison. . . .
The world was another world to me. All things were
seen from a different viewpoint and there was a halo
of beauty over all."[32]

A son of Ira O. Knapp, Director of The Mother
Church from 1892 until 1910, relates in his privately
printed recollections [33] this family history:

Mrs. Knapp, after thirteen years of ill health, had become
a helpless invalid ; the son had developed a supposedly incurable trouble, while Mr. Knapp had a slight indisposition.
The skill of the physicians . . . had been exhausted. Her
sister . . . advised Mrs. Knapp to try Christian Science.
Mr. Knapp remarked laconically, "Well, we will try one
more humbug."

Mrs. Eddy assigned one of her students to the
Knapp family ; and, after absent treatment had been
given, the student was asked to visit the Knapp home.
On getting off the train, she inquired of the station
agent if Mrs. Knapp had come to meet her. Overcoming his surprise that such a question should be
asked about a woman crippled for so many years, the
agent answered gently : "Mrs. Knapp will never come
to this station again." Later, however, when the
Christian Scientist was leaving her hotel, "a handsome, fresh-faced young woman came up the steps,"
inquiring for the guest. It was Mrs. Knapp herself.
"The first time," says one of her sons, "she walked
to the home of her nearest neighbor, about a quarter of
a mile away, the children all went too, dancing around
her in the joy of seeing her able to walk again." [34]
The practitioner remained only four days with the
Knapps. She healed one of the sons and also the
father. The Bible promises then became in the light
of Christian Science so engrossing to the father that,
as the son writes, he literally wore out the big family
Bible.

Another Director of The Mother Church (1888–

1909), William B. Johnson, became interested in Christian Science after exhausting all surgical, medical, and dietetic treatment for rupture and also for a legacy of diseases brought on by bad food and insanitary conditions during his three years of service in the Civil War. The expert who, one day in 1882, was making him a special truss, felt regretfully compelled to tell him that he could promise him no permanent relief, except possibly in Christian Science. In sheer despair, Mr. Johnson called in a student of Mrs. Eddy. When she came, she found her patient writhing on the floor in agony. His response, however, to treatment was immediate. His wife also was cured of tumor and catarrh.

Captain Joseph Eastaman, later a Director of The Mother Church (1892–93), brought his wife to Christian Science in a last effort to save her life. Boston doctors had declined longer to give encouragement. In a desperate "nothing to lose and everything to gain" spirit, he turned, in his discouragement, to Mrs. Eddy who put the unexpected and astounding question to him: "Captain, why don't you heal your wife yourself?" Spellbound with amazement, he entered Mrs. Eddy's class, proved an apt student, and soon, he said, "as I understood the rudiments, I began to treat her [his wife]; and, so quickly did she respond to the treatment, that she was able to avail herself of the kind invitation of the teacher to accompany me to the final session." [35]

In a recent talk with Mr. Joseph G. Mann, for several years at Pleasant View, the author's attention was called to the remarkable story of his first experience with Christian Science. He had been accidentally shot, and the diagnosis of the four physicians, called to his bedside, revealed the ball from the thirty-two caliber revolver lodged in the inner layer of the pericardium of the heart. After a final consultation, the doctors agreed that the case was hopeless. Turning to Christian Science, his restoration to health was almost instantaneous.[36] This testimony would seem the more convincing because it is credibly reported that the community then believed the healing genuine.

But Christian Science healing, contrary to general opinion, includes the spiritual and mental as well as physical, and Mr. Albert F. Gilmore, writes:

I joyously recall a testimony given in The Mother Church one evening which appealed to me so greatly that I have since remembered it. . . . He told of having been ill, in poverty, friendless, and hopeless, in the very depths of misery and despair. Someone told him of Christian Science. The appeal was immediate and he took up the study and sought the aid of a practitioner, with the result that he was soon healed of disease, was restored to an active business, and his friends returned. In the intervening years he had experienced a fullness and joy of life which he had never known before; and said he, "On more than one occasion so plentiful has been God's bounty, I have been tempted to say, 'Not quite so fast, O Lord; You are giving me more than I can take care of.'" To him the regenerating truth had been revealed; he had seen the perfect man with the result that, in goodly measure, he had come into his own; that is, he was laying hold and making use of the blessings which God has bestowed upon all His beloved sons.

Almost as soon as Mrs. Eddy could get settled in her Boston home the wisdom of her decision to locate in the larger city was amply justified by events. To her Sunday preaching and her Thursday lecturing, was added a correspondence which grew so rapidly as to become almost unmanageable. The classes in attendance were soon overtaxing 571 Columbus Avenue, and there was continued growth even after Mrs. Eddy moved, in 1887, to 385 Commonwealth Avenue.

As references to her in the newspapers became more frequent people came her way more and more to see what she was like. Casual contacts occurred with Frances Hodgson Burnett, Louisa M. Alcott, and Rose Cleveland. Many unacquainted or ill acquainted with her teachings felt constrained to attack her in print; but, she was ever ready at a moment's notice to back up the faith to which she had given all allegiance, and it was not her wont to delegate the business to others.

Even when she was busiest, she made time to meet her critics face to face. A few still living recall how she looked and acted when she appeared in person one March Monday morning after pulpit attacks by the Reverends A. J. Gordon, Joseph Cook, and L. T. Townsend, to speak for herself in Tremont Temple where one of the then famous Monday lectures of Reverend Joseph Cook was in progress. To Dr. Townsend she replied in *The Christian Science Journal* of April, 1885:

Because of the great demand upon my time, consisting in part in dictating answers through my secretary, or answering personally the numerous inquiries from all quarters, having charge of a church, editing a magazine, teaching the principles of Christian Science, receiving calls, etc., I find it inconvenient to accept your invitation to answer you through the media of a newspaper; but for information as to what I believe and teach, would refer you to the Holy Scriptures, my various publications, and my Christian students.

Already with that prescience which gives her high place among constructive organizers of all time she was reaching out from Boston, through *The Christian Science Journal*, the first issue of which appeared on April 14, 1883,[37] to the victims of failure and frustration and low vitality on the isolated farms and in obscure communities from coast to coast. It was plain to her that neither the austere theology nor the periodic revivals then popular had substantial significance to those in greatest need of vital and inspiring faith.

In the opening editorial of the first issue of the *Journal*, she broadcast her proclamation of comfort and release to the drab legions for whom the *Journal* had a cheering message: "The purpose of our paper is the desire of our heart, namely, to bring to many a household hearth health, happiness and increased power to be good, and to do good."

Having recently studied the early issues of the *Journal*, the author is convinced that but little reason exists to doubt the strength of its appeal to the handicapped. Hosts of those in trouble of soul or mind or body were evidently helped by reading the healing testimonies straight from the heart and also by the successful union of Mrs. Eddy's monthly contribution of the didactic and the practical. Her editorials are sometimes sermons, oftener "leaders," comparable in their power to get their message across to those which made the fame of Charles A. Dana in the *New York Sun* and Horace Greeley in the *New York Tribune*, Lyman Abbott in the *Christian Union*, and John Fulton in the *Church Standard*.

Both as to substance and style, Mrs. Eddy is

thoroughly at home in the good company of those who write as freely as they talk and with the same effectiveness. Her style has coloring too, which is rarely found elsewhere and which makes a spiritual appeal to those outside her circle as well as in. This extract from her fifteen hundred word "leader" in the *Journal* of September, 1886, is illustrative and representative:

He alone ascends the hill of Christian Science who follows Christ, the spiritual idea who is the Way, the Truth, and the Life. Whatever obstructs this way, causing mortals to stumble, fall, or faint, Divine Love will remove, and uplift the fallen and strengthen the weak, if only they will forsake their earthweights, and "leave behind those things that are behind, and reach forward to those that are before." Then, loving God supremely, and their neighbor as themselves, they will safely bear the cross up the hill of Science.[38]

When "Dear Gilbert," as Mrs. Eddy fondly called her husband, passed away in 1882, like Lee when Jackson fell at Chancellorsville, Mrs. Eddy thought she had lost her right arm. If she had needed Asa Gilbert Eddy in Lynn, there was more need of him than ever with the increase of responsibilities in Boston. To a student of this period, she once said, "I could be happy with him in a hut, but God means that I shall rely on Him alone."[39]

There had to be a helper at hand whom she could trust in little things as well as great, to relieve her of details as well as large responsibilities, to stand between her and those who, with good intentions, would yet use up her increasingly valuable time, and to assure her the conditions necessary to carry on at all. When Calvin A. Frye came in 1882 to remain —

as it proved—with Mrs. Eddy until the end, he was still under forty. Reticent, retiring, devoted to what became his life work, he went his tirelessly methodical way for almost thirty years. Asking nothing and receiving only modest compensation, his loyal service was beyond all valuation to Mrs. Eddy. No one did more to ensure her the proper conditions for successful leadership, even protecting her from physical discomfort. He was perhaps as nearly indispensable to Mrs. Eddy as any one could be. No task was too large, or too small, for him to undertake as she directed. He made her appointments for her when she could see people, and her regrets for her when she could not. He assisted in looking after her finances and her mail, and also copied her priceless manuscripts.

He lived to see responsibilities overtake her beyond his foreseeing when he joined her staff; but he never spared himself in helping all the while. As others came into her group, Mr. Frye maintained his habitual single-mindedness, always doing his utmost and his best, always illustrating the memorable words of the third Gospel: "He that is faithful in that which is least, is faithful also in much."

The maternal instinct was always strong in Mrs. Eddy. When definite word came of her son, a man well on in the thirties and with a growing family in the Northwest, she brought him East by telegram in 1878. Again in 1887, he came East with his family to see his mother. Both tried, at that late date, to forget those years of almost total severance and to make vital the blood relationship. But it was too late. With some of the essential characteristics of his mother, he was, however, too rough and too undisciplined after so long a break, to fit into her complex life. A mining prospector, with the prospector's instinct to venture over much, he was always wanting money, not so much for his family as to sink another shaft in search of silver and of gold.[40] Against her will, Mrs. Eddy had at last, in 1888, to recognize that much as she desired him by her side, she could not make a place for him in her ménage and her widening plans, without wrecking all she had built up. He simply did not fit, and knew not how intelligently to try to fit.

Yet she needed a son's comradeship, a son's cooperation.[41] A certain Dr. Ebenezer J. Foster, who came her way about this time, was different from her son, different also from Mr. Frye. Turned forty, he was a slight man with a gentle disposition and kindly manners. He rarely offered counsel when it was not asked. He never interfered with what she thought or planned. Years later for the life of him he could not remember ever having crossed "Mother" in anything. Graduated, some years before, from the Hahnemann Medical College in Philadelphia, Dr. Foster represented much that she desired. He never forgot the tenderness with which she greeted him. Her love for him—a true mother love—led her to desire that he become a son according to the law. No longer young and strong, she needed such a staff on which to lean. Those near her were not adequate to meet her deeper needs. From that moment his heart instinctively went out to her, and he remained with Mrs. Eddy until 1896.

On November 5, 1888, by legal adoption, he became

Ebenezer J. Foster-Eddy; and in her petition to the court Mrs. Eddy touchingly divulged her maternal yearning in the avowal "that he was associated with her in business, home life, and life work, and that she needed his interested care and relationship." [42]

Now sixty-seven years of age Mrs. Eddy depended on her son-by-law, since her son-by-blood had not turned out dependable. Dr. E. J. Foster-Eddy called her "Mother." He did much for her. He taught in her college. He succeeded William G. Nixon in looking after certain of her publishing interests. He was given various responsibilities. On many he made a pleasing impression. But in a few years he disappeared from the picture to reappear for a moment as a valuable witness for The Mother Church in the litigation against the Board of Directors which ended in 1922. Now in his old age living, like many whom Mrs. Eddy loved, on a generous remembrance, he tenderly recalls that "no one ever heard me say one word against her." [43]

As the eighties drew on towards the nineties, this industrious woman was more industrious than ever. She kept her hand on everything from the incessant revision of her book to the production in those years of such books as *The People's Idea of God*, *Christian Healing*, *Retrospection and Introspection*, *Unity of Good*, *Rudimental Divine Science*, and *No and Yes*.

Mrs. Eddy was always starting something new. Scarcely was she settled at 569 Columbus Avenue, when she placed on the front door a large silver plate, bearing the words, "Massachusetts Metaphysical College." During the seven years of its existence, it succeeded on a big scale, training hundreds of

Feb. 11. 1897.

Dear Mrs. Eddy.

How feeble, at times, are words to express the innermost feelings of the human heart! How true it is that acts speak louder than words! Your many words of kindness have, more than once, been put into a tangible form that verberate your gentleness and sweetness of soul! May the good God continue to bless You and make You happy!

Your generous gift on Tuesday last of $500.00 sent a thrill of surprise and of delight through my heart that will never cease to thank You through Him the Giver of all.

Truly Yours John Wilson

John Wilson, head of the Cambridge Press, was Mrs. Eddy's publisher in her Boston years and later, and also her loyal friend. This letter illustrates her generosity to a friend in financial need.

students to heal the sick, and bringing in large returns.

In those days, busy as she was, her labors on revisions of her book were unremitting. By 1890 *Science and Health* had reached its fiftieth edition. Few books ever written reach their fiftieth printing and fewer still, perhaps none, have produced a tithe of such results in so short a time. From the small beginnings in 1882 when she came to Boston, and with twenty-six members held services in a small hired hall, the movement grew till at the end of this period it numbered two hundred and fifty trained practitioners at work throughout the land, twenty incorporated churches, ninety societies not yet incorporated as churches, and thirty-three academies and institutes.

Even before Mrs. Eddy's removal to 385 Commonwealth Avenue, Christian Science was rapidly pushing its frontier line to the Pacific. Strong centers were developing in various cities, particularly in Chicago, to which she paid her first visit in 1884.[44]

In 1888, came a pressing call to revisit Chicago,[45] which already, as Lyman J. Gage a few years later wrote, "ambitious to excel in everything,"[46] was becoming a favorite convention city. Thus the National Christian Scientist Association had shown wisdom in planning for its first nation-wide convention in Chicago. Delegates from every state were sure to be present, for Mrs. Eddy had so worded her appeal as to make it irresistible. "Let no consideration," she said, "bend or outweigh your purpose to be in Chicago on June 13."[47] It was a virtual summons to meet her there.

Thousands, who in one way or another had felt the widening outreach of her thinking, longed inexpressibly to go to the convention that they might look upon the face, touch the hand, hear the voice of the one woman in all the world whose prayer, thought, and published words—especially in *Science and Health* and at that time also in the *Journal*—had been used of God to restore to sound health of body as well as mind many long regarded by themselves, and often also by others, as incurable.

As delegates began to arrive by every train headlines in the Chicago papers greeted them with the assurance that their "prophetess" would appear. When, on the second day, the doors of Central Music Hall opened, eight hundred delegates and many more were there, packed so closely that every inch of room was taken. Impatient to set eyes upon the woman of their dreams, many were all but ready to greet her with such lines as Auslander's:

> Balboa of your fate, you stared
> On a Pacific none had dared.

When Mrs. Eddy stepped upon the platform, the audience rose to its feet as one man. Not expecting to speak, not specially prepared — as was Bryan [48] when his hour struck in the Democratic Convention of 1896 — Mrs. Eddy hesitated for a moment. Those nearest detected the instinctive recoil of head and hand. Then, Mrs. Eddy walked down to the front of the stage, at her best as always when the unexpected challenged. A hush fell on the crowd as, confident, serene, and smiling, she offered as a text, extemporized for the occasion, the first verse of the ninety-first Psalm: "He that dwelleth in the secret place of the Most High, shall abide under the shadow of the Almighty."

Without a note to aid her, without an abstract even in her mind, a pentecostal flow of golden eloquence began to pour from her lips. The substance of that sermon is in print.[49] Though superior to the published report of Bryan's Cross of Gold speech, the report we have is of small assistance in accounting for the effect of the sermon on that congregation. Some still alive who heard it become inarticulate when they attempt to describe the occasion. *The Boston Traveler's* account [50] is this:

> The scenes that followed when she had ceased speaking will long be remembered by those who witnessed them. The people were in the presence of the woman whose book had healed them, and they knew it. Up they came in crowds to her side, begging for one handclasp, one look, one memorial from her whose name was a power and a sacred thing in their homes. Those whom she had never seen before — invalids raised up by her book, *Science and Health* — attempted hurriedly to tell the wonderful story.
>
> A mother, who failed to get near, held high her babe to look on their helper. Others touched the dress of their benefactor, not so much as asking for more.
>
> An aged woman, trembling with palsy, lifted her shaking hands at Mrs. Eddy's feet, crying, "Help, help!" and the cry was answered. Many such people were known to go away healed. Strong men turned aside to hide their tears, as the people thronged about Mrs. Eddy with blessings and thanks.
>
> Meekly, and almost silently, she received all this homage from the multitude, until she was led away from the place, the throng blocking her passage from the door to the carriage.

Back to the Palmer House [51] Mrs. Eddy was taken for a little rest and quiet. But for once she was not to have her way. Rich and poor had preceded her and were waiting there, bent on seeing her again. They would not be denied. To touch that healing hand, to hear again that captivating voice, the people hemmed her in on every side. Crushing the flowers with which the Palmer House had in her honor hurriedly been decorated, they sought to press in closer to her. Heedless of torn silk sleeves and mussed lace collars, unmindful even of the precious jewelry they trampled under foot, the crowd grew importunate to the point of inconsiderateness.

As usual, Mrs. Eddy was gracious. She yielded to this astounding claim of personality. The rich wine of recognition of her teachings was warm and welcome after all those arid years in Tilton and in Lynn, and the earlier years in Boston. She was deeply gratified to have the truth which she represented receive recognition. But, as always in her notable career, looking ahead she feared that in the afterglow, preoccupation with her personality would prove to have been a disservice to the truth.[52] She foresaw — some friends outside believe — that the tide of popular favor, now surging full and free, would as likely as not a little later ebb as fast away. The situation was not to her liking. In fact, in the Palmer House, she was overheard to say: "Christian Science is not forwarded by these methods."[53]

On her return to Boston, Mrs. Eddy found her worst fears justified. Dissension long growing within had at last turned into revolution. Outside, the Dressers, after their return to Boston in 1883, had been developing a mental science movement of their own, shading off into New Thought.[54] The books of Reverend Warren F. Evans, more and more were being read. Arens's feeble and impertinent attempts to build up a personal business by displaying, as his own, goods which were really Mrs. Eddy's, were feeding a discontent now ready to break out. Almost under her eyes, Mrs. Sarah Crosse, whom she had trusted, was turning to other interests. Mrs. Gestefeld in Chicago, Mrs. Plunkett and Mrs. Hopkins were starting something in several western cities which they could not finish.

Before Mrs. Eddy could get back from Chicago, the "boring in" tactics of malcontents, endeavoring to dilute the larger faith of Christian Science and divest it of its wider implications, had turned into open rebellion already delivering its master stroke. A little group of thirty-six had obtained possession of the Association's books to facilitate the break they planned with Mrs. Eddy, without the danger and the degradation of expulsion. The Association's loyal Secretary, Mr. William B. Johnson, who had Mrs. Eddy's entire confidence, endeavored to induce the thirty-six conspirators to desist, reasoning with them that "now is the only time for us to meet in Christian love and adjust this great wrong done to one who has given all the best of her years to heal and bless." Nevertheless, the thirty-six would-be usurpers stood out a whole year, won at last their letters of dismissal, and went their way to oblivion.

But, those long and anxious months were for Mrs. Eddy months of close thinking. She was meditating on the implication of events. She was testing various inferences which might be drawn from such occurrences. If it were possible for a revo-

lution of such dimensions to break out within the
camp at the moment when her movement, far from
having a setback, was becoming national in scope,
changes — at least in the machinery — seemed to
be indicated. The stabilizing influence of her book,
published in 1875, had saved the cause shortly before. More now was needed, Mrs. Eddy was convinced, to conserve her Boston work by gearing it in
irreversibly to the developments appearing in the
West. The hour had struck to rally the far to
support the near, and thus to give the leader the
larger status obtainable only from a Christian
Science becoming nationalized, and on its way to
being internationalized.

Mrs. Eddy perceived the logic of the situation.
She fearlessly accepted the facts observable at their
face value. With a courage perhaps unsurpassed in
history, with an indestructible confidence correspond-
ingly unique in her central conviction, this woman,
sixty-seven years old, dismantled the machinery
which, out of tears as well as hopes, she had for years
been building up. She closed her college. She gave
up her active teaching. She retired from the editorial
supervision of the *Journal*. She disorganized the
Association.[55] Most significant of all, Mrs. Eddy definitely, even sharply, ordered those who followed in her
train to stop their at times sentimental and often unwise adulation of her personality. She charged them
peremptorily to turn their eyes away from her, and to
fix them on the truth. Then, to end the possibility of
her becoming a storm center, in the future more dangerous to the Cause than to herself, she ordered published in the *Journal* these Seven Fixed Rules.[56]

1. I shall not be consulted verbally, or through letters, as to whose advertisement shall or shall not appear in the *Christian Science* Journal.

2. I shall not be consulted verbally, or through letters, as to the matter that should be published in the JOURNAL and *C. S. Series*.

3. I shall not be consulted verbally, or through letters, on marriage, divorce, or family affairs of any kind.

4. I shall not be consulted verbally, or through letters, on the choice of pastors for churches.

5. I shall not be consulted verbally, or through letters, on disaffections, if there should be any between the students of Christian Science.

6. I shall not be consulted verbally, or through letters, on who shall be admitted as members, or dropped from the membership of the Christian Science Churches or Associations.

7. I am not to be consulted verbally, or through letters, on disease and the treatment of the sick; but I shall love all mankind — and work for their welfare.

Many years had passed since that evening on the streets of Lynn when, as though inspired, she said to young George Clark, "I shall have a church of my own some day." [57]

Now starting life anew as she neared seventy, Mrs. Eddy set her feet firmly on the path that led to the reorganization of The Mother Church, one day to include members from all parts of the world as well as Boston.

CHAPTER VI

AT PLEASANT VIEW

It was during the sixteen years between 1892 and 1908 that Mrs. Eddy, in retirement at Pleasant View, came to the fullness of her powers and the widening of her influence. Freer there than in Boston from ceaseless demands, often importunate, upon her time and her vitality, Mrs. Eddy, turning threescore years and ten, could at last, by careful planning, obtain a larger measure of the ordered life which she had become convinced must be hers to discharge her rapidly expanding responsibilities.

To two of her friends, who were holding positions of importance in the Publishing Society, she indicated in July, 1898, that what she now was doing they too could do if they seriously set themselves to the task, even under less favorable conditions in Boston, of commanding the time which real thinking requires, and also of developing the ability to say "No" to unwarranted encroachments on their busy lives:[1]

You can take my method, bar your doors, and then hold your solitude with moral dignity by meeting the merciless selfishness of callers with a *fixed rule* and the divine imperative Principle to be alone with God and never break this rule till you have your interval of study and prayer. I am an exception to all peace on earth — but not to "good will." The mail and the male and female claim undisputed powers to break my peace and rob me of all individual exemption from labor. But you have no need of thus surrendering your rights for others. I have written this in bed in the still hours while others sleep, — after 3 o. c. in the morning.[2]

No other woman so far along in life — and only a few men like Thomas A. Edison and Mr. Justice Holmes — are on record as having paid such a price for an opportunity to serve the public, as Mrs. Eddy had to pay even after she withdrew to Pleasant View on the edge of Concord, New Hampshire.[3]

Her day was laid out with precision. At six in summer and by seven in winter, Mrs. Eddy was accustomed to arise. Her hour for reading and for meditation she habitually observed. Of this one of her household tells us:[4]

Often she would preface some morning Scripture-reading with the confiding invitation: "Come and hear what God said to me this morning," and then she would read as God's ambassador, or as the good God speaking indeed. There was nothing of the assumed or artificial in all her reading; she read with the unaffected grace of a heart overflowing with humility and understanding, even as she spoke from demonstration, — as one who had suffered and who had a right to speak.

Another says, who was with her those ripe years:[5]

It was Mrs. Eddy's custom when she came into her study in the morning to open her Bible and *Science and Health* and read the verse or paragraph on which her eyes first rested. Sometimes after she had read aloud the selections to those in the room with her she would call the other students and give them a little lesson from what she had read or instruct them as to what it was necessary to handle at that particular time. During the first days I made a few notes of the lessons she gave which I will copy here. They may not be her exact words as they were written after the lesson.

July 15, 1907. Opened to Romans 14:22, "Hast thou faith? Have it to thyself before God. Happy is he that condemneth not himself in that thing which he alloweth."

Mrs. Eddy said, "We should allow nothing which we can-

MRS. EDDY SPEAKING, JUNE, 1903, FROM THE BALCONY
OF PLEASANT VIEW TO 10,000 CHRISTIAN SCIENTISTS

not justify. He who sees sin and condemns it not will suffer for it. Can we work out a problem correctly if one figure is not in accord with the principle of mathematics? Can I enter the kingdom of heaven if I allow one sin? Will not that destroy the whole problem?"

Meals were served on the minute, and any member of her household who was late was invariably regretful. Practical and artistic, Mrs. Eddy set a table well furnished and attractive. Her standpoint in this regard is clearly indicated in her remarks:[6] "To stop eating, drinking, or being clothed materially before the spiritual facts of existence are gained step by step, is not legitimate. When we wait patiently on God and seek Truth righteously, He directs our path."

Her attention to the kitchen[7] was as minute as that she gave her study. On occasion she herself could cook.[8] An expert housekeeper of the best New England type, even in her difficult days at Lynn, she was once found by a noted visitor in dust cap and apron, doing her housework and without apology even scrubbing down the steps. To-day the Chestnut Hill house, kept as she left it, is a model which any housewife would approve.

Because her life was lived according to a fixed routine, often there was time for little extras. Every morning as she walked through her home, she had a cheery word for cook and laundress, maid and friends. Sometimes she stopped a moment to rearrange some trifle on the whatnot or the mantel. Almost till the last, Mrs. Eddy could trip lightly down the stairs; or, as Mr. Joseph G. Mann has told the author, "come floating through the corridors like a young girl."

In the pitch and toss of wit and humor, she was always quick on the catch and the return; both in hearty commendation of good works, and in the sharp reproof of slackness, she never failed.

In fair weather after an outdoor walk, sometimes around the artificial pond which her students had caused to be built for her, Mrs. Eddy would receive her secretary with the morning's mail. As the years went by, larger discretion was given him in sorting it over, with the help of others, to decide on what, in the light of his experience, he felt Mrs. Eddy would wish to see. Many of her letters she wrote with her own pen; and, those dealing with the church or publishing concerns, were likely to be sent by special messenger to Boston.

Dinner was at twelve o'clock, ending invariably with ice cream which she specially liked. One at least of her household recalls the welcome sound of the grinding of the freezer at eleven o'clock each morning.[9]

The daily drive immediately followed and the coachman reported many evidences of Concord's friendly interest in its most distinguished citizen. For everyone, Mrs. Eddy had a friendly greeting or a smile. They might be friends or strangers, adults or children. In every case, she measured up to the cultural test which John Cowper Powys sets in the memorable phrase: "No one can be regarded as cultured who does not treat every human being, without a single exception, as of deep and startling interest."[10]

Though she had left Boston, she had not forgotten the city where she saw her work expand, and

MRS. EDDY LEAVING PLEASANT VIEW FOR HER
DAILY DRIVE

Mrs. Sargent and Mr. Frye accompanying her.

Taken in June, 1900.

she would have visited it more frequently had her busy life permitted.[11] On the visit unannounced of April 1, 1895, she spent the night in the room designed for her in the new church. It was on this first visit to her church that:

She asked to have the lights turned on in the auditorium; she first walked down the center aisle and stood a little while nearly under the dome. Then she came back and went down on the right aisle to the platform and knelt on the first step for a few moments as if in silent prayer. She arose and went to the steps at the left and up to the first desk, where she repeated audibly the Ninety-First Psalm, then over to the next desk and repeated:

Guide me, O Thou great Jehovah!
Pilgrim through this barren land:
I am weak, but Thou art mighty,
Hold me with Thy pow'rful hand.
Bread of heaven! Feed me till I want no more.

Open is the crystal fountain,
Whence the healing waters flow:
And the fiery, cloudy pillar
Leads me all my journey through.
Strong Deliv'rer! Still Thou art my strength and shield.[12]

Although before she left Boston to make her home at Concord, New Hampshire, Mrs. Eddy had given the land for the new church, she was as always more concerned to win her followers to the spiritual life. Most of the organizations formed in early years were by this time broken up, to encourage concentration on things more lasting than material forms.[13]

The teacher, regarding with concern the growing tendency to give her adulation, had removed herself from the center of activity that her teaching might be taken at its own intrinsic value. To a student in a position of responsibility she minced no words in indicating her position : [14]

First. Let my works, and not my words, praise me if I am worthy of praise.

Second. I always detested flattery.

Third. What is being said and written in such profusion of reference to, and praise of, me is not Christian Science and I hereby forbid its publication in the *Journal*.

Practically Christian Science is manifested by moderation, meekness, and love. "He shall not strive, nor cry; neither shall any man hear his voice in the streets. A bruised reed shall he not break, and smoking flax shall he not quench, till he send forth judgment unto victory. And in his name shall the Gentiles trust."

Never did Mrs. Eddy lose her business sagacity. The "Optimist" [15] of Philadelphia, who interviewed her in 1907, was impressed with it. Anyone who tried to outwit her in business was not unlikely to regret his zeal. The following incident [16] is one which Mrs. Eddy had delight in telling; it recounts an instance of her effective dealing with an avaricious neighbor.

With the improvement of Pleasant View in mind, Mrs. Eddy wished to purchase a little strip of land on which stood an unsightly barn. The old man who owned the objectionable adjoining half-acre seemed willing to accept Mrs. Eddy's tempting offer, but for some unknown reason raised his price as often as Mrs. Eddy agreed to meet his advancements.

At last Mrs. Eddy divined that a crafty neighbor, for his own benefit, was secretly manipulating the old gentleman.

She at once sent for this intriguing neighbor and, enlisting him in her behalf, engaged him to buy the property for her. She invited him to set his valuation on the barn in question which he cunningly placed at two or three hundred dollars. He then named the price for which he thought Mrs. Eddy might buy both lot and barn.

An agreement was made whereby he was to deliver to her

the deed for the property after which she was to make him a valuable present in lieu of commission.

The transaction went through smoothly ; the deed, accurate and safe in her hands, Mrs. Eddy said to her neighbor agent, "Now I will make you a present of the barn, and you may move it off as soon as you can."

The barn, really, was comparatively worthless, and Mrs. Eddy's would-be deceiver had deceived himself.

Mrs. Eddy laughed heartily when she told of teaching this schemer the lesson of his life, in letting him fall into the pit which he had dug for her.

While still worshiping in Hawthorne Hall, some of her students tried to raise a fund for the building of a church. Always alert, Mrs. Eddy was as often warning them,[17] "let there first be a Church of Christ in *reality* — and in the hearts of men before one is organized." As though to justify her warning, that first small fund was lost; but later another nucleus was raised, and a site was chosen. Even yet the money was not adequate and a mortgage had in consequence to be placed on the lot. When the mortgage fell due and Mrs. Eddy found her students could not pay it off, she bought the lot herself and had it conveyed to the Board of Trustees to hold for the church to be.[18]

In spite of their good intentions those associated with her in the enterprise again fell into financial difficulty, and again she took the lot over to save the project. In September, 1892, it was reconveyed to four of her students, "thereby constituting them the Christian Science Board of Directors." This Board was bound by the deed of transfer to hold the land in trust for the whole body of Christian Scientists in accordance with a law which had been discovered that permitted property to be held in this way.

By the end of 1894, the way was open, without the aid of church suppers or church fairs, to secure with dignity and dispatch funds ample for the completion of the church.   Built of gray Concord granite the church seated eleven hundred people, and the first service was held on December 30, 1894.   In the next month's issue of *The Christian Science Journal* (January, 1895) after thanking all who had helped to bring the enterprise to success, the treasurer requested that, after January, 1895, since the fund was sure to be completed and the books closed that month, no further contributions be sent.

In developing her great idea and adapting it to widening opportunities, Mrs. Eddy more and more became a jealous guardian of her time.   Too easily accessible while she was in Boston to every chance inquirer, at Pleasant View, an honored citizen of Concord,[19] with Mount Monadnock offering in the southwest a dim but lovely background, she found it easier uninterrupted to command the hours which she required to dream her dreams, to see her visions, and to express them all in print, in organization, and in stone.

To have written all she wrote between 1892 and 1907 would have taxed any genius.   Few newspapers could match her record.   In addition she started, in 1897, The Christian Science Publishing Society, perhaps the most successful organization of its kind in the world to-day; in 1898 *The Christian Science Sentinel*,[20] which every week continues to carry its message to many thousands; and somewhat earlier *The Christian Science Quarterly* containing the Lesson-Sermons which every Christian Scientist studies daily.

To this period also belongs her *Miscellaneous Writings*, which for a year took the place of class teaching; and, in addition to being a graphic guide-book, contains the substance of such addresses as that made by her in Chicago in 1888. As early as 1895 followed the *Church Manual*, to all Christian Scientists the most vitally useful book, next to *Science and Health*, which this woman of "The Vision Splendid" ever wrote:

> To lift to-day above the past,
> To nail God's colors to the mast.[21]

At Pleasant View, Mrs. Eddy also found the detachment she required to think ahead. As her teaching increasingly touched the hearts of her followers everywhere, her vision splendid included a larger building as cosmic as her teaching. But she would not be hurried. She would have her people "strong enough in God to stand." [22]

Ten years she had been living at Pleasant View before she suggested to the Church in Boston the need of a larger building. At the Annual Meeting in June, 1902, on motion of Edward A. Kimball, the Church was formally committed to the enterprise.[23]

In 1903, the land adjacent to the earlier building was acquired. The next year the corner-stone was laid. Then, in June, 1906, thirty thousand Christian Scientists from many lands came to share in the dedication of a church seating over five thousand, costing two million dollars, paid in advance — a church not incorporated by any state law because it was designed for world use, a church not unworthy to be compared with the cathedrals of the Old World.

The Christian Scientists who had come to Boston to see The Mother Church dedicated remained to attend the Wed-

nesday evening meeting at which testimonies of Christian
Science healing were given. The great temple was crowded
from floor to dome, and overflow meetings were held in the
original Mother Church and in four public halls. Many who
were not Christian Scientists were amazed listeners to the
outpouring of testimonies from every part of the great auditorium. Men and women arose in their places on the floor of
the church and in the first and second balconies. As each
arose he called the name of his city and waited his turn to tell
of the miracle of health and virtue wrought in his life as a
result of the study of Christian Science. The names of the
cities called up the near and the far of the civilized world —
Liverpool, Galveston, St. Petersburg, San Francisco, Paris,
New York, Atlanta, and Portland. There were negroes as
well as white men in that audience; there were French,
German, and Scandinavian; there were army officers from
Great Britain, and members of the British nobility, Americans
of great wealth, jurists, former doctors and clergymen, teachers, clerks, day laborers. It was like a jubilation of an army
with banners. And not only of the vanquishment of cancers,
consumption, broken limbs, malignant diseases, and paralysis
did these votaries of Christian Science testify, but of poverty
overcome, victory gained over drunkenness, morphine, and
immoral lives. It was a triumphant assertion of the health
and power of spiritual living.[24]

Home from Cuba, with his Rough Riders, Theodore
Roosevelt had just been elected to the Governorship
of New York State and an honorable peace was being
made in Paris, after our little unpleasantness with
Spain, when Mrs. Eddy, on November 20, 1898,
began to teach the last of all her classes.[25] Its membership was of her own choosing. Only those were
admitted who were specially invited by letter or by
telegram. Before the sixty-seven arrived, none knew
who else was included — each invitation having
evidently been marked "confidential." Her pride

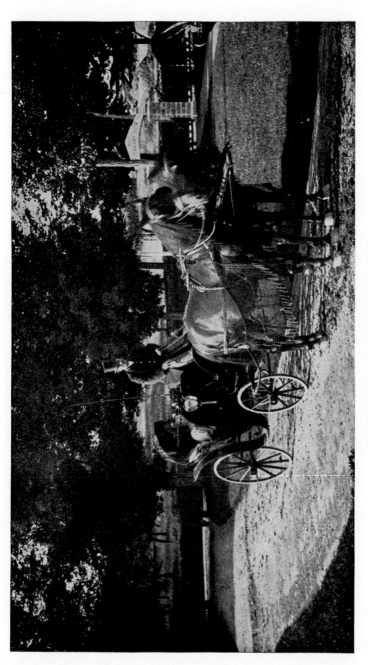

RETURNING TO PLEASANT VIEW

Mr. Frye on the box.

in them she expressed later by saying she was "glad to give to the world such men and women to demonstrate Christian Science." [26]

The recollections, written or oral, of several members of the class [27] are now before the author. United States Senator George H. Moses — not a Christian Scientist — says of the leader, "She was exactly the sort of woman I should have liked my grandmother to have been." [28] None have been found to differ from Mr. George Wendell Adams that, though well on toward eighty years of age, Mrs. Eddy appeared much younger — "a mature woman," vigorous, vivid, and so highly spiritual that one member will "never forget the heavenly look upon our beloved Leader's face." [29]

"Escorted by Mr. Frye," Mrs. Eddy "came into the Hall that Sunday afternoon with her quick, graceful, gliding step, and took her place on the platform. She looked from one to another over the whole class . . . with the most sweet, tender and happy expression." [30] Out of the richness of her spiritual experience, now at its maturity, Mrs. Eddy gave the Class of '98, already well grounded in Christian Science, perhaps the best instruction which any class received during her many years of teaching. She increased their confidence in their power to heal. She showed them how to improve their technique. She convinced them that the Sermon on the Mount [31] can be demonstrated in our everyday concerns. She bade them "run and not be weary," no matter how hard the way might seem, how baffling some of the cases which they wished to help. She emphasized the necessity of living the life they would have others

live.   The value of humility in all their relationships,
she indicated by a personal experience which she once
had at the bedside of a sick child.   "In my anguish
I bowed my head until it touched the floor, and when
the assurance came again of the loving presence and
healing power of God, the child responded instanta-
neously." [32]

Asked:

"Should we ever permit ourselves to speak harshly?"
"Oh," she replied, "there is a tight place.   We *must* separate
Truth and error."   Then slowly and sadly she said: "That
has cost me more suffering than anything else.   I have had
to see error when I most wanted not to see it." [33]

Their minds were every instant concentrated on
her words.   Their emotions were deeply stirred.   But
she was an expert.   She knew how to ease the strain,
as in reference to that day, when, a tiny girl, amid
the laughter of the other school-children, she said
she meant to write a book.   She knew how to use the
timely story; as, at the expense of the more austere
literalists, one day she said:

Some men were employed on a farm to hoe.   After working
some time one of the men laid down his hoe and started toward
the house.   Another asked him why he was leaving his work,
and the reply was that the man was thirsty and was going
for a drink.   "But," argued the second man, "that is not
according to the Bible."   "How so?" asked the thirsty man.
"Why, the Bible says, 'Ho, every man that thirsteth.'" [34]

She took a humorous fling at conventional philosophy in the story:

A tanner of hides bored a hole through his front door and
put a fox's tail through it, letting the bushy part hang outside.   People looked and wondered what it meant.   One man
passed the house many times, and finally the tanner asked him:

"Are you a minister?"   "No, I am not that."   "Are you a lawyer?"   "No, I am not that."   "Well, may I ask what you are?"   "I am a philosopher, and I have been wondering how that fox ever went through that hole." [35]

Aware of their unusual privilege, the Class of '98 learned that, first and last:

there was but one God, and consequently, there could be but one full reflection, which of course was the compound idea, man. She dwelt at length on the point that there could be but one full or complete reflection of one God, and that fact must be the basis for all scientific deduction. She indicated that only as her students grasped the fundamental fact that one God could have but one full reflection did they have the right basic sense of Christian Science, and know that there is no other starting point. [36]

Every religion with "bite" in it reckons with the devil. As Goethe [37] pointed out, man's way to heaven leads through hell, and in hell he meets the devil. Men may try to ignore the devil or to cut his acquaintance after they have met him; but, as Faust discovered, this is a large assignment. "The backward pull" is strong on all of us. Honesty compels agreement with St. Paul that "when I would do good, evil is present with me." [38]   More than once, Jesus indicated that his business here was to beat the devil, and to transmit to his disciples the power to do the same. [39] St. Paul's "thorn in the flesh" he once described as "the messenger of Satan." [40]   The Church Fathers debited the devil with all their erroneous doctrines as well as evil practices. In the Castle of Wartburg the stain on the wall, from the ink bottle which Luther is reported to have flung at the devil, still awes an occasional pilgrim.

Some of the substantial pious in the Valley of the

Connecticut were disquieted when, in 1741, in the most telling sermon which he ever preached, Jonathan Edwards multiplied the minions of the devil to his heart's content, and adjured his shivering people to believe that "the devils watch them; they are ever by them, at their right hand; they stand watching for them like greedy, hungry lions that see their prey and expect to have it." [41]

Mrs. Eddy was not the first defiantly to face the devil, or to doubt his power over souls. Nor is it surprising that, with the term "animal magnetism" so loosely used by many a tongue on both sides of the Atlantic that Disraeli said London was "mad" with it, Mrs. Eddy, when she was developing her teaching, should have coined the special name of "malicious animal magnetism," and in her correspondence abbreviated it to "M.A.M."

It was natural for Mrs. Eddy, with her insight into things spiritual, to understand the apparent attractiveness of evil which she, like others, was thought at times to personalize. There was nothing unnatural in her solicitude in season and out, to keep those around her on their guard against the subtlety and insidiousness of evil. Miss Shannon [42] says:

Mother explained to us what that was, and her explanation of evil indulged in was indeed terrifying. She showed us that, if we neglected to do our duty and did what was wrong without detecting, correcting and overcoming error, but continued repeating the same mistakes and justifying ourselves, the suffering which would result would be simple interest, which we would have to pay; then, if Christian Scientists refused to see the error *when it was shown*, and wilfully or maliciously continued to repeat it, allowing their thoughts to be governed by hate, malice, jealousy, or any of these subtle conspirators,

1898

Mrs. Eddy, as she looked at the time she taught her last class in 1898. This picture was presented by Mrs. Eddy to Mr. George Wendell Adams, who was a member of that famous class. It is from this that Timothy Cole made his engraving. (See illustration facing page 268.)

this would result in moral idiocy, and would bring compound interest. Then the experience of hell would ensue.

Miss Lucia C. Warren wrote in *The Christian Science Journal*, June, 1930:

Hers was the tender sensitive consciousness of the mother who must discipline and counsel her young, must feel responsible for their welfare and future attainments, must guard them from outward and contrary influences, must fit them to encounter alone, and without her, the billows of mortal experience, and to encounter them triumphantly.

Jesus set the precedent. He bade his disciples avoid the very appearance of evil. In the prayer Jesus offered as a model for us all to use, occurs the counsel: "Lead us not into temptation, but deliver us from evil." Jesus realized that most of those with whom he had to deal were apt to go to sleep when there was the greatest need that they should keep awake. It was, unhappily, the three closest to him who all but missed his transfiguration on the Mount because they were sleepy headed; and in Gethsemane — in spite of his pathetic plea — they could not keep awake one hour when:

> Into the woods my Master went,
> Clean forspent, forspent.
> Into the woods my Master came,
> Forspent with love and shame.
> But the olives, they were not blind to Him,
> The little gray leaves were kind to Him,
> The thorn-tree had a mind to Him,
> When into the woods He came.[43]

Slow of comprehension, many associated with Mrs. Eddy had to be treated like irresponsible children inclined to make something out of nothing.

Even that Class of '98 had the arresting question put to them by a teacher who left nothing unsettled: "Why make so much ado about nothing? Error is no more than a row of ciphers added from one wall to another, unless you place a unit with it and make something of it." [44]

But she paid them the distinctive compliment of saying nothing about M.A.M. Years later she herself wrote that she had not referred to it in teaching them.[45] Valuing beyond price what they had learned at Concord, the Class of '98, from none of whom Mrs. Eddy would accept any compensation, went their way to promote harmony among Christian Scientists and also to teach with more authority.

At Pleasant View the days for all passed quickly. Everyone was busy. By her own devotion to the duties which each day brought, Mrs. Eddy furnished an example which her household were keen to follow. Save for the daily drive, she allowed herself no recreation. Always engrossed in her work, she was never too engrossed to be kind. Painters working outside in the winter might feel the cold. Though Mrs. Eddy herself never drank coffee, she saw to it that her workingmen had coffee in abundance, steaming hot.[46] She expressed the tolerant views which she illustrated with the painters in a letter to General Charles H. Grosvenor: "Upheld by divine Love man can make himself perfect but he must not attempt this too rapidly with his neighbor." [47]

With many still living among those employed at Pleasant View and later at Chestnut Hill, the author has talked. All tell the same story of a woman unlike anyone else whom they ever knew and indescribably attractive. Their heartful recollections bring tears to the eyes and a sob to the throat. Several eminent citizens of Concord — not all of her faith — have put themselves on record. A former Mayor expressed the well-considered conviction that Mrs. Eddy was "keen of intellect and strong in memory." [48] "Reserved, deliberate, just," an editor [49] observes. And a lawyer was impressed by her "physical activity not ordinarily to be found in persons many years younger." [50]

Even from the small details of the lives around her she did not hold aloof. She spoke the word that helped, whether in admiration or in admonition. Never was she above the sharing with them of her intimate experiences, the entering fully into theirs. Says Mrs. Grace A. Greene: [51]

She would often say to me, "I make *my* pumpkin pies thus and so," or "I make puddings like this." One day I said, "Mother, can you really make pies and puddings?" She replied, "Of course I can." And then she told me of making herself a bonnet and dress when she was too poor to hire them done, although she had never done such a thing in her life before. She finished by saying, "If you are an ordinary cook, dressmaker, or milliner, Christian Science will make you *perfect* in any of these lines, and everyone should seek to perfect himself *wherever* he is, or *whatever* his calling."

As for her enemies, she was quick to detect and resourceful to checkmate any move to hurt her Cause. But the evidence abounds that her settled policy was, "Love your enemies, bless them that curse you, do good to them that hate you, and pray for them which despitefully use you, and persecute you." [52]

Even those who had once been close to her, and

then went away and sometimes "willfully or mistakenly perverted her teaching," [53] she kept on loving.
But she always drew the line between sin and the
sinner, and once with gravity and regret she indicated what might in some cases prove the natural
result of sinning: "Nothing except sin, in the students themselves, can separate them from me.
Therefore we should guard thought and action, keeping them in accord with Christ, and our friendship
will surely continue." [54]   Because she did love humanity, she was quick to reprove the errors which she saw
in individuals, obscuring the perfection of the real
man.   No matter how she made others suffer, she
suffered more herself.   Hers was that vicarious
suffering, more terrible to bear than that of persons
on whom, for their good, she felt obliged to inflict
pain.

Never did this woman of much loving, speak more
from the heart than when she said: [55]

There is a flower whose language is "I wound to heal."
There is a physician who loves those whom He chastens.
There is a woman who chastens most those whom she loves.
Why?   Because like a surgeon she makes her incisions on the
tender spot to remove the cold lead that is dangerous there.

Even a small part of her letter writing at Pleasant
View would have taxed the time of the modern
woman.   The collected masses of letters, mounting
up into the thousands, which she wrote with her own
hand, are bewildering to examine.   Her secretaries
helped her all they could in correspondence routine;
but there were many burdens which she alone could
carry, and these she carried with dignity.   As back
in her girlhood. when she was writing to Augusta

Holmes about the thousand and one things that
interest young people, so in the days at Pleasant
View, her mind now teeming with projects for the
benefit of millions, Mrs. Eddy became a great as well
as a voluminous letter-writer, unsurpassed in the
range of topics covered, in the widening sweep of
her vision.

Says Miss M. Louise Baum, sometime on the editorial staff of *The Christian Science Monitor:*

Even as the English Bible stands as the great monument of
English style for the centuries until now, and even as Dante
made Italian speech by epitomizing it in his fervent poem,
even so the writings of Mrs. Eddy are certain to stand as
models of twentieth century style, of direct actual saying the
thing itself, with every ornament inherent in the thinking,
never a piece of verbal trickery or tracery added from without,
with every sweeping passage of eloquence borne on the
actual high tide of spiritual revelation.   Mrs. Eddy's word is
yea, yea, and nay, nay.   She is herself what she says.   She
has lived it out, and so it is that her words live and kindle life
in others.

All through her letters runs that Victorian disposition to lend to duty an inexorableness for which
present-day behaviorism is a poor substitute in the
conservation of the higher things of life.   Friendship-love, based on a faith in God as well as man,
which every age requires, appears in her letter of
March, 1896, to Judge Hanna: [56]

Words fail to tell how much comfort your letter gives me.
It sometimes almost overcomes the sense of being to breast
the storms of mortal mind.   Then to hear such a bird note,
then to see such a ray divine of light and love coming from
human pen — O, is it not comforting?   I thank you, God loves
you, that is enough.   He will finish and furnish all that remains to be felt and known by us and all poor sinners.   Yours

and Camilla's photos are in my album side by side; but on
my mantle your face and Gen. Baker's are face to face. That
is the way you are in my heart. For I know you to be two
of the most genuine characters I have ever known, and I have
known grand and glorious ones.

Though Mrs. Eddy did direct The Mother Church,
she was habitually wise in training others to bear
responsibility. February 12, 1895, she writes: [57]

My beloved Students:

I cannot conscientiously lend my counsel to direct your
action on receiving or dismissing candidates. To do this, I
should need to be with you. I cannot accept hearsay, and
would need to know the circumstances and facts regarding
both sides of the subject to form a proper judgement. This
is not my present province, hence I have hitherto declined to
be consulted on these matters, and still maintain this position.

These are matters of grave import, and you cannot be in-
different to this, but will give them immediate attention and
be governed therein by the spirit and the letter of this scripture: "Whatsoever ye would that men should do unto you,
do ye even so to them."

I cannot be the conscience for this Church. But if I were
I would gather every reformed sinner that desired to come,
into its fold, and counsel and help them to walk in the footsteps of His flock. I feel sure that as Christian Scientists you
will act relative to this matter up to your highest understanding of justice and mercy.

Businesslike, forethought for the Church is also
shown in her constant regard for the observance of
all legal requirements. July 28, 1892, she wrote the
clerk: [58]

Remember dear student, that this Church must be properly
chartered, and its Constitution and Bylaws correctly made,
and accepted, and the whole proceeding be strictly legal.
Then, we have complied with civil law (and I always recommend this being done, wisely done) and then, every Church of

MRS. EDDY PRESENTS A PICTURE TO THE BOARD

Christ, Scientist, will have a precedent to follow whereby to establish the Gospel of Christian Science.

In an emergency she took the helm herself, and issued her commands in words too plain to be mis-understood. On September 29, 1893, with the plans well along for the original edifice of The Mother Church but one detail after another delaying the beginning of the work, she wrote the Directors: [59]

My dear Students,

Do not delay one other day to lay the foundation of our Church, the season will shut in upon you perhaps, and the *frost* hinder the work. God is with you, thrust in the spade, Oct. *1st* 1893 and advertise in next No. of Journal that you have begun to build His temple a temple for the worship and service of Divine Love the living God.

With great love   Mother
M.B.G.E.

Man as he was, St. Paul tried to mother each little group of converts which he left behind in town and city on his missionary tours. When visiting in those pre-airplane days was not practicable, he wrote them letters aglow with mothering counsel for their nurture in the Christian Faith.

In the founder of Christian Science, also, that mother instinct was strong. It included those near, those far, and those to follow in her train in all the years to come. There is nothing, perhaps, in all the history of womankind quite like Mrs. Eddy's loving forethought, flowing out toward all her spiritual children. As she looked back even to the sixties when she was building up her book, she realized that it had always been the invasion of wrong ideas, mortal mind,[60] into the circle around her that disturbed, unsettled, detached, sometimes took from her those who needed most the guidance which she gave. It was specially for them that she wrote in *Science and Health:*

The lame, the deaf, the dumb, the blind, the sick, the sensual, the sinner, I wished to save from the slavery of their own beliefs.[61]

It was for them she began in 1883 to publish *The Christian Science Journal*, in 1898 the *Christian Science Sentinel*, and in 1908 *The Christian Science Monitor*. Monthly, weekly, daily, she would have the members of her church read what she was convinced would make them immune to error. But, besides all her many books and papers, from *Science and Health* in 1875 to *The Christian Science Monitor* in 1908, something was needed for the complete mothering of her people, for the binding of them up so closely to the church that nothing could steal from them her revelation of 1866, — which for forty years and more she had been emphasizing, interpreting, enlarging, and widening as new problems came and pressed for a solution.

That is the reason why, among Christian Scientists, the *Manual* of The Mother Church to-day ranks next to *Science and Health*. They see in it the discoverer and founder of Christian Science, mothering her flock long after she had passed on, protecting them from ills when she had gone from sight, forestalling temptation and misunderstanding, and earnestly endeavoring to continue in the spirit — through the *Manual* — to protect them from their own mistakes and from the hurts which others might inflict.

To Miss Susie M. Lang she said on August 2, 1896,

DEDICATED IN 1895

This picture hangs in the Directors' room for which purpose Mrs. Eddy presented it.

"I was compelled by a sense of responsibility to put up the bars for my flock." [62]   Miss Shannon loves to recall that:

The first time that Mrs. Eddy saw the need of a manual for The Mother Church was in connection with teaching, and she told me to write to Mrs. Adams and Mrs. Webster of Chicago, whom she used to call "the twins." She wanted to see them to explain to them the need that she saw to preserve the teaching of Christian Science pure and unadulterated for future generations, and the wisest way she could see at that time was to have a Manual on teaching Christian Science. They came, and she showed them the right thing to do was to have a Committee of her old loyal students, with themselves, and for them to compile a set of by-laws in connection with teaching. This was done. Afterwards, God showed Mother that it was wise to make by-laws to govern all church members as well as teachers, which ultimately developed into the present Manual of The Mother Church, which includes articles and by-laws for teachers and teaching, as well as for Church discipline. [63]

In *The First Church of Christ, Scientist, and Miscellany* (230), we read, "Notwithstanding the sacrilegious moth of time, eternity awaits our Church Manual, which will maintain its rank as in the past, amid ministries aggressive and active, and will stand when those have passed to rest."

Rising to a more official relationship, Mrs. Eddy, on February 27, 1903, addressed The Christian Science Board of Directors:

Beloved Students: I am not a lawyer, and do not sufficiently comprehend the legal trend of the copy you enclosed to me to suggest any changes therein. Upon one point however I feel competent to advise namely: Never abandon the by-laws nor the denominational government of the Mother Church. If I am not personally with you, the Word of God, and my instructions in the by-laws have led you hitherto and will remain to guide you safely on, and the teachings of St. Paul are as useful to-day as when they were first written.

The present and future prosperity of the cause of Christian Science is largely due to the by-laws and government of "the First Church of Christ, Scientist" in Boston. None but myself can know, as I know, the importance of the combined sentiment of this church remaining steadfast in supporting its present by-laws. Each of these many by-laws has met and mastered or forestalled some contingency, some imminent peril, and will continue to do so. Its by-laws have preserved the sweet unity of this large church, that has perhaps the most members and combined influence of any other church in our country. Many times a single by-law has cost me long nights of prayer and struggle, but it has won the victory over some sin and saved the walls of Zion from being torn down by disloyal students. We have proven that "in unity there is strength." [64]

The *Manual* was issued during the very year that her flock began to worship in the new building of The Mother Church. When Mrs. Eddy was no longer visible, the *Manual* was her representative. Through its By-Laws she still speaks in preservation unadulterated of her teaching, in the government through the Board of Directors of her Church, and in the regulation of its services. Over her own signature the six Tenets of The Mother Church appear as follows:

1. As adherents of Truth, we take the inspired Word of the Bible as our sufficient guide to eternal Life.

2. We acknowledge and adore one supreme and infinite God. We acknowledge His Son, one Christ; the Holy Ghost or divine Comforter; and man in God's image and likeness.

3. We acknowledge God's forgiveness of sin in the destruction of sin and the spiritual understanding that casts out evil as unreal. But the belief in sin is punished so long as the belief lasts.

4. We acknowledge Jesus' atonement as the evidence of divine, efficacious Love, unfolding man's unity with God through Christ Jesus the Way shower; and we acknowledge that man is saved through Christ, through Truth, Life, and Love as demonstrated by the Galilean Prophet in healing the sick and overcoming sin and death.

5. We acknowledge that the crucifixion of Jesus and his resurrection served to uplift faith to understand eternal Life, even the allness of Soul, Spirit, and the nothingness of matter.

6. And we solemnly promise to watch, and pray for that Mind to be in us which was also in Christ Jesus; to do unto others as we would have them do unto us; and to be merciful, just, and pure.

MARY BAKER EDDY.[65]

Before ever big business or nations, in peace or war, had learned how to mold public opinion through the press, Mrs. Eddy provided in her *Manual* for a Committee on Publication, now found in every state and every land where Christian Science has organization, "to correct in a Christian manner impositions on the public in regard to Christian Science, injustices done Mrs. Eddy or members of this church by the daily press, by periodicals or circulated literature of any sort." [66]

As recently as last year the Board of Directors, with the *Manual* before them, broadcast the announcement,[67] "We assert the right to defend and protect our religion and persons connected with it from public misrepresentation"; and, as usual, they based their right on the specific words of Mrs. Eddy, "A lie left to itself is not so soon destroyed as it is with the help of truth-telling." [68] But they also counseled discretion, using their leader's very language. "Meekness and temperance are the jewels of love set in wisdom. Restrain untempered zeal." [69]

It was the multitudinous contacts with the public
through the press in carrying out her mothering
program, which made Mrs. Eddy a mystery woman to
many outside her fold and at last drew upon her
the light of pitiless publicity. Democracy is im-
pulsive. Democracy resents privacy. Democracy
wants to know it all. Regardless of the Declaration
of Independence, which declares for all "Life, Liberty,
and the pursuit of Happiness" — by reason of which
the United States Constitution promised for all time
to secure to us the right to worship God in our
own way — democracy worked itself up into an un-
seemly and even passionate curiosity to learn what
Mrs. Eddy really was like, by what means she had
amassed a competence reported to be large, and how
she had built up a church which was thrusting its
searchlight, as the Marquis of Lothian has lately
said, "past what all the greatest teachers have
recognized to be the transient and unsubstantial
phenomena of mortal existence into the eternal
reality which is the kingdom of God." [70]

With the opening of the twentieth century, the big
stick was in full swing and the muckrake was
plied busily, seeking the unsavory in public life.
"Tainted" money became a slogan with professional
reformers, and upon many of them Mr. Dooley's
humorous suggestion that the final proof of tainted
money with some is "'taint mine" was lost.

Any man with sufficient brains and purpose to
lift his head above the mass ran the risk of being
listed with the "scamps." Although there was
much public indignation at the inhuman treatment
which French procedure meted out to Dreyfus, a

growing disposition was in evidence to substitute for the Anglo-Saxon habit of assuming innocence until guilt was proved, the French habit of taking guilt for granted and requiring the accused to prove his innocence.

Great things were already on record to Mrs. Eddy's credit. Her book was long since built. Her church, too, was built and was becoming news to the whole world. Men of consequence, here and there, were observing that Christian Scientists did seem to be bearing the fruits of the spirit. Mark Twain dropped his jesting for a moment to predict that "Christian Science is destined to make the most formidable show that any new religion has made since the birth and spread of Mohammedanism."

But Mrs. Eddy's withdrawal from publicity to the privacy of Pleasant View, her success in so ordering her life as to secure the freedom needed to carry on her work and the quiet in which to hear the voice of God, tended to make her practically unknown, not only to America at large, but also to many of her followers whom she was constantly urging to put Principle before personality, her teaching before her visible self. Nor did the few pilgrimages, made at her invitation to Pleasant View, alter the case, no matter how much pleasure they brought the pilgrims. On the occasion in 1903, when ten thousand went by special trains to Concord, Mrs. Eddy spoke to them from the balcony outside her window. However, rumors continued to gain credence that the head of the Christian Science Church, overcome by physical infirmity, had "fall'n into the sere, the yellow leaf"; that she was at last in the power of a little selfish coterie who were managing her vast interests as they chose and concealing her not only from the public but even from her son, her adopted son, and her former intimates.

Big city newspapers were beginning to wonder whether, after all, Mrs. Eddy was still alive, whether she had not actually passed away, and whether a substitute, her face hidden behind a parasol, was not now in Mrs. Eddy's stead driving out every afternoon to deceive the world.

In May, 1905, departing from her custom, Mrs. Eddy granted an interview to a representative of the *Boston Herald*, whose write-up of the interview seemed so satisfying that Mrs. Eddy wrote the editor a message of appreciation. The next year, however, America gave an exhibition of that national inquisitiveness which Owen Wister characterizes as "peculiarly disagreeable" and "a perfectly unwarrantable invasion of one's privacy."

With the opening of October, reporters of a New York daily came prepared to spend some time in Concord, commissioned by their paper to find out whether Mrs. Eddy was alive or not. A few weeks later, on Tuesday, October 30, 1906, representatives of the Associated Press, the Publishers Press, and all the larger daily papers of Boston and New York — numbering fifteen — arrived at Pleasant View to interview her again. The report read that, though not conspicuously strong, Mrs. Eddy was very much alive and evidently capable of attending to her work.

Individual journalists, also, of the type of Arthur Brisbane and William E. Curtis visited her soon after, and a critical reading to-day of their impres-

WORKS ON CHRISTIAN SCIENCE
BY
REV. MARY BAKER G. EDDY.

325

Address all inquiries to JOSEPH ARMSTRONG, C. S. D.,
95 FALMOUTH STREET, BOSTON, MASS.

Pleasant View.
CONCORD, N. H.

Dictated.

Feb. 27, 1903

Christian Science Board of Directors.

Beloved Students:

I am not a lawyer, and do not suffic-
iently comprehend the legal trend of the copy you enclosed to me to suggest any
changes therein. Upon one point however I feel competent to advise namely: Never
abandon
change, the By-laws nor the denominational government of the Mother Church. If I
am not personally with you, the Word of God, and my instructions in the By-laws
have led you hitherto and will remain to guide you safely on, and the teachings
of St. Paul are as useful to-day as when they were first written.
prosperity
The present and future, of the cause of Christian Science is largely due
to the By-laws and government of "The First Church of Christ, Scientist" in Boston. None but myself can know as I know, the importance of the combined senti-
Church
ment of this, remaining steadfast in supporting its present By-laws. Each of
these many By-laws has met and mastered, or forestalled some contingency, some
imminent peril, and will continue to do so. Its By-laws have preserved the sweet
unity of this large church, that has perhaps the most members and combined influence of any other church in our country. Many times a single By-law has cost me
long nights of prayer and struggle, but it has won the victory over some sin and

(over)

"NEVER ABANDON

WORKS ON CHRISTIAN SCIENCE

BY

REV. MARY BAKER G. EDDY,

325

Address all inquiries to JOSEPH ARMSTRONG, C. S. D.,
95 FALMOUTH STREET, BOSTON, MASS.

Pleasant View,
CONCORD, N. H.

(2)

saved the walls of Zion from being torn down by disloyal students. We have
proven that "in unity there is strength."

With love as ever

Mary Baker G Eddy

N. B. I request that you
print this letter uppon
our church records

MBE.

THE BY-LAWS''

sions gives them even a more convincing finality than when they were first published. Arthur Brisbane almost naïvely said, "Nobody could see this beautiful and venerable woman and ever again speak of her except in terms of affectionate reverence and sympathy."[71] William E. Curtis, as skillful in his day in interviewing world celebrities as was Isaac Marcosson later, had just returned from China. Accompanied by a local Concord editor, he was received by Mrs. Eddy, to whom he explained in some detail the then recent Boxer Rebellion, and

made a statement about affairs in China, touching which Mrs. Eddy asked for more detailed and definite information, and quite unconsciously, seemingly, she took the topic entirely out of his grasp, and for more than an hour, dwelt on the details of the Chinese situation, with such a wonderful insight and with such intimate knowledge of its social, political and economic conditions, as to quite confound the man.

When she had closed her quiet talk, she rose, and after answering briefly some conventional questions, the audience was ended.

As we were leaving the room, Mrs. Eddy halted us and said facetiously,

"I hear I am not the person who goes for a short drive each day. If you wish to remain outside for a few minutes, you will see me enter my carriage and drive away."

We did as directed. In a short while, Mrs. Eddy stepped thru the doorway and into her carriage, smiling recognition at us as she passed.

As we drove from Pleasant View, Mr. Curtis marveled how a woman who so completely excluded the world could possibly know so much about the world's affairs, and particularly how she could have acquired such accurate and comprehensive acquaintance with the history and national habits of the Chinese, a people so little known, and with the court customs and the unpublished intrigues of its rulers. As we parted, he said, 'Just one more surprise, one more instance of where we came to preach, and remained to pray." [72]

Through 1907 and well into 1908, magazine articles which attracted much attention were exploiting her life story, based on such information as could then be unearthed and written with much journalistic skill. But at last the most incredulous were having to admit that Mrs. Eddy was at least alive.

However, a new flock of rumors was let loose — that she might as well be dead, that she had fallen into unfriendly hands, and was no longer altogether capable of caring for herself and her friends. With an adroit change of tactics the suggestion was put forward that it would be only kind, in the distressing circumstances, to invoke the law in Mrs. Eddy's best interest, to bring her legally into court that all the world might learn her real condition and join the law in saving her from her "household," and in turning her over to responsible guardians, described in law as "next friends." Although without large business experience the "Next Friends" seemed quite willing to assume responsibilities, vast and complex, for the management of the millions which they appeared to hope Mrs. Eddy possessed.

Her nearest heir was her son George, who was still in the Northwest, hoping prospector-like to strike pay-dirt in his paternity, and thus break into the ranks indicated in Madison Julius Cawein's line:

Some shall reap that never sow.

Without undue prodding, George's memory recalled a letter Mrs. Eddy once wrote him in which, mother-like, she confided, "I am as lone as a solitary star."

To his mining enterprises he had added risky building projects; and, because of them, he more easily
remembered that her replies to some of his requests
for money with which to experiment had not been
precisely what he could have wished. He was not
the first son to attempt to cajole a mother into being
too indulgent for his good, nor the last son to turn
against a mother who denied him for his good.
George W. Glover, together with his wife, required
but little coaxing to become the flying wedge in the
"Next Friends" game, the success of which would
give him, he hoped, some opportunity to share in the
handling of his mother's fortune, including obviously
valuable copyrights.

Among the increasing number of requests which
came to Mrs. Eddy for financial aid, there were
letters written by a nephew, whom she could personally have known but little. Only son of George
Sullivan Baker and his wife, "Mathy," of whom
Mrs. Eddy in her Tilton days had been fond, George
W. Baker, also, developed a grievance. His letter,
offering to sell some family heirloom to his aunt,
had been answered by a secretary at a time when the
task of personally attending to her vast correspondence was out of the question. A small-town mind
possibly could not be expected to understand how
one could be so busy; nor was it surprising that
George W. Baker was willing, at any inconvenience,
to come down from Maine and do what he could, in
his small way, to save his rich aunt from those she
knew and trusted, but who were scarcely even names
to him.

With an array of notable lawyers, led by ex-United

States Senator William E. Chandler, "The petition of Mary Baker Glover Eddy who sues by her next friends George W. Glover, Mary Baker Glover and George W. Baker *against* Calvin A. Frye, Alfred Farlow, Irving C. Tomlinson, Ira O. Knapp, William B. Johnson, Stephen A. Chase, Joseph Armstrong, Edward A. Kimball, Hermann S. Hering, and Lewis C. Strang" [73] was presented on March 1, 1907, to the Superior Court at Concord, for the appointment of a receiver for Mrs. Eddy's business interests.

The petition alleged that Mrs. Eddy was incompetent to care for her property, and questioned the loyalty of the "men and women near her." [74] The distinguished chief counsel appeared to expect little difficulty in winning the suit. To court he brought his considerable legal ability, wide experience, and more than local prestige. Nevertheless, in his very opening statement, in which he endeavored to draw a distinction between medical and legal insanity, he fell promptly into the old pitfall of trying to prove too much; for if in following his line of argument he established the insanity of Mrs. Eddy, he would inferentially establish the insanity of countless thousands sharing her views. Since no court, State or Federal, has ever yet regarded seriously any effort to draw an indiscriminate indictment against any large body of people in good standing, the Honorable Frank S. Streeter, leader of the opposing counsel, had little difficulty in persuading the court to dismiss that part of the case during the first day's session.

Next, an effort was made to bring into court by summons Mrs. Eddy in person possibly with the expectation that her age might place her at a disadvantage. But this scheme also failed, and the court took advantage of the opportunity promptly to raise the level of the proceedings by appointing three Masters to take her testimony — Dr. George F. Jelly (the noted alienist), Judge Edgar Aldrich of the United States District Court, and Hosea W. Parker of Claremont. By appointment, on August 14, the Masters, with the senior counsel on each side, came to call on Mrs. Eddy in her library at Pleasant View.

A woman past eighty-six, her restless fingers indicating awareness of the object of their visit and perhaps of a situation unparalleled in American Court procedure, received with grace and dignity her odd visitors, the strangest, perhaps, who ever crossed her threshold. Throughout the proceedings, the Masters were considerate. Lifting his kindly face a bit, Judge Aldrich at the outset requested Mrs. Eddy to give notice if, at any moment, she began to feel fatigued. At her best, as usual, in a crisis, Mrs. Eddy answered, "I can work hours at my work, day and night, without the slightest fatigue when it is in the line of spiritual labor." [75]

The purpose of the visit was disclosed in the question — which needed no explanation — next courteously put by Judge Aldrich: "What would be a sound investment of money that comes from life insurance or anything else?" Her answer, and the succeeding questions and answers which it called forth, made it evident to all that Mrs. Eddy was qualified, out of court as well as in, to make sound investments, and even to give instruction to others in their handling. Questions and answers are therefore given in full as contained in a volume, suppressed without general circulation, to which the author has had access:

Replied Mrs. Eddy:[76]

Well, I should invest it in the hands, at my age, of trustees that I could vouch for from my own knowledge. And why? Because, when I found my church was gaining over 40,000 members, and the field demanding me all over the world, I could not carry on the letters, make answers to inquiries that were made of me. Then I said, "Which shall I do, carry on this business that belongs to property, or shall I serve God?" And I said — and it came to me from the Bible — "Choose ye this day whom ye will serve. Ye cannot serve God and Mammon." Then I chose, and I said, "So help me God," and I launched out, and I gave my property — I gave $913,000 to the trusteeship, to others for the benefit of my son — no, not for the benefit of my son, but — $913,000 into the trusteeship for myself. For my son I gave $125,000 into trusteeship for himself and for his family.

Q. (By Judge Aldrich.) Where did that idea of putting your property into the hands of trustees originate, with yourself or somebody else?

A. Utterly with myself. It came to me in an hour in this room, and I think the first one that I named it to was Laura Sargent, and I said to her, "Do not speak of it, but I feel impressed that it is my duty."

Q. When was that?

A. That was in February, 1907.

Q. Last winter, you mean?

A. I do.

Q. Now this is all interesting and useful, but still I have not quite made myself understood. For instance, without regard to your trusteeship now, if you had a hundred thousand dollars to invest to-day, and we will lay aside for the purposes of this question the matter of trusteeship, what kind of investments would you consider sound, municipal bonds, or government bonds, or bank stock, or what?

A. I prefer government bonds. I have invested largely in government bonds, and I prefer bonds to stocks. I have not entered into stocks.

Q. Why?

A. Because I did not think it was safe for me. I did not want the trouble of it, that was all. Perhaps I was mistaken, but that is my business sense of it, and the only time I took the advice of a student and went contrary, I lost ten thousand dollars by it.

Q. What was that?

A. That was an investment that was made in property in the West, where the land, they said, was coming up and going to be a great advancement in value, and I lost it, and I never got caught again. I always selected my own investments.

Q. How do you select them now?

A. Now?

Q. Yes.

A. I leave them to my trustees.

Q. Before that?

A. I will tell you. I have books that give definitely the population of the states, and their money values, and I consult those, and when I see they are large enough in population and valuation to warrant an investment I make it.

Q. Well, now, upon what philosophy do you base your calculations upon population? Why do you take population as the standard?

A. Because I think they can sustain their debts and pay them.

Q. Well, I should think that was pretty sound. Would you go West for municipal investments, or would you rather trust yourself in the East, in New England we will say?

A. I would rather trust my trustees now. I do not take those things into consideration.

Q. Dr. Jelly desires that I should ask you, laying aside for the present the matter of trusteeship, what would be your idea, whether there was greater security of investment in Eastern municipalities or Western?

A. The East I should say.

After this, by request, Mrs. Eddy began to tell the story of the rise and development, and to explain the teachings of Christian Science. But something had happened. The atmosphere had changed. Never altogether at their ease, during an hour over long for them, though Mrs. Eddy was, as usual, courteous and kindly, the visitors were ready to go home. Her answers to the questions put the "Next Friends" suit into a parlous state. As Senator Chandler and a friend hurried down the stairway to the front door, the Senator was overheard, half to himself, to say, "That woman is smarter than a steel trap."

Through an ordeal, which perhaps few women in their prime could undergo, Mrs. Eddy had borne herself with engaging simplicity and sincerity. As always, she had dressed specially for the occasion. "She wore," says Miss Still, "a black grenadine dress with a white chiffon vest and collar and white ruching in the neck and sleeves." [77] As she was waiting for her visitors, she was serene, and even merry. Looking out toward Mount Monadnock, more visible than ever on that bright August day, Mrs. Eddy casually observed, "The 'Nexters' have fine weather for their trial." Miss Still, who was near her at the very moment Masters, attorneys and others came into the library, has lately told the author that "as one looked at her that hot afternoon there was no sign of fear expressed, but her face was calm, clear, and confident, and the moment that the opposing lawyer saw her sitting there in her study, he knew that he hadn't a ghost of a chance of winning his case."

But the experience hurt to the heart a noted

woman, whom Theodore Roosevelt[78] once compared
with other religious leaders decidedly not to her discredit.

To one of her household she confided, "If I were
a man they would not treat me so." [79]   Never was her
good sense more evident than when she said : "'During forty years I have had many trials and when this
came up I was not disturbed. If the world says I
am a fool, that does not make me so.'" [80]

While the suit was still on Mrs. Hulin — she tells
the author — once found Mrs. Eddy looking depressed, and heard her sadly say as if thinking aloud,
"I don't know, perhaps they will have their way."
Mrs. Hulin replied, "Mother, they will not. We
love you. You will win." Then Mrs. Eddy brightened up, and was herself again. She was not a
woman to take chances which she could avoid, or to
fail to take precautions against further annoyances.
Of one of her lawyers she inquired : [81]

If you let this case remain as it now is could the "next
friends" take possession of my person? If they could not
then is it not better to let this suit stand *as it is?* I fear if
you press it they will get Judge . . . to decide it against me
and give my person to my enemies (called "next friends")
and they will take me away from my real friends, students,
and thus *get rid* of me by such means, then fight over my last
will.

But not even this bitterest of all experiences that
ever came into that many-sided life could distract
her from her daily study and habitual revision of the
book, from her habit of meditation and persistent
praying, and also from her loving thought for others.
In the midst of this strange invasion of her busy life,

she gladdened one worker, just home from the field, by expressing the pleasure it gave her to learn of the proposed building of his little church. She added, "'I like those small beginnings. First, the right thought, then right words, and words proved by the hands.'" [82]

Michael Meehan, the capable and cultivated editor of Concord, though of another Christian fold, was, from the beginning, closely identified with the litigation of 1907. The participants on both sides, he personally knew. At the request, afterwards, both of Mrs. Eddy and of Boston friends, Mr. Meehan prepared a book for publication intended to preserve for all time the salient facts of a case which might one day become as famous in legal history as that other New Hampshire suit, the Dartmouth College case, which, some years ago, Alfred Russell stated had been cited more frequently in judicial decisions than any other case in American law reports.

Of *Mrs. Eddy and the Late Suit in Equity* — a costly book to publish — five thousand copies were that next spring off the press. The first copy was promptly sent to Mrs. Eddy. Till far into the night she sat up reading it. Next day she wrote its author that she wished the book withheld from sale and circulation. Perceiving and accepting the moral obligation involved, she added : [83]

You will render me a statement of all expenses to which you have been put. Make liberal allowance for those who have aided you in the work. Put a value upon your own time and service while engaged on it, and when you have done this, double the value you have placed on your own work, and double it again, and then send me the bill.

Mr. Meehan says:

I did this, and as soon as a complete bill was rendered, she wrote out a check in full of account, amounting to many thousands of dollars.

At the moment when most of us would have wanted to put before the public a permanent vindication from such unworthy charges as lay in the "Next Friends" suit, Mrs. Eddy was thinking of larger and less personal interests. Years before, in 1896, she had written Mr. William P. McKenzie, "Love unselfed, love of one's enemies, humility, moderation, strength, are the cardinals of Christian Science." Again she was practicing what she preached.

This book which to-day appears to at least one privileged reader to be in many respects a model of successful refutation Mrs. Eddy feared would "keep alive a memory of bitterness and discord, where obedience to God's law of harmony should be the aim of all." [84]

And so, under God, the "Next Friends" suit collapsed. And under God, Mrs. Eddy, nearing the advanced age of eighty-seven, moved on unhindered to her next world-vision task, the establishment of *The Christian Science Monitor.*

CHAPTER VII

"THE FULL GRAIN IN THE EAR"

On Sunday afternoon, January 26, 1908, as bright a day as ever May could bring, Mrs. Eddy with the ease and grace of a much younger woman,[1] walked across the platform and stepped aboard the special train scheduled to leave Concord at two o'clock.

To help a woman, even the youngest, into a railway coach is the courtesy which gentlemen are expected instinctively to volunteer. But Mrs. Eddy was in the car before anyone could efficiently give aid. There was good reason, too, why she did not desire assistance, even though she was in her eighty-seventh year. However, the "faithful John"[2] was allowed to walk beside her across the platform from the train shed. But that was all.

In defiance of the facts, rumors of infirmity and abnormality had long persisted; and always mentally alert, always looking ahead, Mrs. Eddy was not the woman to confirm erroneous accounts of her condition. What the merely curious and irresponsible might say to injure her, mattered less to her than the possibly evil effect of some carelessly spoken word upon the Cause she loved. Her concern, in consequence, was to insure that if anything were reported to the hurt of Christian Science, it should have no true basis, slight as it might be; that untruths, however studiously circulated, should without delay be known for what they were — sheer fabrications.

Besides, never, perhaps, in all history did another woman appear to understand as clearly as Mrs. Eddy the unreality of error, the transitory nature of untruth. Never, could there have been a woman who looked forward more steadily than did Mrs. Eddy past the individual erroneousness of the present to the general truthfulness of the ultimate.

Seldom could death have been in Mrs. Eddy's thought. When, on August 14, 1907, the "Next Friends" suit precipitated upon Pleasant View a group of unwelcome visitors as ill at ease as they were glad at last to bring their curious visit to a close, one of them referred to life insurance, Mrs. Eddy promptly answered, "God insures my life." [3]

Less than the robust Gladstone, passing at eighty-eight, did Mrs. Eddy almost as old either favor herself or ask those near to make allowances for her. At Chestnut Hill, she took an hour's rest each afternoon, sometimes dozing off a bit. But she was not unlikely to awake at three the next morning, to jot down a new idea or even to write a confidential letter.[4] With her rapidly increasing work, while she followed the routine approved at Pleasant View, she was more engaged than ever. She wasted no time on the unnecessary. She gave no thought to curious contemplation of the future. Her faith was reaching and outreaching, till at last — in Dante's phrase — it "eternalized" her life. No one more triumphantly than the joyous sage of Chestnut Hill agreed with St. Paul, "Death is swallowed up in victory." [5]

If, earlier, anyone had intimated that as 1908 opened she would be saying farewell to Concord, she would have given a retort characteristic and unmistakable.

Not all Concord citizens were Christian Scientists, but almost all held in high esteem — many in deep affection — the woman who had made the capital of New Hampshire more widely and lastingly known than ever Emerson, Thoreau, and the Alcotts had made the Concord of Massachusetts. She identified herself with Concord by little nameless deeds of kindness, timely gifts of shoes to scores of poor children, thoughtful gifts of flowers and fruits to neighbors and to strangers, and by a large generosity in promoting matters of great moment to the city, and by a liberal support of all worthy Concord enterprises.[6]

An evening or two after Mrs. Eddy said goodby to Concord, a group of men at the Wonolancet Club — as reported in the *Manchester Mirror* of February 3, 1908 — made an effort to determine what Mrs. Eddy's stay of almost twenty years among them had brought financially to Concord. The most conservative figures the evening produced ran as follows:

The Christian Science church, —	
Mrs. Eddy's gift	$ 225,000.00
Charitable donations	25,000.00
For good roads	25,000.00
Miscellaneous gifts and contributions	25,000.00
Pleasant View estate	40,000.00
Household expenditures	100,000.00
Income from special privileges granted to Concord manufacturers and business men	40,000.00
Granite contracts for Christian Science churches obtained because of Mrs. Eddy's residence and through her influence	1,000,000.00
Other known expenditures	90,000.00
Total	$1,570,000.00

The City Council was prompt to pass resolutions of unfeigned regret at her departure, and Mrs. Eddy wrote in appreciation:

To the Honorable Mayor and City Council, Concord, N. H.

GENTLEMEN :— I have not only the pleasure, but the honor of replying to the City Council of Concord, in joint convention assembled, and to Alderman Cressy, for the kindly resolutions passed by your honorable body, and for which I thank you deeply. Lest I should acknowledge more than I deserve of praise, I leave their courteous opinions to their good judgment.

My early days hold rich recollections of associations with your churches and institutions, and memory has a distinct model in granite of the good folk in Concord, which, like the granite of their State, steadfast and enduring, has hinted this quality to other states and nations all over the world.

My home influence, early education, and church experience, have unquestionably ripened into the fruits of my present religious experience, and for this I prize them. May I honor this origin and deserve the continued friendship and esteem of the people in my native State.

Sincerely yours,
MARY BAKER G. EDDY[7]

But the hour to go had struck. Larger plans, requiring that she be nearer Boston, engaged her interest. She was also ill at ease about those " Next Friends," who might, she suspected, let their chagrin lead them to make more trouble for her.[8] Slow in getting into court, the suit was also slow in reaching final settlement. Though she filed no complaint, she — with others — felt that a grave defect had been laid bare in the laws of her native and much loved state, or it could not have been so easy for designing men to persecute a citizen — a woman, at that — to feed avarice, to make "news," or to satisfy a merely

morbid curiosity. Her years alone should have suf-
ficed to protect her.[9] Massachusetts might furnish
conditions more auspicious for her expanding use-
fulness. She could hope to have more peace of mind.
Whatever the reason, the hour to go had struck.

The trip[10] from Concord to Chestnut Hill was
almost uneventful. Save her own party, none were
at the station in time to see her off. Comfortably
settled in her stateroom, Mrs. Eddy was an interested
traveler, appearing at the journey's end as fresh and
animated as when her train pulled out of Concord.

Dr. Alpheus B. Morrill traveled with her; but as
the nearest kin at hand, rather than as her physician. Mr. Frye and Mrs. Sargent were on duty.
Mr. McLellan was with her and also Mr. Tomlinson,
who recalls her cheeriness along the way. Mr. John
C. Lathrop was, as usual, ready to render such
secretarial assistance as might be needed.

Arriving at Chestnut Hill Station, one of Mrs.
Eddy's carriages, sent on ahead from Pleasant View,
was awaiting the train. As others of her party
entered the "hacks" ranged along the station platform, Mrs. Eddy walked quietly to her carriage and
at once started to drive the last mile to the new home.

As her carriage drove into the grounds, Mrs. Eddy
detected in front of the house a group of newspaper
men, notified by telephone from Concord after she
had left, that she was on the way. In the last
"hack," John Salchow also observed them, jumped
down, ran up to Mrs. Eddy's carriage as she was
ready to step out. She said, "John, can you get
me into the house?" He answered, "I surely can."

Then, before the newspaper men could guess his

intentions, John gathered Mrs. Eddy up into his stout arms, pressed through the bystanders, and carried her straight into the house. Up the stairs he bore her, set her down in a comfortable chair, and then her joyous laugh rang [11] through the hall. The only explanation of the episode which the papers of the next day had to give was that, "A huge Swede grabbed Mrs. Eddy and ran off with her."

The new house at Chestnut Hill had some time before been unobtrusively bought for her by the trustees, and as unobtrusively remodeled to meet the needs of Mrs. Eddy and her expanding household. Mrs. Eddy's own suite, at her request, had been made as like as possible to her familiar rooms at Pleasant View. Mount Monadnock and her birthplace, Bow, were no longer within sight; but from her sunny study window Old Orchard Road lined with well-kept estates was visible, and the hazy outline of Blue Hills.

At Chestnut Hill, the Pleasant View ménage was continued. If possible, however, more care than ever, under the *Manual*,[12] was exercised in selecting those fitted to give Mrs. Eddy the special aid she required to keep up with the multiplying calls upon her time and strength. By this time, it had become a highly prized distinction to be called to spend three years in Mrs. Eddy's household. Those summoned, eagerly, gladly, humbly complied, although the material compensation was a mere trifle. However, Mrs. Eddy sometimes reminded the friends near her that "trifles make perfection, but perfection is no trifle." There was, too, the Scriptural uplift:[13] "Every one that hath forsaken houses, or brethren, or sisters, or father, or mother, or wife, or children,

or lands, for my name's sake, shall receive an
hundredfold, and shall inherit everlasting life."

Mrs. Eddy required of those nearest her a literal
interpretation of the command of Jesus,[14] "Watch
and pray." On May 29, 1930, one[15] of them says:

With the penetrating spiritual luminosity which shone
through her as from out the heart of God's allness, Mrs.
Eddy untiringly reiterated to her household, and to a benighted
world, the Master's warning; — "Watch." The Godliness
of her ever alert being exemplified her own Godly watch —
and she loved her household as she loved herself by her
indefatigable call to them that they have oil in their lamps,
and watch to keep them trimmed and burning, — so that
evil's serpentine machinations be foreseen to the forestalling
of its workings through their sleepiness, their unwariness, or
their insufficiently spiritual aliveness.

When, now and then, Mrs. Eddy gathered her
"experts" for an intimate talk, she made short shrift
of sluggards. All were made to understand that
their watching and their praying were to be taken as
seriously as Mrs. Eddy took her own. She knew no
God *emeritus;* and those with her were permitted to
know none. To her, as she wrote in her textbook,
"God is infinite, therefore ever present, and there
is no other power nor presence,"[16] and in the name of
such a God — the Only God — she bade them
"Watch and pray."

"You can't alter meteorological forces by words,"
observes Dr. Shailer Mathews,[17] Dean of the Divinity
School of the University of Chicago. "I'm almost
sure of that — almost. . . . If I were in a storm at
sea, so severe it seemed we should sink, I'm pretty
sure I'd pray. . . . If only to get peace, courage,
inner unity."

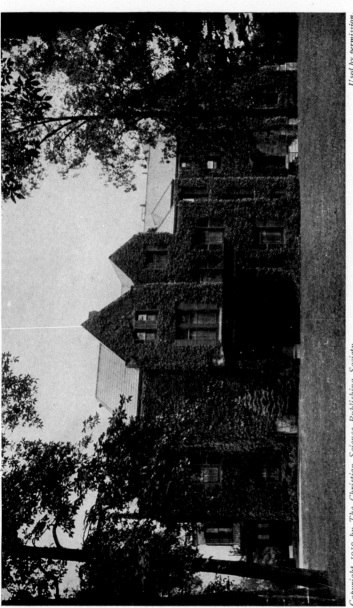

THE CHESTNUT HILL RESIDENCE

From the upper bow window at the left Mrs. Eddy looked out upon the distant outline of Blue Hills.

Mrs. Eddy set no limits to prayer. She prayed as Jesus bade us pray, assured, as Jesus was, that with God all things are possible. She even sought through prayer, intelligently offered, to bring about more harmonious weather conditions. Hers was a deep confidence in the efficacy of prayer, God willing, to control the weather. Perhaps it is worth noting that prayers of the same type are still found in the Protestant Episcopal Prayer Book, twenty years after Mrs. Eddy has passed on.[18]

The faithful Mrs. Laura Sargent specially "attended to the weather." But Mrs. Eddy would have her entire household understand what "attending to the weather" involved. No nonsense would she tolerate with regard to praying. One day she called several of them into her sitting room, made them stand up before her like school-children, and, going down the line she asked, pointing her finger at each in turn:[19] "Can a Christian Scientist control the weather?" Each answered, "Yes, Mother." Sharply, even scornfully, she said to each and all, "They can't and they don't. They can't, but God can and does. . . . A Christian Scientist has no business attempting to control or govern the weather any more than he has a right to attempt to control or govern sickness, but he does know, and must know, that God governs the weather and no other influence can be brought to bear upon it." Every Christian Scientist must pray in faith, and leave the rest to God.

Years never staled her sense of humor. Even her sharpest admonition was likely to be softened by a loving smile. A playful twitching of the lips would

reveal "the funny side" of a situation, which sometimes suggested a schoolboy frightened in the presence
of his teacher. Under severe correction, her students
one day were promising that next time they would do
better when, with a ripple of mirth, Mrs. Eddy said:

I am afraid you are like the Irishman that used to work
on my father's farm. He was so useless about the place
that my father finally called him and said, "Mike, I shall
have to let you go. You're not earning what I am paying
you and it is not right for me to keep you under the circumstances." Rather than be discharged, the Irishman pleaded
to be kept in my father's employ. He said, "If you'll only
keep me, sir, I will work for my week's board." "But,"
replied Mr. Baker, "you don't earn your board in a week."
"Well, sir," he said, "if I can't earn it in one week, I'll do it
in two." That is what your promises sound like to me. You
are not doing your work as you should, and you protest that
if you haven't done it heretofore, you will hereafter.

Upon another occasion, seeking to illustrate the
tendency of mortal mind to misrepresent, Mrs. Eddy
spoke of a neighbor in New Hampshire who wanted
to sell her father a horse. He represented the horse
as perfectly sound, gentle in disposition, and having
all the qualities of a family carriage horse.

My father said, "I am afraid he is too skittish for me. My
family needs a quiet animal that would not be frightened at
anything." "Oh," replied the neighbor, "Mr. Baker, you
couldn't scare this horse, no matter what you did." My
father replied, "Why, that horse would jump if you were to
say 'boo' at him." The man stoutly denied this and offered
to put the case to a test. The arrangement was that while
Mr. Baker crouched behind a large stump in the field, the
owner was to ride the horse by the stump, and Mr. Baker was
to jump out, and shout "boo." All was ready. The horse
loped past the stump. Mr. Baker jumped out, threw his

arms up in the air and yelled a vigorous "boo." The horse made a sudden lunge, threw his rider, and dashed across the country. The Irishman got up, brushed the dirt from his clothes and said, "Well, Mr. Baker, that was too big a 'boo' for such a small horse."

Never was Mrs. Eddy more human than in the ordinary give and take of social contact. She affected nothing. She abhorred all stiltedness in conversation, all pretentiousness in bearing. She put everyone at ease, and knew how to bring out the best in those around her. With her lovely voice often, in those later years, she joined her household in singing such old favorite songs as "Auld Lang Syne," "Comin' Through the Rye," "Annie Laurie," and "The Old Oaken Bucket"; such familiar hymns as "Nearer, My God to Thee," "Guide me, Oh Thou Great Jehovah," "Jesus, Lover of My Soul," and "I Love to Tell the Story." [20]

While she was still at Pleasant View Mr. John C. Lathrop [21] and his mother gave her that music box which she carried with her to Chestnut Hill, and often played. It was during the first winter there that the new Victrola came. The superior music, which it furnished, delighted Mrs. Eddy. Her joy was like a child's; it bubbled over. For a time she played her Victrola every day; and, when the new record — "Home, Sweet Home" — came, she had her household accompany the Victrola in singing it for her. As the last strain died away, playfully she addressed the Victrola, as though it were a human being, "Thank you, Mr. Singer Man, but I prefer my own choir to the choir invisible." Then turning serious, she meditated aloud to those present, "Home is not a place. It is a power. Going home is doing right. If you cannot make home here, you cannot anywhere. I am glad to have you, so many are going with me homeward and we will all meet there. Blessing immortal, eternal, infinite, comes not from personality, but through understanding of Principle." [22]

Those were the days when in cities and at remote crossroads the big news was the discovery of the North Pole. With his right to the discovery at last confirmed, Admiral Peary was in demand by publishers and lecture bureaus. One description, which he gave of his experiences in the far North, was turned into a record. After listening, all intent to it, Mrs. Eddy, in her inimitable way, quietly observed, "Why, it is matter talking."

William E. Curtis was not the only globe trotter to find Mrs. Eddy, whose travels ordinarily extended no farther than her library, unexpectedly well-informed about countries distant as well as places near. Other guests at Chestnut Hill departed full of the wonder which Mr. Curtis felt after contact with a stay-at-home mind as accurate as it proved well-furnished. Lady Mildred Fitzgerald of England relates in March, 1930, that on her several visits to Mrs. Eddy she had been specially impressed with Mrs. Eddy's "grasp of world affairs" and with her untiring efforts to bring England and America together by closer bonds. But those with her every day had the most substantial reasons for respecting her world-mindedness. When after a time at Chestnut Hill John Milton's birthday came, on December 9, she made Milton's line, "They also serve who only stand and wait," the subject of an extemporaneous

THE PORTRAIT OF MRS. EDDY PAINTED IN HER LATEST YEARS

talk on "Timeliness," which one to-day recalls for its vividness and impressiveness, closing, as it did, with the unforgettable sentence, "The right thing done at the wrong time is no longer the right thing."

The author, in the course of his researches, has met many of her Chestnut Hill entourage. All have added to the totality of the steadily accumulating impressions of Mrs. Eddy's genius for attaching the rightly disposed to her by her unfeigned interest in human beings.

One of them says, "I loved to hear her laugh, — a wonderful laugh when she had time to laugh." [23] He also recalls the physical agility of this extraordinary woman long after she could be called young. She loved sometimes even to slip nimbly up into her desk chair, curl her feet under her in tailor fashion like a college girl to-day, and go merrily to her work. He remembers her intimate familiarity with the details of the life around her, an insight into everyday existence which grew more penetrating with the passing years. "When she looked me in the eye," one says, "she seemed to look clear through me." One of the faithful seemed one day a bit depressed, and he still carries in his heart the little note she wrote him after he had left her house:

Dear Student
   You looked sad to-day. Is anything not right that troubles you? If so what is it? I thought it might be something about Maggie's stay here. Perhaps I can help you. With love   Mother.[24]

Another tells how she "scared him almost out of his wits" when, in reply to her inquiry, "Are you doing your work?" he answered, "I am trying to do it"; and she came back at him with this quietus for his irresoluteness: "Don't try, do it." Off he hurried to his room to attack more vigorously the work to which he had been assigned. Within the hour, he was summoned to her study, and was received with smiles and tenderness and praise. She knew, before he spoke a word, that he had pulled himself together and actually done his work.

And how she missed her loved ones when any of them had to be away! Sometimes she felt the separation so poignantly that she could scarcely bear it. With her, all through her pilgrim journey, to say farewell was a great grief. Eyes would, indeed, be dry that could not shed a tear when told how their beloved leader, finding one of her helpers would have for a time to be away, would hide her face in her hands, unable to say goodby. On one of these occasions Mrs. Eddy called the faithful round her and tenderly remarked, "We are all one family, and when my parents would go away we children used to get together and say to each other, 'Now you will be good to me while they are gone, won't you?' So we must all be good to each other while one of us is away."

Her love for those who gave her help embraced all dear to them. It extended even to the household pets — their cats, their dogs, their horses. A little note, written shortly before to one of her faithful helpers, reads:

My Darling Son:
   Pull up the strawberries — they are not in the proper place. Give my love to Pauline and greetings to *Kitty*. Mother.[25]

To-day "Sam" Shoemaker is contributing much

to the development of a technique for the maintenance of genuine personal religion. Perhaps no feature of his technique is more significant than the emphasis which he places on self-disclosures in associating with those who are hungry for the riches of the inner life. Jesus loved to talk his heart out to his comrades by the way. He wanted them to realize that he, like them, was human, and had to solve the same problems which came to them. No open minded reader of Mrs. Eddy's writings can misunderstand either the general drift of her teaching or such forthright and downright words as these: "To think or speak of me in any manner as a Christ, is sacrilegious."[26] As early as 1902 she was counseling her people: "Follow your Leader, only so far as she follows Christ."[27]

Feeling the responsibility to safeguard herself against excesses of adulation, or any other disposition to set her apart from her fellow human beings, she was ever on the alert. Many-sided and ample as was her personality, there was no room in it for spiritual conceit. St. Paul had no exclusive copyright to the thought, decidedly hers as well as his:[28]

Brethren, I count not myself to have apprehended: but this one thing I do, forgetting those things which are behind, and reaching forth unto those things which are before, I press toward the mark for the prize of the high calling of God in Christ Jesus.

But her humility found its choicest expression in the outpouring of her heart to those who knew her best: "Oh what a reward for the 'cup' it is to know that God has made me, me, so poor, so nothing in my sight the means of telling His power and grace and glory!"[29]

The final settlement of the lawsuit was not effected until November 10, 1909. Even though the ultimate victory, now as usual, was hers, she soliloquized, "For every mistake Mother has ever made, she has suffered, and suffered, and suffered." [30]

Christmas Day dawned clear and cold in 1909 in the gray stone house on the hill. Always up by seven in the winter, the leader that day entered her study earlier than usual. As, responding to her call, the happy household came with a smile into the room, she greeted them with, "A cheery, Holy Christ Mass to you all."

Never in the years that followed could they recall a day when she seemed more alive mentally, more vigorous physically, more gracious in manner, or more tender in word. None needed to be told, although all were keen to hear:

I love to observe Christmas in quietude, humility, benevolence, charity, letting good will towards man, eloquent silence, prayer, and praise express my conception of Truth's appearing.

The splendor of this nativity of Christ reveals infinite meanings and gives manifold blessings. Material gifts and pastimes tend to obliterate the spiritual idea in consciousness, leaving one alone and without His glory. [31]

To turn Christmas Day into a riot of extravagant giving never made any appeal to Mrs. Eddy. She would keep the holy season true to its profounder meaning, and members of her household still recall the impressiveness with which, on that last Christmas Day, she said, "A holy, uplifting sense of Life, Truth, and Love is the true Christmas."

Though none foresaw that it was to be her last Christmas Day with them, her next word sounded grave: "By another Christmas there will be great changes.   See that you make them for the better."

Before noon, again the faithful were called round her, and Mrs. Sargent read to them what the beloved leader had just written on a sheet of letter paper lying on her desk:

My *Household*
Beloved :
    A word to the wise is sufficient.   Mother wishes you all a *happy Christmas*, a feast of Soul, and a famine of sense.
Lovingly thine
MARY BAKER EDDY.

To this woman of the spirit, Easter brought a happier opportunity than Christmas Day to speak her supreme message.   The Easter couplet was of her own writing : [32]

Joy — not of time, nor yet by nature sown,
But the celestial seed dropped from Love's throne.

Her lifelong love of flowers reappears in her proclamation to the children of her faith to gather "Easter lilies of love with happy hearts and ripening goodness."   Though she discouraged careless giving, she always took into account the motive.   One of the friendliest of her Easter messages was written to Mr. Edward A. Merritt, a member of the Board of Directors of The Mother Church :

Your Easter memory expressed by this most *beautiful* and unique design is prized by me quite beyond words to express. Accept my heart's thanks for this priceless pin.
    I will wear it in memory of you at the throat of my best gown. [33]

To Mrs. Eddy, Easter had one overwhelming meaning, and one only : "Mortality's thick gloom is pierced. The stone is rolled away. Death has lost its sting, and the grave its victory. Immortal courage fills the human breast and lights the living way of Life." [34]

One of the faithful reports the substance of the little Easter sermon she preached to her household. The text has slipped from memory, but the context would indicate it was from Ephesians IV: 22-24:

That ye put off, concerning the former conversation, the old man, which is corrupt according to the deceitful lusts; And be renewed in the spirit of your mind; And that ye put on the new man, which after God is created in righteousness and true holiness.

As this member of her household noted at the time, Mrs. Eddy first gave the true meaning of Easter. Next she spoke of putting off, not keeping, "the old man." Then she said in substance: [35]

We have but one Mind; and to abide in this perfect freedom of individuality is the resurrection, —is to have risen above material or lower demands. The resurrective sense is positive; it is "yea, yea and nay, nay." The resurrective sense does not listen compromisingly to error. It is *always* about its "Father's business,"—reflecting Principle. Jesus' whole life was resurrective; that is, his life was a constant conscious rising spiritually above sin, sickness, death; and his resurrection from the grave was to sense a type of divine Love's final triumph over the human belief that matter is substance, or has power to impose limitations to Mind or man.

Like the *Manual, The Christian Science Monitor* was a product of the leader's mothering instinct.

My Household

Box G. Brookline, Mass. Dec 25, 1909..

Beloved: A word to the wise is sufficient. Mother wishes you all a happy Christmas, a feast of Soul, and a famine of sense. Lovingly thine

Mary Baker Eddy.

A HAPPY CHRISTMAS

She would have the minds of those she loved immune every day, as well as every week and every month, to the evil influence which she believed newspapers exerted. Long had this peril been in her thoughts. When as early as 1883, she was establishing *The Christian Science Journal*, she wrote:

Looking over the newspapers of the day, one naturally reflects that it is dangerous to live, so loaded with disease seems the very air. These descriptions carry fears to many minds, to be depicted in some future time upon the body. A periodical of our own will counteract to some extent this public nuisance; for through our paper, at the price at which we shall issue it, we shall be able to reach many homes with healing, purifying thought.[36]

All through that first spring at Chestnut Hill, she was preparing to launch her daily paper. In July, she took the Board of Directors into her confidence. Businesslike as ever, she held back, however, till the last of the indebtedness on the Publishing House was cleared. But the very next month, on August 8, 1908, she wrote the Board of Trustees:[37]

It is my request that you start a daily newspaper at once, and call it the [38] *Christian Science Monitor*. Let there be no delay. The cause demands that it be issued now.

You may consult with the Board of Directors, I have notified them of my intention.

The reply of the Trustees, dated August 11, is one of the most important letters in the Chestnut Hill files. It runs:

Beloved Leader:

Your letter of August 8th was delivered to us yesterday. The announcement contained in your letter is good news. We are confident that this move is timely; that the Monitor will be a mighty instrument for the promotion of Christian

Science; and that it will be a success from a business stand-point. We rejoice to have this additional opportunity of assisting you in your plans for the welfare of humanity.

As soon as we received your letter we immediately began the work of starting the new Daily and we shall proceed with it without delay. To-day we consulted with the Board of Directors. To-morrow and next day we will confer with two practical newspaper men from Pittsburgh and Chicago whom Mr. McLellan has called here as advisers.

Gratefully and lovingly yours,
Wm. P. McKenzie
Thomas W. Hatten
Clifford P. Smith
Trustees of the Christian
Science Publishing Society.

The mere intimation that Mrs. Eddy was starting a newspaper at once brought in almost four hundred thousand dollars, which was enough both to buy the land required for the enlargement of the Publishing House and to construct on it the building necessary. While the construction was still in progress and Boston reporters were working overtime to find out what actually was happening, the new presses were placed; and, on October 17, 1908, an editorial in the *Sentinel* announced that:

With the approval of our Leader, Mrs. Eddy, The Christian Science Publishing Society will shortly issue a daily newspaper to be known as *The Christian Science Monitor*. In making this announcement we can say for the Trustees of the Society that they confidently hope and expect to make the *Monitor* a worthy addition to the list of publications issued by the Society. It is their intention to publish a strictly up-to-date newspaper, in which all the news of the day that should be printed will find a place, and whose service will not be restricted to any one locality or section, but will cover the daily activities of the entire world.

It will be the mission of the *Monitor* to publish the real news of the world in a clean, wholesome manner, devoid of the sensational methods employed by so many newspapers. There will be no exploitation or illustration of vice and crime, but the aim of the editors will be to issue a paper which will be welcomed in every home where purity and refinement are cherished ideals.

For this new publication, Mrs. Eddy took the full initial responsibility. No one wished to snatch it from her, few to share it with her. No one envied her such brave initiative. There was no precedent to guide her. For her novel task, she had no special training. In her eighty-seven busy years there had been no spare time to learn to run a daily paper. No religious organization whatever had before that made a success of a daily paper. Most of the weekly denominational journals were then — and many still are — run at a deficit when they are not actual failures.

Some loyal Scientists, not the Trustees of the Publishing Society, hoped that the two words *Christian Science* would not be in the title of the new paper. Why add to the obvious difficulties? When before its first appearance she named the paper *The Christian Science Monitor* and even stressed the *The*, some had misgivings which proved too strong to conceal. She was earnestly solicited, at the very last, to recall her decision. When the first copy of the *Monitor* came off the press, it was taken out to Chestnut Hill for Mrs. Eddy to approve. With trepidation, Mr. Archibald McLellan,[39] who had definite convictions about the matter, went into the leader's study to make one last appeal for the abbreviated title. Almost as soon as he disappeared, he reappeared, disappointment and dejection in his habitually cheerful face. "It is no use," he said, "the name will have to remain *The Christian Science Monitor.*"

In spite of the counsel of some friends, and the expectations of some enemies, she gave her paper the name it bears to-day, directed that the cover should be "illustrated with a pretty design," and placed on the editorial page the motto: "First the blade, then the ear, then the full corn in the ear." [40] Even the first style type font, best of its day for newspaper use, was of her selection. Later, at the request of the Board of Trustees, she expressed in print the desire that Christian Scientists should subscribe to the new paper. Every wish of Mrs. Eddy was, and is, a command to loyal Christian Scientists. In every detail, her interest was constructive and constant. One of the first editors a few years later wrote: [41]

No wonder Mrs. Eddy was an ever-inspiring Leader to work for, and no wonder there grew up around her a body of devoted assistants. No matter how hard they might work, she worked harder still; and for months and years, while they were receiving her constant and incisive instructions, they read with mingled amusement and amazement the stories of her mental incapacity and the failure of the movement, which then, very much as now, constituted in the Press the news of Christian Science.

The Christian Science Monitor made its bow on November 25, 1908, the day before Thanksgiving. The editorial leader was from Mrs. Eddy's pen. It struck the keynote of a policy unchanged in all the years: "The object of the *Monitor* is to injure no man, but to bless all mankind."

From that first issue, the author has made it his business to record impressions and collect opinions about the *Monitor*, in newspaper offices on either side of the ocean. He recalls his talks, during the Great War, with editors of daily papers in London, Paris, New York, Chicago, Kansas City, Denver, San Francisco, Los Angeles, and other cities of the new world and the old, and the frequent tributes which he heard paid by eminent newspaper men to the *Monitor*. Of a certain substantial college in New England, a representative has observed that it is the second choice of more graduates of other colleges than any other institution in the land. It might be first choice were some starting new. No higher praise could be desired. Among newspapers, the *Monitor* would seem to occupy somewhat the same position as that college. Every editor is loyal first to his own paper. Practically all the many with whom the author has discussed the *Monitor* speak next for it. Last May the *Monitor* was singled out by Batten, Barton, Durstine, and Osborne for first place as a national advertising medium, with no other daily paper even a close second.

There is, perhaps, no field in which success is achieved with greater difficulty than in journalism. Certainly no service which the Christian Churches could render is potentially superior to the establishment and the maintenance of high-grade newspapers, standing for the best things in public life. But the author is here but faintly echoing professional opinion of more importance than his own. An editorial in German in *The Christian Apologist* of December 25, 1929, published by A. J. Bucher,

Methodist Editor at Cincinnati, pays this impressive tribute to the *Monitor*: [42]

Regardless of what one may think of the health society which terms itself The Church of Christ, Scientist, we must at least concede them one thing, and that is they have brought forth what all the Christian churches in the United States combined have thus far failed to produce, namely, the publication of a daily newspaper edited in a thoroughly Christian spirit. Their *Christian Science Monitor* stands high above our American daily papers, both as to contents and form. It carries good and dependable information concerning the most important incidents of the day, both domestic and foreign. Each issue contains an excellent and dignified leading editorial on some question or topic which stands in the foreground of public interest. Christian Science doctrine is held entirely in the background. Shouting headlines, found on the front pages of our daily papers, are entirely missing, as are also the sensational and the professional newspaper fiction. Each good reform movement is observed and is vigorously supported. The paper takes its place resolutely on the side of law and order, as for example, on the prohibition question. A good clean atmosphere pervades its sections of light literature. It serves the most varied needs and interests of an intelligent group of readers. With its handsome proportions, excellent paper and print, the *Monitor* presents a distinguished appearance.

If all those in the American Federation of Churches would lend a hand, there is no doubt but that we could publish a Christian daily newspaper — and that, too, with a large measure of success — which is one of the most crying needs of the present time. This would be a newspaper which would not consciously and deliberately lie, but would give out the truth, which would not serve sensation but information, which would not be in the pay of alcohol interests nor stand in political cross currents, and which would keep from its pages the immorality through which we must wade in the average daily paper. It would be a newspaper that we would not be afraid to have our children read. Here would be an opportunity to put on record the fact, which we stress so zealously, that we Protestants, with all our differences in minor points, are nevertheless one in essentials. It is high time that we had such a newspaper in America. When will it appear?

Not even those days, crowded with details necessitated by the launching of the *Monitor*, were free from the characteristic annoyances which seemed ever at the heels of this woman of expanding interests. With opera glasses, a young woman in the neighborhood was spying much on her, growing bolder as Mrs. Eddy started for the drive which she missed only once in all her days at Chestnut Hill.[43]   To reprove outsiders was not Mrs. Eddy's habit. She reserved reproof as a compliment to those for whom she felt immediate responsibility.[44]   But love, unclouded by resentment, almost always proved effective in her dealing with strangers.   At last, when the intrusion had degenerated into rudeness, Mrs. Eddy sent her driver to the girl with an overflowing basket of delicious peaches and her card on which she wrote a brief word of kindly interest.   Curiosity turned at once into respect, and the young woman is reported to have come to like Mrs. Eddy.

Never was any Christian Scientist more assiduous in the daily study of the Bible Lessons than was the founder of the faith.   Each of the many thousands devoted to the cause has his own hour, or hours, for studying the Bible and his textbook.   Business men and women are often up at five o'clock to devote two hours before breakfast to the study of their Bible Lessons.   Some busy home-keepers steal an hour from their work in the morning or the afternoon for the same purpose.   A few sit up late at night to do

their work.   Whatever hour they choose, they study
their Bible Lessons every day.   This is a spiritual
phenomenon to which Christians everywhere may
well give increasing heed, and by which there may be,
as years go by, profit beyond all estimating to the
Church of Christ.

Mrs. Eddy's reliance on the Bible was absolute.
The well-thumbed and much-marked copy which she
used at Chestnut Hill, the author has had the privilege of using in the preparation of this chapter.   Out
of the Old Testament, she drank deep of spiritual
truth.   Not morbid and yet not unmindful of the
claims which advancing years were making, the
author finds her one day in 1909 meditating on Isaiah
XLVI : 4 : "And even to your old age I am he : and
even to hoar hairs will I carry you : I have made, and
I will bear ; even I will carry, and will deliver you."

But her favorite in those days was Philippians IV :
8–13 :

Finally, brethren, whatsoever things are true, whatsoever
things are honest, whatsoever things are just, whatsoever
things are pure, whatsoever things are lovely, whatsoever
things are of good report ; if there be any virtue, and if there
be any praise, think on these things.

Those things, which ye have both learned, and received,
and heard, and seen in me, do : and the God of peace shall be
with you.

But I rejoiced in the Lord greatly, that now at the last
your care of me hath flourished again ; wherein ye were also
careful, but ye lacked opportunity.

Not that I speak in respect of want : for I have learned,
in whatsoever state I am, therewith to be content.

I know both how to be abased, and I know how to abound;
every where and in all things I am instructed, both to be full
and to be hungry, both to abound and to suffer need.

I can do all things through Christ which strengtheneth me.

He would indeed be unresponsive who failed to feel the uplift which this woman of large faith received as she gave to the Scriptures such interpretations as the following words which I find marked, in 1909, from the last copy of *Science and Health* which she used :

1. God is All-in-all.
2. God is good.   Good is Mind.
3. God, Spirit, being all, nothing is matter.
4. Life, God, omnipotent good, deny death, evil, sin, disease. — Disease, sin, evil, death, deny good, omnipotent God, Life.[45]

Even in the gathering twilight no joy was so great to Mrs. Eddy as studying her Bible Lessons.   There were times, indeed, when, with all her heart and soul, she wished she could be a member of the Lesson Committee ; and thus have a larger share in the spiritual education of the people of her heart, rather than in "settling impending difficulties, the effects of mortal sin." [46]

Until the very last, she was editing and reëditing her book.   In each new edition she made minor changes, and occasional larger alterations, as she was convinced the Spirit led her more deeply into the truth.   Her command of words grew.   No changes except those authorized by Mrs. Eddy have been made in the book since Mrs. Eddy passed on. But her own copy employs a vocabulary of ten thousand vital words, which has been assayed thus :

Every word means something.   Not one is thrown in as a makeweight or as a padding.   The weight and fluency of her style inheres in her thinking. There are no extra words to veil thought or to cover vacancy. She has achieved the great thing; her thinking stands forth in its naked sincerity as if she had done away with the medium of speech and had brought forth the Word itself which is one with thought and deed.

At Chestnut Hill, while Mrs. Eddy had secretarial help, yet with her own pen she still wrote many a letter. Ruthless in planning the hours for those around her, Mrs. Eddy was yet more ruthless in planning her own program so as to insure an extra minute here and there for the work which, in no circumstances, could she bear to neglect. This quaint note in Mrs. Eddy's own handwriting speaks for itself: "Maid one half hour to dine at noon. Mrs. Eddy has twenty minutes." [47] She knew the secret of finding time for everything important, and once observed, "'just a little duty performed each hour and each day, and at length symmetrical unity.'" [48]

Some of her letters bear marks of the pressure under which they were written. But not one is recalled which is marred by indiscretions or retaliations. What John Hay in his advancing years admitted, there was no need for Mrs. Eddy farther on in years to admit: "Every day I still write notes filled with indiscretions, and I can't help it." Mrs. Eddy could, and did help it.

Motherly in conversation with those around her, she was as much so in correspondence:

Your sweet letter at hand. I am *sensible* of the zeal and good works of dear Mrs. . . . and you. But none can know *my necessity* to *reprove*, rebuke, exhort, but the loving Father and Mother of us all. You all are babes in Truth and Love and the older you are the more the Mother sees to *love*, and

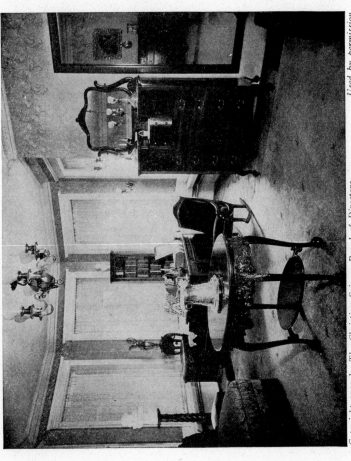

MRS. EDDY'S STUDY, CHESTNUT HILL

This room resembles in some detail the study she occupied for sixteen
years at Pleasant View.

to *reprove*. Why? because you *attempt* more, and each endeavor is an experiment with a student; whereas it is an old and proven effort with me and I know just how it will come out. The danger to the student is popularity and power, selfseeking instead of self abasement I have washed their feet and continue to do thus, and they must wash one anothers feet instead of elbowing each other, or they never can follow the example of our Exemplar.[49]

How considerate she was! To the Board she wrote:

Mr. F. . . . is carrying too big a burden. His salary does not pay his rent and clerks! Please vote to amend the By-law to read instead of three thousand dollars annually for the Pub. Com. not less than three thousand dollars. Then vote to increase his salary to five thousand dollars annually.[50]

To sacrifice herself was an instinct:

After forty years in your service I need more of my time to watch individually. I have neglected myself for others; now help your Leader by helping yourself. This is all I ask of a student; and is it too much, and will you not grant my request?[51]

Mrs. Eddy was not arrogant or pretentious. When in 1907 she began to look about for another home, she wrote:

I give up the thought of the estate in . . . for several reasons, one of which is I dislike *arrogant* wealth, a great show of it, and especially for one who *works* as well as preaches for and of the nothingness of matter.[52]

In business matters she was always strictly honest. To a student she said:

In doing business I am careful to account for all I take or appropriate, and I require this of my students. I may give them all I please, and they have that privilege with me, but I *demand honesty* of myself and of others — and strict accounts.[53]

Mrs. Eddy came even closer than that disciple who inquired if it was his business to forgive as much as seven times, to an understanding of the inexhaustibleness of the Christ spirit of forgiveness. To one long dear to her, and then for a time estranged, at last Mrs. Eddy wrote:

This lovely morning I wish I could see you and put my arms round your neck and tell you how much I love you. I never can feel so happy as when thinking of you in the old way and asking God to bless my child that so many years I have been accustomed to do, and must continue to do as long as memory lasts.

I have forgiven you in years past, and can and do again, because I love you and I cannot hold any enmity against one who has done the good that you have done; or even if they had done much that was wrong I must love all, because I cannot help it. I *feel* it and cannot feel otherwise.[54]

She did at times grow weary. Once she wrote:

Give oh give me peace — for one 24 hours in 30 years! You dear one, are fresh in the conflict I an old soldier weary of battle.[55]

But on she pressed until the very end, deserving Chesterton's inspiring lines:

So, with the wan waste grasses on my spear,
I ride forever, seeking after God;
My hair grows whiter than my thistle plume,
And all my limbs are loose, but in my eyes
The star of an unconquerable praise;
For in my soul one hope forever sings,
That at the next white corner of a road
My eyes may look on Him!

Her foreign correspondence brought Mrs. Eddy special joy. When the new Mother Church was dedicated three years before, in June, 1906, delegates had come from many countries, their very presence testifying that at last Christian Science had put a girdle around the globe. Even so, an eminent London surgeon was then predicting that in another quarter century, the edifices of Christian Science in London would be turned into music and lecture halls. But he was one of many in that time who needed to meditate upon the wisdom of the humble humorist who said, "Never predict unless you know"; for in June, 1909, news came that the First Church of Christ, Scientist, in London had not only paid for, but also dedicated, on June 13, 1909, a new building at a cost of four hundred thousand dollars. In addition, it had sent a thank-offering of some seven thousand dollars to the Publishing House.

Scarcely had Mrs. Eddy's joyous letter of congratulation gone overseas to her London followers when, in November, Christian Scientists of Scotland announced that they were ready to begin the building of the First Church of Christ, Scientist, in Edinburgh. To them she wrote a letter ringing with the peculiar satisfaction which such news as they had sent her must have brought to one whose ancestors had been Scotch : [56]

Beloved Christian Scientists :

Like the gentle dew of heaven and the refreshing breeze of morn, comes your dear letter to my waiting heart — waiting in due expectation of just such blessedness, crowning the hope and hour of divine Science, than which nothing can exceed its ministrations of God to man.

I congratulate you on the prospect of erecting a church building, wherein to gather in praise and prayer for the whole human family.

Lovingly yours,
MARY BAKER EDDY.[57]

As she drew near her earthly end, the woman of the stars seemed to be living in two worlds at once. Day by day she drew closer to God. At times she seemed to think aloud to Him. She advised her maid to speak to God about her own personal problems.[58] To one of her secretaries she casually observed "I'll tell you what God has told me to-day." Once, after making a remark which she wished at once to recall, "She placed her finger to her lips and said, 'That was Mary talking, now let God talk.'"[59] In emergencies, she gave her household special spiritual directions which they needed in their work.

Before any public appearance, however minor, she prayed to God to use her in His own good way. Once, at the end of a day filled with vexations, she prayed aloud, "Oh, Father, we turn like tired children to Thee; Thou wilt not leave us comfortless."

Mrs. Eddy accepted literally the account which Christ Jesus gave of himself: "I and my Father are one." But she said, "I cannot be a Christian Scientist except I leave all for Christ."[60] She never doubted that the familiar promise would be kept: "Lo, I am with you alway, even unto the end of the world." Jesus was her Way-shower.

Her eagerness to know what Jesus would do, if he were in her place, was sometimes very touching. Once, in approaching a problem, she remarked to a friend, "I wonder what Jesus would do." On another occasion it comforted her to observe, "Jesus would know what I am going through." Perhaps no leader of her time had better right to quote the lines attributed to St. Patrick:

Christ, as a light
Illumine and guide me!
Christ as a shield o'er-shadow and cover me!
Christ lie under me, Christ be over me!
Christ be beside me
On left hand and right!
Christ be before me, behind me, about me,
Christ this day be within and without me!

Never had she been quite so naïve, so childlike, as in those final weeks. "One night," says one of her helpers, "she called me to her bedside. She talked about the work. At last she had me tuck her in. But somehow she was not comfortable. She tossed about. She 'fussed' a bit. Then quieting down, with the smile we loved to see, she looked at me and said: 'Forgive me, Dear. I always was such a Betty.'" [61]

Happy Pilgrim of the Infinite, Mary Baker Eddy grew quieter as the days grew shorter. After supper, seated in her study, she would look down the driveway, watch the light come in the electric globes on either side the gate; then tell out the stars as, one by one, they brightened up the sky. Thinking of the things invisible, she would often glance a moment at her blessed Bible or her own *Science and Health* lying open on the desk.

Until the end she took her daily drive. The frosty fingers of an early winter were, with the coming of December, reaching out to touch the window panes, the woods, the hills. As she stepped into her carriage on the first afternoon in December, a heavenly smile was shining from her face and eyes. Each happy band of children, waiting here and there along the road to greet their "dear old lady," waited not in vain. Returning home, she rested a few moments in her study. Then, at her request, a pencil and tablet were brought to her. Hesitating a moment, Mrs. Eddy stooped slightly forward, and on the tablet wrote these words:

God is my life.[62]

Next day she was up and about. Her household gathered in her study, and she talked with them. They realized that she was failing. They had, however, so often seen her rally from a weakness even greater that, though foreboding, they were not over-anxious. All through the day, however, as they worked and prayed, they were ill at ease.

On December third, a half hour before midnight, her faithful household group around her, Mrs. Eddy passed quietly away.[63]

The final services, on December eighth, were as she would have had them. Across the snow-clad lawn at Chestnut Hill came, on that Thursday morning, about fifty guests. At eleven o'clock Judge Clifford P. Smith [64] read the ninety-first Psalm, which had furnished the text for the historic sermon in Chicago in 1888, together with portions of the Gospel of St. John, Chapters thirteen and fourteen. Mrs. Carol Hoyt Powers, Second Reader of The Mother Church, read Mrs. Eddy's poem, "The Mother's Evening Prayer." [65] The Lord's Prayer was recited in unison. Then the casket was taken up on the shoulders of affection, borne through the open gateway, and carried to Mount Auburn near Boston; and over the last resting place of this woman of the stars, the stately oaks now keep watch in solemn dignity.

A LAST WORD

CHAPTER VIII

"BY THEIR FRUITS"

Throughout her vivid life, Mary Baker Eddy often figured in the news columns. She paid the price which always must be paid for startling complacency or for breaking with conservatism. There were long stretches when room for some new depreciation or disparagement was about the only space she was allotted in the daily papers.

Only after she was gone, did Mrs. Eddy "make" the editorial page — a steeper grade to make than the news page. At last appreciation displaced the depreciation of earlier years. The adulation, against which in her lifetime she never ceased to warn her chosen, won readers from dark disparagement. Now that she was beyond the touch of idle gossip, not a few wondered why anything but praise could have been spoken of a woman who had kindled in the hearts of uncounted many a spiritual fire which showed no sign of dying out.

In her beloved Boston, the editor of the *Globe*, commented on her passing that: "Present day testimony must be one of respect for a woman of remarkable mind and of unusual ability." The editorial reference to her in the *Post* was a tribute to her for reviving primitive Christianity and adapting it to present day conditions. The editor of the *Evening Transcript* put Mrs. Eddy in the company of Julia

Ward Howe, who some weeks before had passed
on after winning earlier in her distinguished career a
well-deserved immortality by the writing of her
famous patriotic poem. Mrs. Eddy's verse is sung
each week by millions round the world; her books
many read; and her newspaper no one from the first
has grudged a place among the most substantial
papers of the time. Hers was a "career," according
to the editor of the conservative *Springfield Republican*, "from which everyone may draw immense inspiration . . . that must come from the spectacle of
astonishing achievement. . . . One may search history from the beginning and have difficulty in
matching Mrs. Eddy's performance, between the
ages of fifty and eighty, in making a million people
accept her at her own valuation."

Outside of New England, where praise or blame
is more outspoken, tributes to the leader of Christian
Science developed into such panegyrics as few persons in all history have evoked. Editors in New
York, Philadelphia, Baltimore, Washington, Atlanta,
Chicago, St. Louis, Kansas City, Denver, San
Francisco, Los Angeles, and many other cities with
one voice placed Mrs. Eddy among those of whom
it has been said that:

> Never to the mansions where the mighty rest
> Since their foundations, came a nobler guest.

If all such tributes to this woman who yearned
more for the praise of God than for any praise of
man be ruled out of reckoning, still no one seriously
doubts that Mary Baker Eddy was born to leadership. Scarcely one of its essentials did she lack.

When he coined his phrase "a prodigious example of insubmission, courage, perseverance, and ingenuity," Maeterlinck might have been painting Mrs. Eddy's portrait. Glimpsing in her girlhood the goal of her life work, she set her feet on a long trail which was to stretch across a century, and she followed on until the end. Her ineffable charm, which the years could never blight, brought many to her. By a process of careful selection and reselection, based on spiritual fitness, she was sometimes making those changes in her entourage which the higher interest of her cause demanded. She let all count with her, but — as Kipling advises — "none too much." To counsel she listened, but she made her own decisions.

When criticism seemed to her in order, she preferred to criticize in private. To praise, when she honestly could, she gave publicity; and never could one call it "the praise of men's forgetting." True, there were times when some charged that she played favorites; but none was ever bold enough to charge that she set her own interests above the cause she loved and those who tried to capitalize any distinction thus conferred upon them to the injury of the cause might find waiting for them round the corner the demotion which their indiscretion merited. She always followed through, and any in her train who failed to follow after were one day likely to discover that they had been left far behind.

Patient, sometimes over many a year, with the shifty and even the disloyal, Mrs. Eddy always drew the line the moment the good of the cause demanded it. Insubordination she never tolerated. To seek a quarrel was not her way; but, when a quarrel was

thrust on her, the regret at the outcome was rarely
hers.   In the life of Mary Baker Eddy, as of Ellen
Terry,[1] opposition called out her highest fighting
power.   More than once, in order to win, with one
stroke of her pen she demolished old machinery
and constructed — it sometimes seemed — almost
over night new machinery better fitted for the
changed conditions.

Many a pitched battle she fought to gain breathing
space in which to write, to discover, to build, to
organize, to construct; and if now and then, in an
almost continuous struggle against handicaps covering some fourscore years and ten, she was stricken,
her spirit remained as unbroken as the Scotchman's
in the ballad :

> Fight on, my men, Sir Andrew says,
> A little I'm hurt, but not yet slain;
> I'll but lie down and bleed awhile,
> And then I'll rise and fight again.

On the far-flung battle line of the faith she founded,
Mrs. Eddy turned a page as new in modern religion
as Einstein's page in modern science.   Some doubted
this while she was here.   A few were certain that her
work would not outlive her.   But even fewer now
worth while think in terms of death of her extraordinary movement.   From Count Hermann Key-
serling's[2] announcement that "every spiritual American who can be considered representative, actually
belongs, whether he knows it or not, to the wider
circle of Christian Science," to the admission of
Harry Emerson Fosdick,[3] "Anything that floats must
have some good timber in it, and Christian Science
never could have floated as it has if there had not

THE LEADER IN HER CHESTNUT HILL DAYS

been sound wood there," agreement has become general that Christian Science lives and grows and must be reckoned with.

Between Mrs. Eddy's discovery and Einstein's, the likeness is amazing. Changes in men's thinking have taken place since two centuries ago Newton conferred on space definite physical reality. Faraday, a century later, developed the "ether" concept to explain the electro-magnetic field. Within the memory of readers middle-aged, matter, once solid as a mountain in men's thoughts, has crumbled into molecules, the molecules into atoms, and at last the atoms into immaterial "particles" of radiation. Yesterday Einstein casually observed that space is "eating up matter," [4] a concept not altogether inharmonious with Mrs. Eddy's concept of God as good since M. K. Wisehart on his return last season from Europe reported Professor Einstein as now convinced that "God is as valid as a scientific argument." [5]

It is, however, in the field of imparting religion, that Mrs. Eddy's leadership excels. She is a literalist, wherever the spiritual teachings of Christ Jesus are involved. Hers is a spiritual technique highly effective. She has set the feet of millions in the path that leads up to the mount where the Ten Commandments are thundered forth to be obeyed and the Beatitudes break in blessings to be lived. The religious services of the Christian Science Churches are well attended, both on Sunday morning and on Wednesday evening. Weather matters little. The author has looked in on nights when it was pouring rain, and The Mother Church was well filled. He has made it his business to test attendance on a very hot night in early summer, and the people were there.

Reasons why Christian Scientists go to church as a matter of course are as evident as they are easy to set forth. For one thing, the details of their worship are so designed and perfected as to hold the close attention of the worshiper. The service is always brief. All present on Sunday share with the two Readers in prayer and join in the singing, which in Christian Science is as distinctive as it is truly congregational. Yet neither in the Sunday nor the Wednesday evening service is any stress laid upon the emotional. Nor is there any "long face" ever in sight.

A great teacher developed the Christian Science service to suit student worshipers. Not even Mark Hopkins on one end, with his student on the other, of that over-ridden log, deserves a higher place among the teachers of America than Mary Baker Eddy. She, too, first taught one at a time; and later, when increasing calls upon her hours obliged her to group her students into classes, she tried to keep the number down so as to give them the maximum possible of individual attention.[6] For all her teaching, she personally made careful preparation, and by the time her Boston Church was going strong she had a Committee at work preparing the Bible Lessons far in advance for all student worshipers.

One can be a Christian Scientist and little heed the magazines and newspapers, but one cannot be a Christian Scientist and omit the daily study of the Bible Lessons. The world over the author knows Christian Scientists, and he has yet to find one in good standing who cannot quote his Bible with a readiness and an accuracy which few outside that faith, even preachers of our day, can match.

The study of the Lesson for the preceding six days acts as a feeder for the Sunday service in which the same Bible passages which the worshiper has been studying through the week, are read from the platform accompanied by correlative sentences from the Christian Science textbook.

Every Sunday congregation, therefore, no matter where assembled, is both a company of worshipers and a group of students met together to receive more light on the studies they have made day by day, through the preceding week. Even in traveling, by land or sea, or in vacation time, wherever Christian Scientists are — however few — they read their lessons. Though no Christian Science Church may be within reach many when Sunday comes have their little service as though they were at home. With the same lessons studied everywhere on week days, and on Sundays read in church throughout the world, there is constituted a democracy, both of study and of worship, going far to explain "the crowded churches" which outside of Christian Science are the fascination and despair of Christian leaders. Rarely, in fact, are they to be found elsewhere save in the case of the few congregations fortunate enough to have a brilliant preacher, and even he must not often take the risk of preaching long.[7]

Every religious fold has some excellence by which other folds may profit, but the approach to it from the outside must be with understanding and with sympathy. Perhaps Rufus Jones [8] has stressed the greatest of all Christian needs, in making the awareness of the presence of God the one essential. Standing for the same eternal principle, Mrs. Eddy worked out a technique which keeps her followers, every one, constantly aware of God. But to this boon, she added practical demonstration of the intrinsic value of the Bible lessons used daily and their reading at the public services on Sunday and a literal acceptance of the healing promises of Jesus.

For a discussion of healing, no apology is made. The interest in the revival of apostolic healing is now widening. Many years ago the late Bishop Brent, while still in the Philippines, wrote the author in approval of Christian healing, and immediately after, on shipboard coming home, he even wrote a book for the author's editing in explanation of what the life of God in the soul of man can do for anyone. No later than last May, Bishop Remington of Eastern Oregon is reported to have summoned the Church to recover the lost art of healing. After twenty and more years of experimenting, started most intelligently by the Emmanuel Movement, the Protestant Episcopal Church has its Nazarene Society helping many; its Commission on Healing carefully studying with the Church's approval the ways and means of restoring what should never have been lost; and its latest General Convention seriously agreeing that "Christian healing has passed beyond the stage of experiment and its value cannot be questioned."

Mr. Frederick Dixon wrote:

People frequently talk of Christian Science as if it were nothing more than a mammoth dispensary; as a matter of fact, that is an almost ludicrous misconception of what its healing means. It means — the eradication from the human consciousness of all those mental causes which produce sin, disease, and death. It means that in order to be healthier every patient must become a better man. It aims not merely at the destruction of sickness and pain, but of sorrow and want, of misery and vice.[9]

The knowledge that the understanding mind does deeply influence for good the body pathological is not confined exclusively to the pages of *Science and Health*. Three hundred years before Mrs. Eddy announced that "Whatever is cherished in mortal mind as the physical condition is imaged forth on the body,"[10] Spenser, in his Faerie Queene, was reminding a believing public:

> For of the soule, the bodie forme doth take,
> For soule is forme, and doth the bodie make.

Some twenty-three hundred years before Mrs. Eddy wrote "Moral conditions will be found always harmonious and health-giving,"[11] Socrates was saying to Charmides, "First then and above all, the soul must be treated if the head and the rest of the body are ever to be made whole."[12]

In making the observation that "When spiritual being is understood in all its perfection, continuity, and might, then shall man be found in God's image,"[13] Mrs. Eddy was simply leading men back to the teachings of Him whom John Charles Earl thus describes:

> He pours the flood of light on darkened eyes,
> He chases tears, diseases, fiends away;
> His throne is raised upon those Orient skies,
> His footstool is the pave whereon we pray.
> Oh, tell me not of Christ in Paradise,
> For He is all around us here, to-day.[14]

While theologians were over-busy speculating about the personality of Christ Jesus, Mary Baker Eddy went to the heart of the practice of Christ Jesus and revived his healing ministry. She never claimed to have originated, but only to have discovered and restored, what had too long lain dormant since the passing of our Lord, and to have furnished a healing technique which all can learn to practice who will take the trouble in both faith and prayer. A study first-hand, with a mind unbiased, of her words and works usually substantiates her claims.

"The gods give thread for a web begun." In her long life on earth, Mrs. Eddy began a web, and in the twenty years which since have intervened, thread has been furnished in abundance to those she designated to carry on when she was gone. After the pattern she set, that web is still a-weaving. What the finished product is to be no one as yet foresees. No prevision is adequate. Those who understand the teachings of their leader are content to make the best use they can of the thread given them. The ultimate they leave to God.

Meanwhile the world at large keeps an eye on Christian Science. Every year it expects more of this faith. "By their fruits" the world is judging Christian Scientists. Some of the fruits of this new faith it is, therefore, now in order to consider.

At first, not all the fruits of Christian Science ripened. Not all, as early as Mr. James A. Neal,[15] of revered memory, brought forth fruit abundantly. Many of the earlier Christian Scientists were plain folk. Many of the men worked in factories, or in the field. The women were housekeepers, often broken on the wheel of drudgery. But they came to Mrs. Eddy. They sat at her feet. Something told them she had a message for them; and in listening to her words a reorientation came to them of which through all their later years they never tired of speaking. To some — as several told and also wrote the author years ago — the days they spent in Mrs. Eddy's class — opened to them a new heaven and a new earth. Not in all cases, however, did this entrancing experience last. The vision which she gave was sometimes allowed to fade out. Some of those earlier followers turned back to the trivial round and found it as trivial as it was before, to the common task and it seemed commoner than ever. But there were others who conserved their vision until the end, and until the end they testified that the healing touch which body and mind had felt lasted, and outlasted, time.

One of the earlier Scientists testified to healing of an illness before she ever met the woman wonderful. So deeply moved was she by her experience that she packed her bag, and hurried to Boston to see her benefactor. Not realizing that Mrs. Eddy had already become a very busy woman, the visitor was disappointed on ringing the door bell, to learn that Mrs. Eddy was too engrossed to see anyone. Not to be entirely frustrated, the well-meaning visitor begged to be shown a portrait which she had heard hung in the parlor. Almost as soon as she was admitted to the room she discovered herself in the presence of the woman she had come to see and thank. With both hands outstretched, Mrs. Eddy stepped forward, put her arm around her visitor, and promptly said,"I was in my study writing as busily as ever I wrote in my life when suddenly I put down my pen and came to this room. I knew not why." Before leaving the house the visitor had become a member of Mrs. Eddy's class, and later proved a worthy student.

Even in these sophisticated days the primitive type of faith persists, naïve and blessed in proportion to its simplicity. Coming down the automatic elevator in a city office building, late one night when the street floor seemed deserted, the author stopped a moment at the hallway desk of the watchman who was not then in sight. But near a low reading light a chair was drawn, and on the chair a book lay open — a little much worn copy of *Science and Health with Key to the Scriptures*. On solitary guard this faithful man, through the still watches of the night, was seeking intently for a clearer understanding of the truths he found in Christian Science. With a curiosity the author hopes is not beyond all pardon, he spied these words on the open page on which the watchman's eyes had rested and which he had marked:

Truth will be to us "the resurrection and the life" only as it destroys all error and the belief that Mind, the only immortality of man, can be fettered by the body, and Life be controlled by death. A sinful, sick, and dying mortal is not the likeness of God, the perfect and eternal.[16]

Dropping in one Wednesday evening at a service in a suburban church, the author heard a plain man tell his story. He was all humility, although for twenty years, as he explained, he had been a persistent student of Christian Science. During all that time he had never faltered, whether on the mountain top or in the valley far below. Some small success had come his way, sometimes also failure. Through the years, however, he had stood firm, and modestly he hoped he could with truth report some headway gained. For all that Christian Science had done for him he was grateful, and to the casual visitor his words rang true.

The testimony of the Christian Science lecturers is significant because, in lecturing to groups, sometimes numbering thousands and including many persons not of their own faith, they have to treat their subject in a generous spirit, of which such words as these are representative:

Christian Science is essentially Christian. It is calm, peaceful, serene, and divinely secure. It resorts to no emotionalism to excite an interest in itself. On the contrary, it appeals through pure reason and logic to the very best in one's nature. It repeats the saying of ancient times: "Ho, every one that thirsteth, come ye to the waters." [17]

The best practitioners have stories to tell from real life which, for spiritual insight, can scarcely be surpassed. Their work is not perfunctory. In emergencies, they remain in the sickroom day and night, denying discord and asserting God's presence and power until the hour strikes for the results to come. Back, therefore, of their calm and measured words, there is a wealth of hard facts to give weight to their words:

Christian Science is vital to men and women, because it presents a scientific explanation by which all may work out their own salvation. It explains all cause and effect as mental; and that sin, disease, and death are overcome by the understanding of the same divine Principle which enabled Jesus to heal the sick and raise the dead. Contrary to popular opinion, this healing is achieved not by any use of the human will or suggestion, but by the understanding of that which is absolutely true in the sight of God. It is indeed the "Spirit of truth," the Comforter which Jesus promised.[18]

The testimony of both the business man and business woman is to the author all the more impressive because he has talked with many of this type, from the expert secretary to the big business man, although it must not be forgotten that in Christian Science there is no small and great. In its spiritual democracy, Kipling's millenial lines find immediate fulfillment:

> And no one shall work for money, and
>   no one shall work for fame;
> But each for the joy of the working, and
>   each, in his separate star.

Of nothing in this book is the author more certain than of business efficiency in Christian Science. Not once has he failed to find the loyal Christian Scientist living up to the high business ideal which insures success. That ideal has been happily expressed by Mr. Charles E. Heitman in the words: "Alertness, worthiness, and love of our work determine its productive value." The Christian Scientist's eye is never on the clock. He wastes no time in loud or idle talk. He is never overtaken by brainstorms. His vitality he does not waste in worry or in hurry. Undercutting and side-stepping the true Christian Scientist never practices. His single-mindedness and happiness of spirit carry over into business life and make his every effort count toward high success. How could it be otherwise, when an hour, often two hours, he sets aside each day — sometimes in the early morning — for the study of the Bible Lessons, which brings the quiet mind, the ordered energy, the poised personality?

Nor is the author without much good company in his opinion. Years ago Michael Meehan — not a Christian Scientist — confirmed it:

Christian Scientists are successful. Why? They are in harmony with the law of the presence of God in all things, as forcibly demonstrated by the Founder of Christian Science; their complete acceptance of God's law makes them quickly responsive to the laws of their country and enhances their value as citizens; they do not gossip — they have neither the time nor inclination; their petitions over wrongs and grievances are not clogging court records; they are never found patronizing questionable resorts, nor are they engaged in questionable practices; they do not meddle in the affairs of their neighbors; they avoid even the appearances of evil.[19]

Mr. Clarence H. Howard, a business man of St. Louis, who long ago became convinced of the value of the tests which Christian Science sets up and which Mr. Meehan describes, successfully applied them in the development of the manifold activities of his Commonwealth Plan, until at last the Commonwealth Steel Company of Granite City, Illinois, of which Mr. Howard was President, has become one of the major industries of the Mississippi Valley.

Another outstanding example of business men who were Christian Scientists was Mr. William Delavan Baldwin, Chairman of the Board of the Otis Elevator Company, who testified:

It is now about forty years since I first became interested in Christian Science, and during all of this time I have been and am a strong and devoted adherent of the teachings of Mary Baker Eddy. Each year brings to me an ever greater appreciation of her wonderful character and the tremendous influence for good her revelations and teachings have had, and are now having with ever increasing force. The world needs the higher spiritual understanding and knowledge of spiritual healing taught by Mrs. Eddy, to solve and heal its complex material problems. Christian Science rests on demonstration.

No field has been more productive of a type of Christian Scientist than the Stage. Perhaps it is because stage folk have to pay a heavier price than most of us for any lowering of vitality. They must keep high their level of efficiency. Competition is so keen and public censure so immediate that if they do not give their best at every performance, they may have to say of the audience:

> They light me once,
> They hurry by,
> And never come again.

Twenty years ago *The Music Master* and *The Lion and the Mouse* were crowding theaters, and winning for their author, Charles Klein, a deserved reputation and also a large income. He overworked. His health broke. Life lost its zest for him. His associates believed him through. Suddenly he snapped back into larger success than ever. Asked to account for such an unexpected resurgence of health and effectiveness, he replied that he turned to Christian Science. In the *Cosmopolitan* for February, 1907, he wrote:

I gradually, indeed almost immediately, recovered my health, my peace of mind, professional and financial success, and happiness far beyond my wildest dream.

Since 1918, when as Vice-President of the Association of American Colleges, the author was brought close to many an institution, he has wondered: "Does Christian Science touch the college mind?" More recently he has listened to many expressions of opinion, talked with representative students, and also read the files of student letters received by The Christian Science Board of Directors, while administering the late Ruggles Educational Fund, established in 1926 under the will of Dr. Georgia Sackett Ruggles of Los Angeles, California, to assist young men and women, not only in this country but also in Canada, England, Germany, Holland, France, Switzerland, and other lands, to complete their education.

Among the distinguished American institutions represented in these reactions to Christian Science are Harvard, Williams, Brown, University of Chicago, Northwestern, and University of Idaho. The author heard a young college man, at a Wednesday evening service, express gratitude for the help which Christian Science was bringing to him in his college life. Not merely had his faith equipped him, he said, to handle better the problems of his daily living; it had also helped him through examinations, by the elimination of fear and its replacement by such a spirit of confidence and serenity as made it possible for him to marshal all his resources, which else would have been scattered.

The author was so impressed with the thoughtfulness of a Christian Science student, senior in another college, in which he was well regarded, that finally there was procured from him this statement in writing:

Of course, the average college man finds his religion up against a severe test when he first meets the cold lights of science and the paradoxes of philosophy, and the general attitude of skepticism which is so prevalent among undergraduates. I have seen many of my friends enormously disturbed as they watch the foundations of a none too objective religious background crumble out from under them. They often have to resort, in case belief in religion is not swept away, to retaining a non-rational and usually emotional faith, which is quite unsatisfactory to their reasoning intellect. For my part, having only just acquired a really workable knowledge of Science when I entered college, I have through college been most interested in putting it to the test under . . . conditions which ordinarily prove severe. I have even gone out of my way to do this as much as possible.

I can truthfully say, Dr. Powell, that there has been no problem that I have found in any of the departments of the college work, which I have not been able to settle definitely by using Science. I am constantly amazed at the completeness of Mrs. Eddy's writing. Using the concordances carefully, the most detailed points in such a highly complex subject as philosophy will be explicitly decided in her writings, with the scientific logic which characterizes the entire system. Or if there is not a direct answer to a given problem, the student can find statements which will enable him to decide for himself. I never have found a question which I could not solve in a way wholly consistent with Science, — to my complete satisfaction. I cannot tell you the value of having a firm and completely stable mental and spiritual system, which I have never known to fail. It means a mental vigor and decision which could come, I think, only from a consistently inclusive Science.

On another occasion, the author was fortunate to obtain from a Phi Beta Kappa man, ten years out of a great university, this thought-provoking opinion:

If I could speak to the college youth of to-day I would say this: the study and the practice of Christian Science will make you a better student with less effort; from my own experience in helping others I can say that there are no conditions of pain or suffering which Christian Science cannot eliminate, that there is no fear which it cannot cast out, no financial problem which it cannot solve; if my words have any weight it is only because they are backed up by proof, proof gained from such persistent evidence that it is impossible to draw any other conclusion except that neither luck nor human sagacity but the operation of a power above and beyond man is responsible for the multiplicity of harmonious results which have followed the application of the principle and rule set forth in the Christian Science textbook, *Science and Health with Key to the Scriptures* by Mary Baker Eddy.

Out of letters in the files of the late Ruggles Educational Fund from students at home and abroad, a few selected sentences are submitted:

As I walked to school each morning I kept saying Divine Mind works harmoniously. "All is infinite Mind and its infinite manifestation." [20] By declaring this I saw that I was not doing the work myself, but reflecting infinite Mind which neither works too fast nor too slow. Immediately my laboratory work speeded up and I caught up with the class and stayed with them to the end.

For the first time in my life I have reached the point where I actually *love* to study and want to forge ahead and learn much more than is actually required in the courses. I am convinced now of the value of a college training if one really wants to get all the good possible out of it, and it seems to me that my understanding of Christian Science is being broadened rather than confused by it. The history either of a country or a literature is so much more explicable and meaningful in the light of Truth, and in studying it one gets rid of false prejudices at the same time that one sees the futility of all systems of thought or action resting on a material basis. Involuntarily I measure any theory or hypothesis with which I come in contact by the rule of Christian Science and value it according as it approaches or falls below that rule. I am all the more grateful for this *absolute standard* of judgment inasmuch as several of my friends have had their orthodox religious views completely upset in college and are now pretty much at sea.

Through holding fast to Truth and denying error I have overcome the difficulties which confronted me. (A German student in a German University.)

While in Berlin, I stood before an examination to last five hours . . . I made it clear to myself that the one infinite Mind alone filled me and that God governs us all : that nothing can be asked of me that I could not do. . . . To my great joy I began to see here too that my right thinking was victorious. (Another translation from a German student.)

There was a time when the attitude of Christian Science toward family life was not everywhere understood. Much ink — most of it perhaps wasted — was spilt in criticism. The simple fact is that Mrs. Eddy literally took her stand with Jesus, as she interpreted him. Jesus preached purity in all the relationships of life. Mrs. Eddy preached the same in somewhat the same language. But she was always practical. Once she observed :

Be faithful over home relations ; they lead to higher joys ; obey the Golden Rule for human life, and it will spare you much bitterness. It is pleasanter to do right than wrong ; it makes one ruler over one's self and hallows home — which is woman's world. Please your husband, and he will be apt to please you ; preserve affection on both sides.[21]

Coming over on the Olympic, Zoe Beckley found Lady Astor with *Science and Health* always near her in her daily writing and "speech-preparing." Zoe Beckley's human interest story in the *Woman's Home Companion* (August, 1930) pictures Lady Astor as charming, vital, sensible, and adds : "She is religious, a Christian Scientist. Motherhood is a

" MOTHER "

The Timothy Cole Engraving.

mania with Nancy Astor. 'I have only six children,' she says ruefully, 'I would like a full dozen.'" Nothing could better illustrate Mrs. Eddy's practicalness than in counseling the individual to live up to his own understanding of the truth before he interferes with the affairs of others. Mrs. Eddy says:

> Great mischief comes from attempts to steady other people's altars, venturing on valor without discretion, which is virtually meddlesomeness. Even your sincere and courageous convictions regarding what is best for others may be mistaken; you must be demonstratively right yourself, and work out the greatest good to the greatest number, before you are sure of being a fit counsellor.[22]

Among the many letters received by the author in twenty-four years from aged men and women who had been with Mrs. Eddy in Lynn and Boston, is one indicative of the blending of the ideal and the practical almost from the first in her experience. In reply to the author's inquiry for the exact truth concerning Mrs. Eddy's opinions on marriage when, in 1875, the writer often talked with her, the word came: "There was nothing at variance" with those lines in her chapter on Marriage in that first edition of *Science and Health* (1875): "Be not in haste to take the vow 'until death do us part' but consider well its obligations, responsibilities, and relations to all your future happiness; judge before friendship,[23] then confide till death."

In the twenty years since Mrs. Eddy passed on, the practical bearing of her teaching has become apparent along with the lowering in the world at large of the high standard of purity set up by her. At a time when marriage seems menacingly unstable, and subject to easy dissolution, Christian Science is securing for it more stability. Christian Science calls the entire family to rally to the unifying standard of purity, unselfishness and recognition of the higher rights of every member. Writes the college-bred mother of one of the many attractive Christian Science families, whom the author has the happy privilege of knowing in their homes:

There has been one sentence that has been like a beacon light to us in bringing up our three children. This was told to some of Mrs. Eddy's students who asked her how they were to protect their little children from aggressive propaganda of mortal mind. The sentence is as follows: "Give the children the truth at home, and then let them go." We have found that in so far as we have lived up to this admonition, teaching them the moral principle found in the Ten Commandments and the Sermon on the Mount, that we could then send them forth into their school and college and social life, trusting them to God's care. We have tried to instill in them the desire for obedience to the spiritual import of the Bible, our text-book, *Science and Health with Key to the Scriptures*, by Mary Baker Eddy, and the *Manual* of the Mother Church, and to awaken in them the sense of the importance of daily study of the lesson-sermon. They have turned to the principle of Christian Science in working out all their problems and have found that, since each one of us must work out his own salvation, it is wise to attempt to solve a problem first through one's own understanding of the truth before turning to another for help.

We are learning through the teaching of Christian Science to treat the children as equals and to share all family problems and experiences with them as far as is practicable. We find that their response to this point of view is astonishing, and contributes to their confidence in themselves, and the progress, interest, and happiness of the home life. The children have been encouraged to have a special interest outside their prescribed school studies, such as athletic sports and music.

Jesus prayed that his disciples should be kept not from the world, but from the evil in the world, and Mrs. Eddy gives us the practical application of this principle in her admonition: "keep your minds so filled with Truth and Love, that sin, disease and death cannot enter them." [24]

We have tried to arouse in the children the ideal of service to mankind in all they do. We discovered that one of them had adopted the plan of saying to himself mentally whenever he met a new friend: "What can I do for you?" A very important lesson for them is obedience to the laws of the land. This obedience to Caesar does not conflict with rendering what is due to God but unfolds the necessary quality of self-discipline in the individual. We have been learning as a family that happiness in the home life is due to the exercise of certain qualities, such as honesty, loyalty, purity, activity, charity and affection.[25]

" Wherefore by their fruits ye shall know them." [26]

TWENTY YEARS AFTER

Almost twenty years have passed since Mrs. Eddy, on the little tablet which a member of the family brought her, wrote her last message to the flock she loved and was about to leave.

Since that December day in 1910, much has happened. Recently the author was one of a little group, a member of which, apropos of nothing, sagely observed: "Christian Science is now on its last legs."

Unless the author has altogether misunderstood and utterly misinterpreted the rich sources open to him first among all investigators, and on which this is the first book to be based, Christian Science, which has more than doubled its churches, societies, and membership in twenty years, far from being on "its last legs," is now going stronger than ever.

The very reserve concerning the publication of statistics by those responsible for the general policy of the movement has increased the author's respect for the management. Again and again, as he has come accidentally upon facts and figures not officially in evidence, he has discovered a systematic policy of understatement rather than of overstatement, and an appropriate spiritual modesty which Mrs. Eddy once called the "jewel" [1] of Christian Science.

While the author is aware that readers of this book will give only such credence to his opinions as they appear to deserve, he confidently believes that his general impression of the strong and steady development these twenty years past of Christian Science, will seem even to the incredulous to be amply justified.

Mrs. Eddy never claimed to have found something entirely new. On the other hand she said,[2] " I have found nothing in ancient or in modern systems on which to found my own except the teachings and demonstrations of our great Master." What Jesus brought to light, and then in the dark ages many lost, Mrs. Eddy brought to light again. No religious leader in all time has ever been more insistent than the discoverer and founder of Christian Science that Christ Jesus kept his promise: " Lo, I am with you alway."[3] No follower of Christ Jesus has ever testified more convincingly than Mrs. Eddy both to the naturalness and the effectiveness of His works.

They are [she says] the sign of Immanuel, or "God with us,"— a divine influence ever present in human consciousness and repeating itself, coming now as was promised aforetime,

To preach deliverance to the captives [of sense],
And recovering of sight to the blind,
To set at liberty them that are bruised.[4]

Objectionable comparisons never interested Mrs. Eddy. Hers was too busy a life to waste time on them. As she came to the fullness of her powers and her fame, not merely did she herself wish all Zion prosperity; but she also spoke thus for her followers: "A genuine Christian Scientist loves Protestant and Catholic, D.D. and M.D., — loves all who love God, good."[5] Incidentally, the author has had abundant evidence that at least once she indicated she would rather see a good Congregationalist than a poor Christian Scientist.

That was natural. Congregationalism had been her cradle, and she never once denied the devoutness and democracy of the Congregational denomination.

If Mrs. Eddy did not specifically praise the "Disciples" (sometime called Campbellites) she illustrated the possibility of putting the Christian fellowship they preached above mere difference of definition.

The woman who wrote "Divine Science derives its sanction from the Bible," [6] was not apt to be at odds with Lutherans, who from the first have kept the Bible at the center of their worship.

Making for itself a large place in history by the substitution of "conversion" for mere "respectability" at the very time that Mrs. Eddy was growing up, Methodism never emphasized "Ye must be born again" more positively than Mrs. Eddy emphasized the thought in such phrases as "The man born of Spirit is spiritual." [7]

The dignity and decorum which give distinction to Episcopal worship are matched in Christian Science through the explicit instructions worked out in the earlier days by its founder.

If as Dr. J. Fort Newton believes, "something is missing in modern religion," it is not the fault of Mrs. Eddy, nor of those to-day who carry on not merely in her spirit but also in obedience to her definite and far-reaching instructions.

On February 27, 1903, Mrs. Eddy wrote The Christian Science Board of Directors:

Never abandon the by-laws nor the denominational government of The Mother Church. If I am not personally with you, the Word of God and my instructions in the by-laws have led you hitherto and will remain to guide you safely on. [8]

Mrs. Eddy was still on earth when one of her critics who turned later to hearty appreciation said:

The power, through loving mercifulness and compassion, to heal fleshly ills and pains and griefs — all — with a word, with a touch of the hand! This power was given by the Saviour to the Disciples, and to all the converted. All — every one. It was exercised for generations afterwards. Any Christian who is earnest and not a make-believe, not a policy-Christian, not a Christian for revenue only, had that healing power, and could cure with it any disease or any hurt or damage possible to human flesh and bone. These things are true, or they are not. If they were true seventeen and eighteen and nineteen centuries ago it would be difficult satisfactorily to explain why or how or by what argument that power should be non-existent in Christians now.[9]

Differ as men in 1930 may about Christian Science, all who have even scant knowledge of the organization agree that Christian Science under the conscientious conduct of a Board of Directors never unmindful of their spiritual responsibility to the founder, has lifted the blight of poverty as well as sickness from many a life and many a home.

Under a technique of daily Bible study of their leader's planning and with her still ever-present help through her writings, Christian Scientists have developed a habit of church attendance and of church financial support which in the minds of many other Christians is evolving out of doubt into aspiration.

Even more significant is the large percentage of Christian Scientists who indisputably — as even casual observers testify — bear those fruits of the spirit which St. Paul listed as "love, joy, peace, long suffering, gentleness, goodness, faith, meekness, temperance."

Not a few outside of Christian Science who recognize its worth, now have little difficulty in agreeing with "Sonny's Father" in Ruth McEnery Stuart's story:

I want to treat 'em white, thet's all. Any sect thet dwells upon the beauty of holiness an' thet challenges every soul to find God in itself has got a great truth, an' there's so much health an' well-bein' in that one reelization thet we might forgive 'em ef their heads gits turned a little an' they become imbued with the idee thet they've got a corner on the Grace of God.[10]

Most of us are quite willing that any group — if they can — shall get "a corner on the Grace of God"; for the only corner possible, in the nature of the case, on the Grace of God is a strategic place from which the Spirit drives us out to share the Grace of God with those who have it not.

If, these twenty years past, under the direction of the Board, Christian Science has actually gotten "a corner on the Grace of God," none need be over-anxious. The best they have Christian Scientists were never keener than they are to-day to give away, without solicitation and also without proselyting, " to them that are far off and to them that are nigh."

What the final judgment is to be on Christian Science, those who direct its course — though giving no evidence of concern — would be the last to venture to predict. They understand that their first responsibility — and that of all other Scientists — is to live the faith to which they bear witness. They know, too, that Clio, muse of history, still stands, as in pre-Christian days, with judicial pen suspended, always waiting — but never over-eager — to write the last word concerning men and movements.

With persecution passing, one peril still remains. It is the peril of prosperity. But even out of that peril, which has proved too much for many a worthy cause, there is a way for Christian Science. It is — as the incoming president of The Mother Church in 1924 clearly indicated — the way of gratitude

to the God of our fathers, who has carried us through this desert to the promised land ; to Christ Jesus, "the author and finisher of our faith" ; to our beloved Leader, Mary Baker Eddy, whose teachings have sustained our faith, and whose Church Manual has kept us in the right path ; and to our Board of Directors, who, through stress and storm, have held our standard aloft without wavering.[11]

So long as Christian Scientists keep in this way, so long also as day by day they try to live up to the teachings of their leader, so long will they take no thought for the morrow. "For the morrow shall take thought for the things of itself."[12]

LYMAN P. POWELL

NOTES

PROLOGUE

1. *Page 3, line 25.* Alfred Farlow.

2. *Page 8, line 5.* One of the staff at Christian Science headquarters, with some pathos, then explained to the author that in order to get through even ordinary routine, he was coming in from the suburbs every morning to be at his desk by seven and sometimes staying late.

3. *Page 9, line 7.* Mrs. Eddy's *Letters and Miscellany*, Vol. 14 : 29 : 1688.

4. *Page 12, line 2.* Vol. III, 526. This passage was read at the annual meeting of The Mother Church in 1929, by Judge Clifford P. Smith, to an audience of five thousand.

5. *Page 12, line 16.* Page 531, 2.

6. *Page 13, line 2.* Andrade's *An Hour of Physics*, 222.

7. *Page 13, line 17.* *Science and Health with Key to the Scriptures* by Mary Baker Eddy, 468. Hereafter when the author refers to *Science and Health* it will be abbreviated thus : *S. & H.*

8. *Page 13, line 28.* Otto's, *The Idea of the Holy*, 158.

9. *Page 14, line 4.* *Scribner's*, December, 1929; *Collier's*, April 19, 1930. In addition, Bishop Charles Fiske of Central New York is thus quoted in *The Living Church*, June 21, 1930: "Church attendance is not an infallible test of religious reality. It is, however, a fairly accurate thermometer by which to record the warmth of Christian loyalty. I have had a count made of the number of worshipers present at the principal Sunday service in some of our churches. The reports are amazing. In one city church having nearly 1,200 communicants, there was a Sunday morning congregation of 250. About the same number was present in a church reporting 1,300 members. In another, with close to a thousand communicants, the congregation numbered 225. In other churches with communicant lists ranging from 800 to 900 and upward, the proportion was about the same. Apparently the smaller churches showed a better record. City and town parishes with 400 to 600 communicants, and over, record an average attendance of about thirty-five per cent. Village and small town churches of 200 total membership, or less, showed about forty per cent. The count in several churches showed an appalling absence of men — about one-sixth of the congregations was all that could be mustered in several parishes, one-seventh in others. These are the facts. I can understand everything about them, save that clergy and laity who know the facts do not seem in the least anxious or concerned about them. The insoluble mystery is that so few of our leaders show serious dissatisfaction at such evident falling away.

"These figures do not reflect special discredit upon our own diocese. I was led to make the count here because of the publication of certain statistics of church attendance in New York City. Fifteen prosperous parishes, leading churches of the city, having a total reported communicant list of 23,196 had on a fair, cool day in summer an attendance of only 2,496 at the principal Sunday morning service. Of course summer attendance is hardly a true test, although even in New York everybody is not away for week-end holidays or enjoying an entire season's vacation for the heated term. A survey made on a fair Sunday at the peak of the winter season showed in the same churches 6,977 persons present, not counting the attendance at early communions, which in several of the churches must have been considerable. Attendance under favorable conditions, therefore, was less than one-third of the reported membership. Unfortunately, the figures do not tell the whole story, because five of the congregations counted were in famous metropolitan churches where there is usually a large proportion of visitors to swell the number of worshipers. Either parish communicant rolls are absurdly overpadded, or the religious habits of church members are tragically lax."

10. *Page 15, line 4.* Everyone should read Channing Pollock's defense of the times in *The American Magazine*, July, 1930. In *Church Federation*, June, 1930, it is recorded that Charles P. Steinmetz, the world's foremost electrical engineer, in his last days, forecast the future in the following impressive words: "I think the greatest discovery will be made along spiritual lines. Here is a force which history clearly teaches has been the greatest power in the development of men and history. Yet we have merely been playing with it and have never seriously studied it as we have the physical forces. Some day people will learn that material things do not bring happiness and are of little use in making men and women creative and powerful. Then the scientists of the world will turn their laboratories over to the study of God and prayer and the spiritual forces which as yet have hardly been scratched. When this day comes, the world will see more advancement in one generation than it has seen in the last four."

As though to call Christians of all types to their coöperative responsibility the Right Reverend James De Wolf Perry, Bishop of Rhode Island and Presiding Bishop of the Protestant Episcopal Church in the United States, said in Westminster Abbey August 10, 1930, in his farewell sermon to the Lambeth Conference as reported in the New York *Times*, August 11, 1930: "Hearts and minds everywhere are uniting in a demand for a way of life to guide them and light and truth to reassure them. Here is a singleness of need that will be satisfied only by the witness of a united voice."

11. *Page 15, line 32.* Renascence.

12. *Page 16, line 8.* The Independent, November, 1906.

13. *Page 16, line 28.* Quoted in *The Living Church*, October 13, 1928.

CHAPTER I

1. *Page 27, line 5.* Matthew xi : 5.

2. *Page 27, line 15.* The author was privileged in the summer of 1917 to share with the late Baron von Hügel the gracious hospitality of the Master's Lodge at Balliol College, Oxford, and to listen entranced to the Baron's now familiar

interpretation of "Christianity as caring" — the very words the Baron uses in his letter to his niece.

3. *Page 27, line 27.* John ix : 25.

4. *Page 28, line 10.* Luke xix : 40.

5. *Page 30, line 3.* Christian Science encircled the globe in Mrs. Eddy's time. Since she passed on, Christian Science has grown so rapidly that twenty-six countries besides the United States are now represented in the advertising columns of the *Monitor.* In London alone there are twelve churches instead of, as twenty years ago, only three, and in other European cities the cause is growing at a substantial rate every year.

6. *Page 33, line 17.* First Reader of The Mother Church, 1902–05; First Reader of First Church of Christ, Scientist, in Concord, New Hampshire, 1906–09; since 1905 he has been a member of The Christian Science Board of Lectureship.

7. *Page 35, line 25.* Quoted by Judge Clifford P. Smith, manager of Committees on Publication, at the annual meeting of The Mother Church in June, 1921.

8. *Page 36, line 31.* *Religion and Medicine,* 10.

9. *Page 40, line 13.* Albert Bigelow Paine: *Mark Twain, A Biography* (1912), Vol. III, 1271.

10. *Page 42, line 18.* The interest taken by Christian Scientists in other lands, other folds, and in all who need, is of the Scriptural type. They are averse to making the left hand acquainted with what the right hand does. Kipling's couplet describes them:

> Help me to need no help from men,
> That I may help such men as need.

At a time when individual Christian Scientists were very generous to the sufferers from the fire of 1906 in San Francisco, the Church itself was criticized for holding aloof by some who did not understand the modesty of Christian Science giving. The criticism was soon silenced, however, by the relief action taken in accordance with their leader's directions by The Mother Church.

All through the four years of the Great War names of Christian Scientists stood high on the honor roll of war relief, not merely in the war zone lands, but also in countries only indirectly hurt by the world tragedy. Nor was their generosity confined to their own people. Beginning with the Red Cross, funds of their contributing were disbursed through the Y. M. C. A., the Boy Scouts, and other relief committees in many lands.

When the earthquake came in 1923 to Japan, The Mother Church was instant in relief, and the Japanese delegation which visited Boston last spring to thank the city for its generosity, on that occasion paid a special visit to the Directors of The Mother Church, bringing letters of appreciation from the Mayor of Tokyo and the bureau of reconstruction of the Japanese Government.

The author has seen letters from Episcopal, Methodist, and Baptist ministers expressing fervent gratitude for Christian Science gifts to them when they were overtaken by the floods, some in the Mississippi Valley, others in Vermont.

It has been said that Christian Science has no paid missionaries and does no systematic missionary work. Such critics, however, disregard the fact that every Christian Scientist is *ipso facto* a non-proselyting missionary: and among the most impressive data to which the author has had access are some — with illustrations — from the Philippine Islands, Brazil, Argentina, Southwest Africa, the Dutch East Indies, and other remote lands indicating that not merely are Christian Scientists doing works of mercy, wherever they may be, but that also in some lands — notably Africa and Oriental countries — Christian Science societies and churches are in consequence automatically resulting.

11. *Page 42, line 23. The Literary Digest*, April 26, 1930.

12. *Page 43, line 2. The Radiant Life*, 11.

13. *Page 43, line 16.* Philippians ii : 12. The conception of the priesthood of democracy grew out of a discussion with Charles E. Heitman, member of the Board of Directors, and constructively helpful to the author.

14. *Page 43, line 33. Miscellaneous Writings*, 154.

15. *Page 44, line 31.* In the *Jewish Tribune*, July 26, 1929, Orwell Bradley Towne says: "Christian Scientists do not put on revivals or conduct campaigns openly or secretly to gain followers, or for funds with which to finance its activities. Christian Science as a religious organization seeks only to serve the cause of humanity as set forth in the Bible. Christian Science is not for any particular class of people, and its membership is not made up of any particular class of people."

16. *Page 45, line 9.* In the report of the United States Bureau of Labor, dated October, 1929, on the "Care of Aged Persons in the United States," there appears (p. 129) a table showing a census of the aged in homes of various religious groups and also the average cost of caring for each resident. Christian Science heads the list with an average annual expenditure on each resident at Pleasant View of 1270 dollars, while the next nearest group is listed as expending only a little more than one-third as much, and some other groups below one-fifth as much.

17. *Page 51, line 26.* J. Roscoe Drummond.

18. *Page 51, line 28.* A suburb of Boston.

19. *Page 54, line 17.* Mary Baker Eddy's *Poems*, 14.

CHAPTER II

1. *Page 55, line 6.* Mrs. Eddy wrote, December 28, 1899, to Rufus Baker that "affection craves legend and relics." From collection of the Reverend Irving C. Tomlinson. For full discussion of Mrs. Eddy's pedigree, see Sibyl Wilbur's *The Life of Mary Baker Eddy*, page 6, long accepted by Christian Scientists as a standard biography. Her closing words run thus: "It is therefore sufficient to state that Mary Baker Eddy's great-grandparents were akin to the McNeils."

2. *Page 55, line 18.* After her passing Reverend Richard S. Rust, D.D., pastor of the Baker family, wrote of Mrs. Eddy's mother: "The character of Mrs. Baker was distinguished for numerous excellencies, and these were most happily blended. She possessed a strong intellect, a sympathising heart, and a placid spirit. Her presence, like the gentle dew and cheerful light, was felt by all around her. She gave an elevated character to the tone of the conversation in the circles in which she moved, and directed attention to themes at

once pleasing and profitable. She appeared no less lovely in the sphere of domestic life. As a mother, she was untiring in her efforts to secure the happiness of her family. The oft-repeated impressions of that sainted spirit on the hearts of those especially entrusted to her watch care can never be effaced, and can hardly fail to induce them to follow her to the brighter world. No sacrifice was esteemed too great, could it subserve their interests. She ever entertained a lively sense of the parental obligation in regard to the education of her children." From Mrs. Eddy's scrapbook.

On February 28, 1891, Calvin A. Frye took down at the wish of Mrs. Eddy some of the early memories of her mother's bedtime visits with her little girl and how she tried to impress on her such maxims as: "Count that day lost whose setting sun finds no good done." Also such wise counsel as: "Now remember child that a word that's flown is in your hearer's power and not your own." (From historical files of The Mother Church.) Also this hymn the mother used with which to sing her little girl to sleep:

> How can I sleep while angels sing,
> And hover o'er my bed;
> And clap their wings in joy to Him
> Who is their glorious Head?

Also the recollections of Miss Clara M. S. Shannon, 26, companion to Mrs. Eddy for several years, for Mrs. Eddy's description of her mother's appearance. "Short and stout; she had golden hair, and beautiful blue eyes; she was a blonde."

3. *Page 55, line 22.* Professor Hermann S. Hering's notes on Mrs. Gault in March, 1919, and several other personal recollections of Mrs. Eddy's emphasis on the significance of this prenatal influence on her life, March, 1930. Also the written recollections of Miss Shannon, that "she (Mrs. Baker) was filled with the Holy Ghost . . . and felt the quickening of the babe."

4. *Page 55, line 23.* Mark Baker was a vigorous and inelastic personality. He sometimes seemed to insist upon agreement with or without understanding in the family circle. As his little girl began early to display the instinct for leadership which later received full expression in the founding and development of the Christian Science Church, intellectual clashes seem to have taken place between father and daughter. But on the authority of Mrs. Eddy's most critical biographer, we are told that her mother and her sisters were usually on Mary's side.

5. *Page 56, line 7. Retrospection and Introspection,* 31; also Miss Shannon and the written recollections of Miss Julia S. Bartlett, who lived with Mrs. Eddy at her Columbus Avenue home for several years, and William R. Rathvon, Mrs. Eddy's corresponding secretary and member of her household from November, 1908, until Mrs. Eddy's passing in December, 1910.

6. *Page 56, line 13.* Rev. I. C. Tomlinson, a member of her household at Concord and at Chestnut Hill, stresses Mrs. Eddy's unusual consciousness of God.

7. *Page 56, line 20.* Professor Hering; Wilbur, 27.

8. *Page 56, line 21. Saint Joan,* by Bernard Shaw, 60. Mrs. H. S. Philbrook, who grew up with Mrs. Eddy, in a letter to her dated April 7, 1901, the original

of which the author has seen, states that she too as a child had heard voices
"scores of times" but never was impressed by them.

9. *Page 57, line 8.* *Retrospection and Introspection*, 13.

10. *Page 57, line 20.* Shannon, 5.

11. *Page 57, line 27.* Wilbur, 26.

12. *Page 58, line 4.* The author recalls on several visits to the Chestnut Hill
home, seeing the bed light Mrs. Eddy used until the last. Sometimes she woke
— says Mr. Rathvon — at three in the morning to make notes on the pad she
always kept on the little walnut table at the side of her bed, still there in her
modest sleeping room, which is unchanged like her study in furnishings and
appointments. Also Mrs. Eddy's *Letters and Miscellany*, Vol. 39 : 74 : 5121.

13. *Page 58, line 17.* E. M. Ramsay's book, *Christian Science and Its
Discoverer*, 4. *Retrospection and Introspection*, 10.

14. *Page 58, line 31.* That Mary Baker was already thus early in life, resourceful, enterprising, and gifted with a sense of humor, is indicated by the
following incident she related to Mr. Rathvon in 1909 : "Mark Baker was insistent that all of the family be present at morning devotions, which he conducted
by reading from the Bible followed by extemporaneous prayer, with all present
kneeling in silence. In his fervor he would sometimes extend his prayer beyond
the limits of the little girl's endurance. On one occasion, after standing it as
long as she could, she took a long shawl pin from the pincushion on the table,
crawled along the floor until she got behind the chair where he was kneeling
and vehemently exhorting, applied the pin at a point where it brought immediate results, and in the confusion that followed made her escape." Mr.
Rathvon recalls that as she told him the story eighty years after, the quiet
smile, to which those near her were accustomed, lighted up her face.

15. *Page 59, line 9.* *Retrospection and Introspection*, 7.

16. *Page 59, line 16.* The business card of Albert, after his admission to the
Bar, shows that he shared Mr. Pierce's office. Franklin L. Pierce was just
graduating from the New Hampshire House of Representatives into Congress
where he supported President Jackson. Six years later he joined Webster,
Clay, and Calhoun in the United States Senate; later served in the Mexican
War; and was elected President of the United States in 1852.

17. *Page 59, line 21.* August 7, 1902, the Reverend Irving C. Tomlinson
wrote Mrs. Eddy that he had learned the following fact "from your loving
neighbor and loyal follower, Mrs. Mary D. Aiken. She was telling me of her
mother, Mrs. Harriet P. Dodge, née Dunklee, who as a girl was well acquainted
with your honored family. . . . Mrs. Dodge says, 'When I was quite a young
girl I cut my finger and Albert Baker tried to persuade me that it did not hurt
me any.' You and your dear brother were so close that these thoughts must
have been your own." See also Mrs. Eddy's letter of April 17, 1837, in
Munsey's, April, 1911, 10.

18. *Page 59, line 28.* Nominated for Congress in 1841 in a district in which
a nomination insured election, Albert Baker died before the polling day at the
age of thirty-one to the grief of relatives and friends.

19. *Page 60, line 33.* Those inclined to think Mrs. Eddy was ever seriously
influenced by Emerson may care to know that in her bold handwriting on the

flyleaf of her copy of Emerson's *Nature*, published in 1836, the author finds the comment: "Emerson put so much reason into Mind and so much philosophy into Science that he lost the true sense of Spirit, God."

20. *Page 61, line 14.* That Mrs. Eddy was not altogether ignorant of English parliamentary speaking a while earlier would seem to appear from a letter she wrote to her friend, Judge Septimus J. Hanna, February 6, 1898: "You have shown yourself our American barrister for the legal rights of C. S. beyond the power of an English Fox that I as a child delighted to take in when reading his eloquent pleadings for equity." Mrs. Eddy's *Letters and Miscellany*, Vol. 39 : 225 : 5209.

21. *Page 61, line 27.* On May 5, 1907, in a talk with George H. Kinter, one of her secretaries, she thus described her memory: "When I was a little girl I could remember whatever I read, never forgot anything, used to be the prompter for the entire family, my father and all of them. We had a chore boy, a good fellow, but one who had had no advantages of books, or schooling, so I used to read the Bible to him, a chapter at a time, and then repeat it to him. I wanted him to go to Sunday School, and my father did too, but he was bashful about it because he could not recite Bible verses as the others did. I adopted this plan, but he would forget it as soon as I had recited it to him, so I hit upon the plan of reading it aloud, and then closing the book, I would rehearse it to him, and then he could remember and did recite it himself in Sunday School."

22. *Page 62, line 2.* Lindley Murray's *Introduction to the English Reader*, 100.

23. *Page 62, line 24.* Ibid., 102.

24. *Page 63, line 19.* Plate and pictures of the Baker family shown the author March 21, 1930, by Mr. Arthur S. Brown in his home at Tilton, New Hampshire, give new evidence of the cultural influences playing round the early life of Mary Baker. Mrs. Brown's father, the late Mr. Selwin B. Peabody, was successor to Mrs. Abigail Tilton in her later years in the management of the large business interests of the Tilton family, and received from her many things of family value, which are now treasured by Mrs. Brown.

25. *Page 63, line 22.* Many lively discussions on slavery appear in the newspapers of the day. In 1839, Albert Baker sat with a select committee, which adopted resolutions on non-interference of slave and non-slave states with each other, rebuked abolition propaganda methods, recommended that Congress should not interdict slave trade between states and expressed the opinion that the abolition of slavery without expatriation of slaves, would prove disastrous.

26. *Page 63, line 32.* Shannon, 5.

27. *Page 65, line 11.* Andrew Gault was the grand-nephew of the unusual woman who read and prayed much with Abigail Ambrose Baker just before the birth of Mrs. Eddy.

28. *Page 65, line 24.* Historical files of The Mother Church. These verses of Mrs. Eddy now appear in print for the first time.

29. *Page 65, line 31.* Paul Leicester Ford in *The True George Washington*, 38, says that Washington in writing to his London tailor for clothes in 1763 directed him to "take measure of a gentleman who wares well-made cloathes of the following size: to wit, 6 feet high and proportionably made — if anything rather slender than thick, for a person of that highth, with pretty long arms and thighs.

You will take care to make the breeches longer than those you sent me last, and I would have you keep the measure of the cloaths you now make, by you, and if any alteration is required in my next it shall be pointed out."

Mr. Ford also says, 62: "To the end of his life, Washington spelt lie, lye; liar, lyar; ceiling, cieling; oil, oyl; and blue, blew, as in his boyhood he had learned to do. . . . It must be acknowledged that, aside from these errors which he had been taught, through his whole life, Washington was a non-conformist as regarded the King's English."

The reader will observe in this chapter the same improvement in Mrs. Eddy's spelling between her fourteenth and her eighteenth year as is usual with young people still at school. Like Theodore Roosevelt, she was a prodigious letter writer. Like him always hard pressed by her duties, she frequently added to, subtracted from, and interlined her letters. All through her life, she sometimes dropped her commas; sometimes she forgot her periods; and in many letters she did not cross her t's. Once she wrote her trusted friend, Judge Hanna: "I long to see you punctuate my matter just as you do your own; that is the modern way but I know no rules for it, and leave this to you. I have changed the poem a little in punctuation and composition which greatly improves it. I wrote it so quickly I had no time to choose words as is necessary." Mrs. Eddy's *Letters and Miscellany*, Vol. 39 : 129 : 5154.

30. *Page 66, line 6.* Marcosson in *Munsey's Magazine*, April, 1911, describes the discovery of these letters in the former home of Mrs. George Sullivan Baker at Tilton, and writes an excellent critique of them. The letters are reproduced here through the courtesy of the Frank A. Munsey Company.

31. *Page 66, line 22.* Ibid., 7.

32. *Page 67, line 15.* Ibid., 8, 9.

33. *Page 68, line 8.* Ibid., 9, 10.

34. *Page 68, line 17.* This appears to be the only reference in her correspondence to the Shakers, and it indicates no special interest then in them. But it is worth noting that it was in 1747 that a revival took place in England in the ranks of the Quakers, out of which emerged the sect of the Shakers. At first Jane and James Wardley were the leaders, then Ann Lee, daughter of a blacksmith. In response to a revelation, "Mother" Ann later removed with her followers to America where a settlement was established near Albany, New York. The first Shaker Society in the United States was organized at New Lebanon, New York, in 1787. As "Mother" Ann herself went about preaching and healing by faith, so her followers made converts with the result that sooner or later societies were established in Kentucky, Ohio, Indiana, and Florida as well as in New England. In 1874 there were fifty-eight Shaker communities, numbering 2,415 souls, but by 1905 the number had shrunk to one thousand. The Shakers were celibates, living apart in their own communities and holding property in common. According to the Encyclopaedia Britannica, they "held that God was both male and female. . . . In Mother Ann . . . the female principle in Christ was manifested, and in her the promise of the Second Coming was fulfilled." Their lives were of the simplest, without adornment in dress or surroundings. They were busy always with their good works and their handicrafts, regarding physical disease as an offense against God.

35. *Page 69, line 3.* *Munsey's,* April, 1911, 10, 11.
36. *Page 69, line 9.* Letter written by D. Russell Ambrose, April 9, 1876, to his cousin, Mrs. Eddy. Historical files of The Mother Church.
37. *Page 69, line 32.* *Munsey's,* April, 1911, 11.
38. *Page 70, line 5.* The letters that follow are from Mrs. Eddy's *Letters and Miscellany,* Vol. 21 : 223-246.
39. *Page 70, line 9.* In the home of Mr. and Mrs. Arthur S. Brown of Tilton now stands the imposing hall clock once in the Holmes' residence.
40. *Page 70, line 32.* Though in her adult years, Mrs. Eddy was given to reading Shakespeare — as the marked copy of her Shakespeare in the author's hands indicates and her allusions to him in her writings confirm — she could scarcely in her girlhood have done so much; for it was not then considered proper for girls to read his plays. Indeed, on this account, Charles and Mary Lamb, in 1807, published their interesting, but innocuous, *Tales from Shakespeare,* especially for girls. In the introduction occurs the paragraph:

For young ladies too it has been my intention chiefly to write, because boys are generally permitted the use of their father's libraries at a much earlier age than girls are; they frequently have the best scenes of Shakespeare by heart, before their sisters are permitted to look into this manly book; and, therefore, instead of recommending these tales to the perusal of young gentlemen who can read them so much better in the originals, I must beg their kind assistance in explaining to their sisters such parts as are hardest for them to understand; and when they have helped them to get over the difficulties, then perhaps they will read to them (carefully selecting what is proper for a young sister's ear) some passage which has pleased them. . . .

But family reading of Shakespeare at least was permitted; for Mr. S. B. G. Corser, son of one of her early pastors speaks of dropping in sometimes "at the Baker homestead, where Shakespeare perchance was the theme of conversation." Quoted from personal letter dated July 17, 1902, to Mrs. Eddy, Chestnut Hill files.

Till her passing, Mrs. Eddy was an omnivorous reader. With her little blue pencil in her hand to mark passages of special interest, and not infrequently to insert in the margin her own original comments, Mrs. Eddy read by day and sometimes after she had gone to bed, with her droplight illuminating book and pillow. Scores of her books, particularly of the last third of her life, the author has handled, and most of them can be found in many a minister's study. They include: Amiel, Arnold (Edwin), Beecher (Henry Ward), Black (Hugh), Browning (Robert and Elizabeth), Bunyan, Burns, Byron, Carlyle, Channing, Conybeare & Howson's *Life of St. Paul,* Dickens, Drummond, Eliot (George), Emerson, Farrar, Furness, Hillis, Hilty, Jordan (William George), Keats, Kingsley (Charles), Longfellow, Mabie (Hamilton W.), Maclaren (Ian), Markham (Edwin), Milton, Munger, Parker (Joseph), Plato (Jowett's Translation), Pope, Ruskin, Shakespeare, Talmage (T. DeWitt), Tennyson, Tolstoy, Trench, Trine, Van Dyke, Whittier. As indicative of her wide ranging intellectual interests, Mrs. Eddy sent to Mr. William Lyman Johnson on February 13, 1905, the newly published *Legends of Parsifal.*

Her guest room and the room for her maid were fittingly provided with devotional books; and to her own desk with regularity came such magazines as

Century, Christian Herald, Contemporary Review, Literary Digest, North American Review, and *The Outlook.*   Many numbers are still preserved.

41. *Page 72, line 3.*   Mary Baker began her church going when as a little girl she was taken by her parents every Sunday to the First Congregational Church at Concord.   She describes in *Miscellany,* 147, 4, how she spent the noon hour between the services under "the grand old elm," which has been recently cut down.   She joined the Tilton Congregational Church when she was seventeen years old.

42. *Page 73, line 6.*   In her scrapbook nature clippings abound and a little later in the cycle of the seasons than maple sugar time, she once broke into a lilt not so very different from some of Browning:

> Who loves not June
> Is out of tune
> With love and God:
> The rose his rival reigns,
> The stars reject his pains,
> His home the clod!
>
> MARY BAKER EDDY'S *Poems,* 57

CHAPTER III

1. *Page 75, line 22.*   Mrs. Sarah C. Turner, niece of the Cheneys, in a testimony embodied in a letter written May 5, 1907, by Albert E. Miller to Mrs. Eddy, recalls that Mary Baker was fair to look upon.   Her eyes were blue.   Her cheeks were richly red.   Soft chestnut hair fell in ringlets to her shoulders.   Grace of manner and a becoming gown gave to these good looks a fascination all observed and few resisted.

The color of Mrs. Eddy's eyes (like her stature, which actually was five feet six inches) has often been the subject of discussion.   The most informing note is furnished by Miss Emma McLauthlin, her friend and household companion at Pleasant View for several weeks late in the nineties.   In her recollections Miss McLauthlin writes: "I asked her as to the much disputed color of her eyes; she put both her hands on my shoulders, and gently pushed me with my back to the window while she faced the light with her eyes looking smilingly into mine, and asked me what color I thought they were.   I said 'They are hazel with such large pupils that they look very dark, I do not see a vestige of blue in them.'   She laughingly said that reminded her of a disagreement between Judge and Mrs. Hanna over the same subject.   The Judge was first called to meet her personally, and when he returned Mrs. Hanna asked him to describe her looks; in doing this he spoke of her eyes as sky-blue.   When later Mrs. Hanna had had an interview with her, she asked her husband why he had told her Mrs. Eddy's eyes were blue, when there wasn't a vestige of blue in them.   Many years later, during a stay with her of several weeks, one day as she sat gazing out of the window with a far-away look, seeing visions unknown to me, standing opposite, I noted with wonder that her eyes were blue as sapphires."

2. *Page 75, line 26.*   Report of Charleston Committee.   *The Charleston Evening Post,* quoted in the *Christian Science Sentinel,* January 26, 1907.

3. *Page 76, line 4.* Gilbert C. Carpenter, once secretary to Mrs. Eddy, with whom the author has talked, recalls that Mrs. Eddy once told him how she first met at the age of ten her future husband: " . . . it was at the marriage of her brother, Samuel Dow Baker to Maj. Glover's sister, Eliza Ann Glover, and he took her on his knee and asked her how old she was. She told him ten years old. He said he would come back in exactly five years, and then said jokingly that he would make her his little wife; whereupon she jumped off his knee and hid herself. He came again in exactly five years, when her sister Abigail married Alexander Tilton, manufacturer, for whom the town of Tilton was named; she expected to see him at this wedding. The third time was at the age of twenty-two in Tilton. She was going along the street and thought it was her brother George, so she slapped him on the back and said, 'Oh, you're dressed up,' and when he looked around she beheld to her mortification it was Maj. Glover." Recollections, 22.

4. *Page 76, line 6.* S. B. G. Corser, son of Dr. Corser, August 4, 1902, wrote: "As Mrs. Eddy's pastor — and for a time teacher — my father held her in the highest esteem; in fact he considered her, even at an early age, superior both intellectually and spiritually to any other woman in Tilton, and greatly enjoyed talking with her. . . . I well remember her gift of expression which was very marked, as girls of that time were not usually possessed of so large a vocabulary. She and my father used to converse on deep subjects frequently (as I recall to mind, from remarks made by my father) too deep for me. She was always pure and good. During my residence of some years, previous to the fall of 1843, in or near the town of Tilton, I never heard a lisp against the good name of Miss Baker but always praise for her superior abilities and scholarship, her depth and independence of thought, and not least, her spiritual mindedness."

5. *Page 76, line 9.* Carpenter, 23.
6. *Page 76, line 24.* Ibid., 23.
7. *Page 78, line 6.* Powell's *Historic Towns of the Southern States,* 259.
8. *Page 78, line 18.* Ibid., 275.
9. *Page 79, line 4.* Lindley Murray's *Introduction to the English Reader,* 151. See facsimile, page 64.
10. *Page 79, line 14.* Shannon 11, 12.
11. *Page 80, line 7.* Farlow 114, quoting U. S. Department of Agriculture, Weather Bureau.
12. *Page 80, line 25.* Shannon, 11. Also William R. Rathvon's reminiscences (1930): "On May 29, 1909, Mrs. Eddy was in a reminiscent mood and speaking to me of her earlier experiences in Charleston, said, 'We found the people of the South generally kind and hospitable, so long as the question of slavery was not raised. My husband had the courage of his convictions and may not always have been discreet in voicing them. As a result he was once challenged to a duel by one who believed the Northerner would not fight. Being the challenged party Major Glover had the privilege of naming the weapons and conditions. He chose pistols "toe to toe, and muzzle in the mouth." These austere conditions settled the question of his courage for all time, and the challenger withdrew his challenge as quickly as he could and my husband was not again disturbed.' Such performances sound strange to us now, but this was in the days when

duelling was the 'gentleman's test of honor and courage' and was approved by such eminent Southerners as Clay, Jackson, Calhoun, and Benton, all of whom fought notable duels."

13. *Page 80, line 32.* Farlow, 115.

14. *Page 81, line 15.* Wilbur, 39.

15. *Page 81, line 24.* The following is taken from a photographic copy of a Card, which appeared in the *Wilmington Chronicle*, August 21, 1844:

Through the columns of your paper, will you permit me, in behalf of the relatives and friends of the late Maj. George W. Glover, of Wilmington, and his bereaved lady, to return our thanks and express the feelings of gratitude we owe and cherish toward those friends of the deceased, who so kindly attended him during his last sickness, and who still extended their care and sympathy to the *lone*, feeble, and bereaved widow, after his decease. Much has often been said of the high feeling of honor, and noble gener- osity of heart which characterize the people of the South, yet when we listen to Mrs. Glover, (my sister,) whilst recounting the kind attentions paid to the deceased during his last illness, the sympathy extended to her after his death, and the assistance vol- unteered to restore her to her friends, at a distance of more than a thousand miles, the power of language would be but beggared by an attempt at expressing the feelings of the swelling bosom. The silent gush of grateful tears alone can tell the emotions of the thankful heart. Words are indeed but a meagre tribute for so noble an effort in behalf of the unfortunate, yet it is all we can award; will our friends at Wilmington accept it the tribute of grateful hearts.

Many thanks are due Mr. Cooke, who engaged to accompany her only to New York but did not desert her, or remit his kind attentions until he saw her in the fond embrace of her friends.

Your friend and obedient servant,

GEORGE S. BAKER.

Sanbornton Bridge, N. H., Aug. 12, 1844.

It was the conscientious freeing of her slaves that sent her home without an income and made her a dependent on the world. But she never counted the cost before she did the right.

16. *Page 82, line 18.* Mrs. Eddy's scrapbook, 37B.

17. *Page 82, line 29.* Wilbur, 40.

18. *Page 83, line 8.* Ibid., 41.

19. *Page 83, line 18.* "When a widow & I sat rocking to sleep my baby boy as I gazed into his sweet face a big tear fell upon his soft cheek & wakened him. Reaching up his little hand to my face & half asleep he murmured 'mama not 'onesome Georgie is comp'ny. Georgie not s'eep.' . . . his little hand fell & he slept on. Those tender words comforted me." Dictated to her secretary at Pleasant View. Historical files of The Mother Church.

20. *Page 83, line 25.* Wilbur, 40.

21. *Page 84, line 15.* *The Ladies' Home Journal*, June, 1911; reproduced here through the courtesy of the editor.

22. *Page 85, line 14.* On January 31, 1863, Mrs. Patterson wrote to Dr. Quimby: "My sister (Mrs. Tilton) and her son will visit you at an early period. She has an abdominal rupture, and I am very anxious for her restoration. She is very useful to her family and community." *The Quimby Manuscripts*, 1921 edition, 149.

23. *Page 86, line 19.* Wilbur, 51.

24. *Page 87, line 27.* Recollections in November, 1911, of Elmira Smith

Wilson, the blind girl, who was Mrs. Patterson's maid in North Groton and Rumney, 1.

25. *Page 88, line 3.* Letter to Martha D. Rand, Munsey's, April, 1911, 12. Mary Baker's autograph album, given her March 21, 1846, indicates many admirers, all writing in the stilted verse of that day.

26. *Page 88, line 5.* James Smith's letter to Mrs. Glover, December 8, 1849. This verse, written by James Smith and pasted in Mrs. Eddy's early scrapbook, speaks for itself:

LINES
Written in a young lady's album.

Air — "The Bride."

I'd offer thee this heart of mine,
If I could love thee less;
But hearts as warm, as soft as thine,
Should never know distress.
My fortune is too hard for thee,
'Twould chill thy dearest joy;
I'd rather weep to see thee free,
Than win thee to destroy.

I leave thee in thy happiness,
As one too dear to love!
As one I'll think of but to bless,
Whilst wretchedly I rove.
But oh! when sorrow's cup I drink,
All bitter though it be,
How sweet to me 'twill be to think
It holds no drop for thee.

Then fare thee well; an exile now,
Without a friend or home,
With anguish written on my brow,
About the world I'll roam.
For all my dreams are sadly o'er —
Fate bade them all depart, —
And I will leave my native shore,
In brokenness of heart.

S.

27. *Page 88, line 16.* See Ch. 2, p. 71. Also autograph album in historical files of The Mother Church.

28. *Page 90, line 6.* *Munsey's,* April, 1911.

29. *Page 90, line 22.* Perhaps it was this failure of the homeopathic doses, given by her husband to help his wife, that led at last to the sentence in her textbook (152): "Her experiments in homeopathy had made her skeptical as to material curative methods." See also *The First Church of Christ, Scientist, and Miscellany,* 345 : 15. The following extract from the recollections of "the blind girl" who lived with Mrs. Patterson at North Groton and Rumney affirms that Mrs. Patterson "read a great deal and studied a large Doctors book on Homeopathy, and there were some of the neighbors that would come occasionally for medicine which she would give them. She always kept under her pillow a little bottle of pellets and one day in making up the bed the bottle fell upon the floor and I stepped on it breaking it. While trying to find and pick up the

little pills Mrs. Patterson noticed what I had done, but she did not scold me, but told me not to mind as they were no good any way." Wilson 3, 4.

30. *Page 91, line 1.* Until the end, Mrs. Tilton's character presents a curious combination of generosity and stiffness. In her will dated May 6, 1886, she bequeathed the Tilton Episcopal Church five thousand dollars on condition that a former rector whom she disliked should not be recalled. Liberal provision was made for her many relatives including her nephew, George W. Glover, but Mrs. Eddy was omitted. Her business associate and his little daughter were directed to occupy the first carriage in her funeral procession; "then my direct family according to their years." Of her sister's attitude Mrs. Eddy wrote, "My oldest sister dearly loved me, but I wounded her pride when I adopted Christian Science, and to a Baker that was a sorry offence." *Christian Science Sentinel,* January 5, 1907.

31. *Page 91, line 19. Retrospection and Introspection,* 20.

32. *Page 92, line 4.* Wilson, 6.

33. *Page 92, line 7.* Mrs. Turner, niece of the Cheneys, stated in May, 1907, in personal recollection of Mrs. Patterson and her little son. Historical files.

34. *Page 92, line 8.* Her sister, Martha Pillsbury, loaned the thousand dollars to buy the sawmill and some land. Wilson, 1.

35. *Page 92, line 26.* Ibid., 3.

36. *Page 93, line 14.* Mrs. Sylvester Swett's recollections in the reminiscence files of The Mother Church. See *S. & H.* 170 and 221 for evidence that Mrs. Eddy early became acquainted with the Graham and Cutter cures for dyspepsia.

37. *Page 93, line 34.* The "blind girl" (Myra Smith Wilson) wrote November 7, 1911, when she was a very aged woman: "Mrs. Tilton, her sister, and myself rode in the carriage with Mrs. Patterson. It was in the spring and the roads were very bad — in spots deep snow — other places mud. As we were leaving, the bell in the church was rung. It was said Joseph Wheat had his son Charles toll the bell. I walked the greater part of the way to Rumney and was very tired & Mrs. Tilton walking with me so that she would not hear the moans and grief of Mrs. Eddy."

38. *Page 94, line 20.* Historical files of The Mother Church.

39. *Page 95, line 21.* Historical files of The Mother Church.

40. *Page 96, line 3.* The author's book of 1907, 43–45, 51; Haggard's, *Devils, Drugs, and Doctors,* 306.

Grimes was a hypnotist and left behind him some crude observations in *Electro-Biology.*

John Bovee Dods, more business man than philosopher, explained his clairvoyant methods in *The Philosophy of Electrical Psychology,* published in 1850.

Andrew Jackson Davis, born in 1826, had extraordinary vogue before the Civil War as a mesmerist. Elaborate pictures of his method are given in *The Magic Staff* (1857). His favorite thesis was there is no mind, only matter; and his cult faded out before he passed on.

Warren F. Evans, too, was enamored of magnetism and in his *Mental Medicine* (1872) declared it to be "the torch by the light of which mankind will explore their way to an all-satisfying faith." He was more than a mesmerist. Having been both a Methodist and a Swedenborgian, the philosophy he brought to

Quimby, to whom he came for treatment in 1863, was a "blend." Quimby's chief service to Evans, in addition to the improvement in his health, was to show Evans how definitely to heal. He described Quimby's method as "an exhibition of the force of suggestion," laying much stress in the last two chapters of *Mental Medicine* on both the value of "psychic force" and on the specific ways of using finger pressure at various points of the body. He began to practice mental healing after his return to his New Hampshire home, later conducted a mind-cure sanitarium at Salisbury, Massachusetts, and between 1869 and 1886 published several books more lucid than *The Quimby Manuscripts* on mental healing, which had a large place in the genesis and development of New Thought. No propagandist, Evans tried simply to give mental healing a place among the curative agencies in life, and in his last book, *Esoteric Christianity* (published in 1886) he described his teaching as largely "occult" and "phrenopathic."

41. *Page 96, line 23.* Mrs. Eddy's *Letters and Miscellany*, Vol. 55 : 199 : 7796.

42. *Page 97, line 3.* This is in Calvin A. Frye's handwriting. Historical files of The Mother Church.

43. *Page 97, line 6.* *Retrospection and Introspection*, 6.

44. *Page 97, line 10.* Farlow, 82.

45. *Page 97, line 15.* Gilbert C. Carpenter states in his recollections, 11 : "To illustrate how easily she wrote poetry, Mrs. Eddy said to me one day, 'I think in poetry,' and without a moment's hesitation, she dictated a poem to me . . . :

> Guide us gently, God,
> Through the cloud or on the sod;
> Be our everlasting stay
> Night or day.

Reminiscence files of The Mother Church.

46. *Page 97, line 20.* Mrs. Eddy's scrapbook, 37.

47. *Page 97, line 23.* Letter to E. Augusta Holmes, April, 1840. Mrs. Eddy's *Letters and Miscellany*, Vol. 21 : 227 : 2681.

48. *Page 97, line 30.* *Munsey's*, April, 1911, 12.

49. *Page 98, line 3.* Mary B. Glover's letter to Daniel Patterson. Historical files of The Mother Church.

50. *Page 98, line 5.* Albert E. Miller's letter of May, 1907.

51. *Page 98, line 17.* H. A. L. Fisher's *Our New Religion*, 44.

52. *Page 98, line 20.* Milmine, 56.

53. *Page 98, line 21.* Even at the age of sixty-four, as Mr. Farlow testifies in his recollections (2), Mrs. Eddy looked about forty.

54. *Page 99, line 12.* *The Quimby Manuscripts*, 1921 edition, 146.

55. *Page 99, line 17.* Ibid., 147.

56. *Page 100, line 3.* Historical files of The Mother Church.

57. *Page 100, line 13.* She perhaps meant "excited."

58. *Page 100, line 18.* *The Quimby Manuscripts*, 1921 edition, 147–8.

59. *Page 100, line 24.* Milmine, 44.

60. *Page 100, line 34.* Wilbur, 86–7.

61. *Page 101, line 3.* Reports another patient: "His mode of treating the sick was to immerse his hands in water and manipulate their heads." Miss Abigail Dyer Thompson recollections, reminiscence files of The Mother Church.

62. *Page 101, line 10.*   Wilbur, 87.   Also Matt. ix : 21; and Powell's *Emmanuel Movement*, 176.

63. *Page 101, line 12.*   *The Portland Courier*, 1862.

64. *Page 101, line 20.*   Letters, January 31, 1863; March 10, 1863; September 14, 1863; May 24, (no year); May, 1864; *The Quimby Manuscripts*, 1921 edition, 149–156.   *See* also Miscellany, 307, where Mrs. Eddy wrote in later years: "At first my case improved wonderfully under his treatment, but it relapsed."

65. *Page 101, line 25.*   *The Quimby Manuscripts*, 1921 edition, 156.

66. *Page 101, line 26.*   Historical files of The Mother Church.

67. *Page 102, line 1.*   *The Quimby Manuscripts*, 1921 edition, 162.

68. *Page 102, line 11.*   Milmine, 58.

69. *Page 102, line 15.*   Abigail Dyer Thompson's letter of January 20, 1930, states: "With regard to the statement made by Dr. Quimby in introducing Mrs. Eddy to my mother, I have heard her tell the entire experience, including that statement, repeatedly since my childhood; and also know that when mother recalled it to our Leader's mind, Mrs. Eddy replied that Dr. Quimby had paid her the same tribute many times during her stay in Portland."   Thompson recollections in the reminiscence files of The Mother Church.

70. *Page 102, line 29.*   *The Quimby Manuscripts*, 1921 edition, 149.

71. *Page 102, line 33.*   John 1 : 9.

72. *Page 103, line 5.*   *The Quimby Manuscripts*, 1921 edition, 164.

73. *Page 103, line 18.*   Matthew xvii : 20.   *Retrospection and Introspection*, 24.   Also Milmine, 61.

74. *Page 103, line 30.*   Till the end George A. Quimby was both jealous for his father's reputation and adverse to Christian Science, but on November 11, 1901, he wrote of Mrs. Eddy: "The *religion* which she teaches certainly *is hers*, for which I cannot be too thankful; for I should be loath to go down to my grave feeling that my father was in any way connected with 'Christian Science.'" *The Quimby Manuscripts*, 1921 edition, 436.

75. *Page 104, line 23.*   This letter is reproduced by permission of Mrs. Julius A. Dresser.   Historical files of The Mother Church; which also indicate that Julius Dresser was somewhat sensitive, and would not willingly become a target of criticism for ministers and doctors.   He spent his time for a while in newspaper work, first in Portland, Maine, and then in Webster, Massachusetts. As his health failed again, he went to California to remain till 1882.   Mrs. Eddy then had attracted a following in Boston, and established Christian Science. The reason Mr. and Mrs. Julius Dresser gave in explanation of their return in 1882 to take up "the Quimby work" was that they "had heard what was going on in Boston" and "they believed the time was now ripe for action."

76. *Page 105, line 19.*   *The First Church of Christ, Scientist and Miscellany*, 306, 307.   In Vol. I of the 10th edition of *S. & H.* Mrs. Eddy wrote : "The only manuscript that we ever held of his, longer than to correct it, was one of perhaps a dozen pages, most of which we had composed."   4.   "Not one of our printed works was ever copied or abstracted from the published or from the unpublished writings of any one."   5.

77. *Page 105, line 23.*   *The Quimby Manuscripts*, 1921 edition, 163.   In later years she spoke of "his rare humanity and sympathy" (*Misc. Wtgs.* 379 : 18),

and also described him as "a remarkable man." *(Miscellany,* 307 : 22)   Just before this chapter went to the publisher the author found by chance that the Rt. Hon. H. A. L. Fisher (27, note) supports the author's thesis after a study of *The Quimby Manuscripts* alone.

78. *Page 106, line 26.*   The earliest names Mrs. Eddy called her teachings were *Moral Science, Christian Healing, Mental Healing, Christian Science Mind-Healing.*   But we read in *S. & H.,* 107, that "In the year 1866, I discovered the Christ Science or divine laws of Life, Truth, and Love, and named my discovery Christian Science."

79. *Page 107, line 4.*   For discussion of its authorship the reader is referred to *The Christian Science Monitor,* February 25, 1927.

80. *Page 107, line 12.   The Quimby Manuscripts,* 1921 edition, Preface VI, indicating that Quimby did not use the phrase "Science and Health."

81. *Page 107, line 22.   Message for 1902,* 16.

82. *Page 107, line 26.*   Love — II Cor. xiii : 11, I John iv : 7, 8, 16.

Spirit — Gen. i : 2; Job xxxiii : 4; John iv : 24; Rom. viii : 16; Eph. iv : 30; I John iv : 13.

Truth — Deut. xxxii : 4; Psalms xxxi : 5; Isa. lxv : 16; Jer. x : 10.

Life — John i : 4, iii : 26; Rom. viii : 2, 10; Eph. iv : 18; Col. iii : 4; I John i : 2; v : 12, 20; Rev. xi : 11.

83. *Page 108, line 3.*   Durant's *Mansions of Philosophy,* 55 ff; Powell's *Christian Science,* 1907, 108.

84. *Page 108, line 7.*   Durant, 58.

85. *Page 108, line 14.   Memoirs of Jonathan Edwards,* 51; and Powell's *Heavenly Heretics,* 22 ff.

86. *Page 109, line 2.*   Dictated memorandum of Mrs. Eddy's talk with Calvin A. Frye in historical files of The Mother Church.

87. *Page 109, line 12.*   Milmine, 62, quoting Mrs. Crosby. Also Dresser's *A Message to the Well,* 88.

88. *Page 109, line 18.*   S. B. G. Corser's letter to Alfred Farlow, August 4, 1902

89. *Page 109, line 26.*   Browning's *Paracelsus.*

90. *Page 110, line 2.*   Letter of December 11, 1909, in files of The Mother Church.

91. *Page 110, line 9.*   The author has a letter which Mrs. Crosby wrote him in her last years, again summing up her indebtedness: "I am sure my experience with Mrs. Eddy gave me a clearer understanding of my own capabilities as well as a better knowledge of the world."

92. *Page 110, line 18.   S. & H.,* 107.

CHAPTER IV

1. *Page 111, line 7.   Human Life,* July, 1907.

2. *Page 112, line 4.*   Asa G. Eddy's letter to James C. Howard, August 5, 1880. The Howard letters were recently acquired by The Mother Church.

3. *Page 112, line 20.   Human Life,* July, 1907.

4. *Page 113, line 2.*   Bartlett, 9, 10.

5. *Page 113, line 5.   McClure's,* April, 1907, 613.

6. *Page 113, line 12.* Memorandum April 11, 1930, from executive offices of The Mother Church.

7. *Page 113, line 18.* One of her hearers — not a follower — left this record: "She is a woman of one idea almost to wearisomeness." — Van Ness, *The Religion of New England,* 168.

8. *Page 113, line 31.* Italics the author's.

9. *Page 113, line 32.* Mrs. Eddy's *Letters and Miscellany,* Vol. 55 : 207 : 7801.

10. *Page 114, line 3.* *McClure's,* May, 1907, 113.

11. *Page 114, line 4.* Dakin, 96.

12. *Page 114, line 9.* Farlow, 88, 89.

13. *Page 114, line 17.* The First Church of Christ, Scientist, and Miscellany, 237. Also the *Christian Science Sentinel,* July 4, 1908.

14. *Page 115, line 2.* Dr. Cushing wrote the author, June 17, 1907: "The *Reporter* is wrong, as she went home in the morning not afternoon." *S. & H.,* 3rd Ed., 155–157, confirms Dr. Cushing's statement.

15. *Page 115, line 5.* Dr. Cushing's affidavit in *McClure's,* March, 1907, 512.

16. *Page 115, line 16.* Ibid., 512.

17. *Page 115, line 27.* Dr. Cushing's letter, June 17, 1907.

18. *Page 115, line 32.* Powell's *Human Touch,* 15, 16.

19. *Page 116, line 13.* Mrs. Eddy's *Letters and Miscellany,* Vol. 55: 199: 7796. See *Miscellaneous Writings* 24:7 for Mrs. Eddy's account.

20. *Page 116, line 22.* *Lynn Reporter,* June 30, 1866. However, six months later, she withdrew her claim.

21. *Page 116, line 33.* The Christian Science Journal, June, 1887. Years later Mrs. Eddy describes as follows the deeper meaning of the fall: "For three years after my discovery, I sought the solution of this problem of Mind-healing, searched the Scriptures and read little else, kept aloof from society, and devoted time and energies to discovering a positive rule. The search was sweet, calm, and buoyant with hope, not selfish nor depressing. I knew the Principle of all harmonious Mind-action to be God, and that cures were produced in primitive Christian healing by holy, uplifting faith; but I must know the Science of this healing, and I won my way to absolute conclusions through divine revelation, reason, and demonstration. The revelation of Truth in the understanding came to me gradually and apparently through divine power." *S. & H.,* 109.

"In following these leadings of scientific revelation, the Bible was my only textbook. The Scriptures were illumined; reason and revelation were reconciled, and afterwards the truth of Christian Science was demonstrated. No human pen nor tongue taught me the Science contained in this book, SCIENCE AND HEALTH; and neither tongue nor pen can overthrow it. This book may be distorted by shallow criticism or by careless or malicious students, and its ideas may be temporarily abused and misrepresented; but the Science and truth therein will forever remain to be discerned and demonstrated." 110.

"After a lengthy examination of my discovery and its demonstration in healing the sick, this fact became evident to me, — that Mind governs the body, not partially but wholly. I submitted my metaphysical system of treating disease to the broadest practical tests. Since then this system has gradually gained ground, and has proved itself, whenever scientifically employed, to be the most effective curative agent in medical practice." *S. & H.*, 111.

22. *Page 117, line 7.* Fisher's *Our New Religion*, 45.

23. *Page 117, line 16.* Farlow, 88.

24. *Page 117, line 23.* In *Retrospection and Introspection*, 24, 28, she calls her experience "The Great Discovery" — that "Mind reconstructed the body, and that nothing else could. . . . It was a mystery to me then, but I have since understood it. All Science is a revelation. Its Principle is divine, not human, reaching higher than the stars of heaven."

25. *Page 117, line 27.* Genesis xxxii : 30.

26. *Page 117, line 32.* This she paid back with interest, amounting to ninety-six dollars, thirty-five years later, in 1899 in reply to an appeal from John Patterson, then eighty years old and destitute. Chestnut Hill files.

27. *Page 118, line 5.* Dr. Cushing wrote the author in 1907 that Dr. Patterson was not even at home when his wife had her fall in Lynn, and had to be brought down from New Hampshire by telegram the next day. He was rarely where he should have been when needed.

28. *Page 118, line 7.* Report in Historical files of The Mother Church.

29. *Page 118, line 13.* Affidavit of R. D. Rounsevel, proprietor of the White Mountain House, Fabyans, N. H., January 18, 1902. Farlow, 119.

30. *Page 118, line 31.* Wilbur, 166, 167.

31. *Page 119, line 4.* Shannon, 26, 27.

32. *Page 119, line 11.* Mrs. Eddy's *Letters and Miscellany*, Vol. 55 : 225 : 7811. Spofford letters recently deposited with The Mother Church.

33. *Page 119, line 22.* Recollections of Mrs. Clara E. Choate, dated October 12, 1914. Reminiscence files of The Mother Church.

34. *Page 119, line 28.* Original letter to Mrs. Anna Kingsbury recently deposited with The Mother Church.

35. *Page 120, line 6.* Bartlett, 9.

36. *Page 120, line 11.* Mrs. Eddy's *Letters and Miscellany*, Vol. 55 : 53 : 7691.

37. *Page 120, line 35.* The Mother's Evening Prayer, Miscellaneous writings, 389.

38. *Page 121, line 7.* He wrote Mrs. Eddy February 24, 1902 that he had had one sheet of the first manuscript typewritten for her that she had written while with him. Historical files of The Mother Church.

39. *Page 121, line 23.* But, as Mrs. Eddy's little notebook before the author indicates, neither the Crafts nor the Wentworths ever paid her any cash, though it is evident that what they received from her came to far more than her "keep," liberally estimated. H. S. Crafts was lifted out of the manual labor class by her, into at least a semi-professional status with income to match.

40. *Page 121, line 27.* Ellis letters. Mrs. Eddy's *Letters and Miscellany*, Vol. 43 : 5663–5670.

41. *Page 121, line 30.* H. S. Crafts wrote December 14, 1901 (Files of The Mother Church) that, though a spiritualist when he began to study under Mrs. Eddy, her teachings changed his views and led him altogether away from spiritualism. The author had the privilege in his youth of spending two days in the home of the daughter of Judge Edmunds, a leader of the spiritualistic

movement in New York in Mrs. Eddy's earlier womanhood, and of observing that the daughter, once his medium, at the time the author in her old age met her was convinced that under emotional strain the Edmunds family had misinterpreted their experiences. Scarcely anyone of intelligence in the middle of the nineteenth century but had at least a passing interest in spiritualism. In fact, with C. C. Helberg's *A Book of Spirit Writings* and Mrs. M. E. Williams's article in the latest issue of *Psychic Research* available, there is as reliable evidence that Abraham Lincoln was a spiritualist as that Mrs. Eddy, with no more than gossip gathered up a generation later to go by, ever had a profound interest in spiritualism.

42. *Page 122, line 5.* Not merely did many of these students receive — as the little notebook shows — instruction without charge but also in some cases, where there was actual want, she loaned them money to live on while they studied with her, — that, too, at a time when to make both ends meet she often added to the ordinary cares of a homekeeper scrubbing the floors and living on a meagre diet. She could never, perhaps, have gotten on at all had she not budgeted her time and strength and means. Among the many evidences in the little notebook that she counted her every penny is the following memorandum:

Sept. 26, 1874   Postage 18 cts.
Sept. 26, 1874   Expressage 15 cts.

also recollections of Miss Emma C. Shipman in the reminiscence files of The Mother Church.

43. *Page 122, line 17.* Mrs. Eddy's *Letters and Miscellany*, Vol. 55 : 205 : 7799.

44. *Page 122, line 22.* Farlow, 94–97.

45. *Page 122, line 26.* Mrs. Eddy's little notebook, in which she kept a careful record of her receipts and expenditures in those days, is a touching revelation of her serious situation. She counted every penny of outlay, as well as of income. Early training may have been a contributory force in this respect, for at Pleasant View she once related to a friend: "When they (the Baker family) were children, in the winter evenings they used to shell corn for food for the chickens, etc. On one occasion little Mary was sitting by the fire, and as she shelled, a grain of corn fell off her lap. She pushed it with her little foot towards the burning log. Her Mother said, 'Mary, get down and pick up that corn.' She answered, 'Oh! Mother, it is only one grain.' 'Never mind,' said her Mother, 'It will help to make a meal for a little chick.' I have not forgotten that lesson." Shannon, 8.

46. *Page 122, line 28.* Church Manual of The First Church of Christ, Scientist, 46.

47. *Page 123, line 9.* Bancroft's *Mrs. Eddy as I knew her in 1870*, 2.

48. *Page 123, line 15.* In addition, without charge, she opened her little home in Lynn to him and his family, setting aside five of her seven available rooms, and unconsciously revealing the wealth of her tenderness in the words: "Now you have a home offered you and no rent to pay for it   So do not be cast down I thank God more for this than anything that I have a shelter if it is humble to go to in an hour of want and to welcome those who need a little time to meet the hour." Letter recently deposited with The Mother Church.

49. *Page 123, line 28.* Mrs. Eddy's *Letters and Miscellany*, Vol. 20 : 11 : 2469.

50. *Page 124, line 5. Retrospection and Introspection, 50.*

51. *Page 124, line 29.* Matthew vi : 33.

52. *Page 124, line 31. S. & H.,* 60.

53. *Page 124, line 32.* Ibid., 89.

54. *Page 125, line 4.* Recollections of Miss Sarah A. Farlow in the reminiscence files of The Mother Church.

55. *Page 125, line 26.* Historical files of The Mother Church.

56. *Page 126, line 3.* Wilbur, 178. He also told the author substantially this in 1907.

57. *Page 126, line 10.* Shipman recollections in reminiscence files of The Mother Church.

58. *Page 126, line 30.* Miss Sarah O. Bagley letter recently deposited with The Mother Church.

59. *Page 127, line 7.* Wilbur, 139.

60. *Page 127, line 14.* He called her Mrs. Patterson. Wilbur, 140.

61. *Page 127, line 19.* Crafts' letter in historical files of The Mother Church.

62. *Page 127, line 28.* Farlow, 106.

63. *Page 127, line 30.* Wilbur, 179. Of the Wentworths Mrs. Eddy wrote : "they are very kind Don't you think they wont take a cent for board and want me to remain as long as I live." Original letter to Sarah O. Bagley recently deposited with The Mother Church.

64. *Page 128, line 22. McClure's,* May 1907, 107.

65. *Page 128, line 29.* Her little notebook contains the full record of her percentage month by month from Kennedy's healing, for a typical year :

June, 1870	$225
July, 1870	200
August, 1870	137
September, 1870	167
October, 1870	90
November, 1870	200
December, 1870	130
January, 1871	147
February, 1871	100
March, 1871	136
April, 1871	110
May, 1871	100
Total	$1742

66. *Page 129, line 3.* Mrs. Eddy's notebook.

67. *Page 129, line 13.* But when personalities faded far into the past, Daniel Spofford, near his threescore years and ten, once in his quiet way indicated to a friend of the author, that what Mrs. Eddy did for him was beyond all estimation.

68. *Page 129, line 19.* How Mrs. Eddy made spiritual preparation to "read out the eight" is such a revelation of her character that Miss Bartlett's personal recollection of the extraordinary experience is given at length :

"In October, 1881, eight students who had allowed error to enter their thought, united in writing a disloyal letter of false accusations to their Leader and signed their names to the same. This cruel letter was read by one of their number at a meeting of the Christian Scientists Association in the presence of Mrs. Eddy who was the President of the Association. She made no reply, and when the meeting, which was held in her house, was closed, she went to her room and all the students went to their homes with the exception of two. These two remained with their beloved teacher to comfort her in her sorrow and anguish. . . . On hearing what had transpired I took the first train for Lynn, desiring to be with my dear teacher and to be of some service in her hour of trial. Dr. Eddy admitted me to the house. I found Mrs. Eddy seated by the table and the two students who had spent the night with her sitting near. I quietly took a seat near them as did Dr. Eddy also, and listened to Mrs. Eddy who was talking with a power such as I had never heard before. They were wonderful words she was speaking while we young students were receiving of the great spiritual illumination which had come through her glorious triumph over evil.

"Just before I had entered the room she was sitting with the others and the burden was still heavy upon her, when all at once she rose from her chair, stepped out in the room, her face radiant and with a far-away look as if she was beholding things the eye could not see. She began to talk and to prophesy of the blessings which would reward the faithful while the transgressor cannot escape the punishment which evil brings on itself. Her language was somewhat in the style of the Scriptures. When she began, the three with her, seeing how it was, caught up their pencils and paper and took down what she said. When she was through speaking, she put down her hand and said, "Why, I haven't any body," and as she came back to the thought of those about her, they were so moved by what they had seen and heard their eyes were filled with tears and one was kneeling by the couch sobbing. . . . Those three days were wonderful. It was as if God was talking to her and she would come to us and tell us the wonderful revelations that came. We were on the Mount. We felt that we must take the shoes from off our feet, that we were standing on holy ground. What came to me at that time will never leave me." Bartlett reminiscences, 16–18. Also see Wilbur, 259 ff.

69. *Page 130, line 21.* George Walter Fiske's *The Changing Family*, 222.

70. *Page 130, line 35.* Wilbur, 205, 206.

71. *Page 131, line 25.* Historical files of The Mother Church.

72. *Page 131, line 34. The Religion of New England* by Thomas Van Ness, 166.

73. *Page 132, line 4. Christian Science Hymnal*, 17, 34, 49, 71, 77, 83, 90, 172.

74. *Page 132, line 21.* Historical files of The Mother Church.

75. *Page 132, line 27. Pulpit and Press*, 5.

76. *Page 133, line 4.* Bronson Alcott's letter to Mrs. Eddy, January 17, 1876, in historical files of The Mother Church.

77. *Page 133, line 8.* Alcott's letter to Mrs. Eddy, March 5, 1876, in historical files of The Mother Church.

78. *Page 133, line 20. Christian Scientist Association Records*, Vol. 1 : 48.

79. *Page 133, line 32.* Alcott's letter to Mrs. Eddy, February 6, 1876, in historical files of The Mother Church.

80. *Page 134, line 29.* Hiram S. Crafts' letter stating that she was not a spiritualist. Historical files of The Mother Church.

81. *Page 135, line 14.* Mrs. Emilie B. Hulin, often with Mrs. Eddy in her Concord days, told the author in April, 1930, that Mrs. Eddy in speaking of this period said that sometimes, as she wrote, her hands would grow so cold she would go down to the kitchen to warm them over the stove.

82. *Page 136, line 4.* Mrs. Eddy's letter to Mrs. Miliken recently deposited with The Mother Church.

83. *Page 136, line 19.* "When," writes Mrs. Eddy in *Science of Man*, 1876 edition, 12, "we commenced teaching this science, we permitted students to manipulate the head, ignorant that it could do harm, or hinder the power of mind acting in an opposite direction, viz.: spiritually, while the hands were at work and the mind directing material action. We regret to say it was the sins of a young student, that called our attention to this question for the first time, and placed it in a new moral and physical aspect. By thorough examination and tests, we learned manipulation hinders instead of helps mental healing."

In further confirmation of the fact that Mrs. Eddy had completely done with Quimbyism, the author, in 1907, was informed by George A. Quimby, that he believed that Mrs. Eddy had finally landed in prayer-cure pure and simple.

84. *Page 136, line 25.* Cambridge History of American Literature, Vol. III, 526.

85. *Page 137, line 6.* The weather report, in and about Boston in 1875, indicates an average temperature of 72 for July, and 71 for August, with a rainfall of 3.93 and 3.50 respectively.

86. *Page 138, line 4.* Shannon, 5.

87. *Page 138, line 6.* George Clark's boys' story of sea life was accepted, and all the way home Mrs. Eddy rejoiced with him, as though she, herself, had not suffered a grievous disappointment. Wilbur, 202, 203.

88. *Page 138, line 19.* The bill itself is in the historical files of The Mother Church.

89. *Page 138, line 27.* Mrs. Eddy's *Letters and Miscellany*, Vol. 55 : 219 : 7808.

90. *Page 138, line 34.* In her personal notebook Mrs. Eddy records: "490 typographical errors in words besides paragraphs and pages wrong and punctuation."

91. *Page 139, line 19.* S. & H., 1st edition, 300.

92. *Page 139, line 22.* S. & H., 43.

93. *Page 139, line 25.* S. & H., 1st edition, 386.

94. *Page 139, line 30.* Since Mrs. Eddy passed away in 1910, no changes have appeared in *Science and Health*, other than those already indicated by her.

95. *Page 141, line 7.* S. & H., 1907 edition, 390. This quotation appears on the same page in the present edition.

96. *Page 141, line 18.* Flyleaf of S. & H., 1907 edition.

97. *Page 141, line 19.* For account of " Next Friends " see Chapter VI.

98. *Page 142, line 1.* Letter from John Wilson, December 18, 1896, in historical files of The Mother Church.

99. *Page 142, line 10.* Wm. G. Nixon was her agent from 1890 to 1892, in seeing the book through the press, but *Science and Health* is still printed by the Cambridge University Press. Mrs. Eddy's letters to Mr. Nixon, Nos. 2242–2282.

100. *Page 142, line 29.* Mrs. Eddy's letter to Mrs. A. H. Whiting recently deposited with The Mother Church.

101. *Page 143, line 4.* John Wilson's letter in historical files of The Mother Church.

102. *Page 143, line 20.* Recollections of William B. Reid dated January 16, 1930, in reminiscence files of The Mother Church.

103. *Page 144, line 9.* William Dana Orcutt's *In Quest of the Perfect Book*, 52–54.

104. *Page 144, line 13.* *The First Church of Christ, Scientist, and Miscellany*, 319.

105. *Page 144, line 14.* Mrs. Eddy's *Letters and Miscellany*, Vol. 18 : 2158–2241.

106. *Page 144, line 28.* *The First Church of Christ, Scientist, and Miscellany*, 318.

CHAPTER V

1. *Page 145, line 3.* The reader who cares for the information is referred to the following descriptions of Boston:

Drakes' *Old Landmarks of Boston;* Ticknor's *Doctor Holmes's Boston;* E. M. Bacon's *Rambles Round Old Boston;* Shackleton's *The Book of Boston;* Powell's *Historic Towns of New England*. Also certain letters written to the author, beginning in 1893, by Oliver Wendell Holmes, T. W. Higginson, Edward Everett Hale, George P. Morris, Charles Carlton Coffin, Frank B. Sanborn, Hezekiah Butterworth, William E. Barton, W. W. Goodwin, Edwin D. Mead, James Schouler, James F. Rhodes, and President Charles W. Eliot.

2. *Page 148, line 8.* Powell's *Heavenly Heretics*, 126.

3. *Page 148, line 20.* "A beautiful spot by the sea where sometimes she loved to go by herself." Bartlett, 10.

4. *Page 148, line 24.* After going the limit in free will service for affection's sake, Barry in a temper foolishly turned to the law to secure him repayment in cash.

Spofford had the distinction of being the only American of his day to have a legal action brought against him for witchcraft; then of disappearing under circumstances so mysterious that a charge was laid against two of his former friends that they had murdered him, which was not dropped until Spofford reappeared in two weeks. He lived to become a kindly old man, who left on record a final opinion that Mrs. Eddy was "the sole author of her famous book."

Richard Kennedy became a respected Vestryman of St. Paul's Episcopal Church in Boston and lived on into the twentieth century. In a conversation with the author in his old age he deplored the pettiness of the men and women around Mrs. Eddy those days in Lynn and observed that it all seemed unworthy of men and women in this work-a-day world of ours.

In jauntily passing off Mrs. Eddy's writings as his own Edward J. Arens seemed to forget what he perhaps had never learned, that they were copyrighted, and that infringement of copyright — a subject on which Asa Gilbert Eddy had made himself an authority — is a serious matter in the eyes of the law; but when the court so ruled, Arens had at last to quit, and dropped into the background.

5. *Page 149, line 13.* Bartlett, 9.

6. *Page 149, line 19.* Mrs. Eddy's *Letters and Miscellany*, Vol. 10 : 111 : 1138.

7. *Page 149, line 24.* Mrs. Eddy's *Letters and Miscellany*, Vol. 17 : 39 : 2059.

8. *Page 149, line 26.* Mrs. Eddy's *Letters and Miscellany*, Vol. 39 : 103 : 5141.

9. *Page 149, line 30.* Mrs. Eddy's *Letters and Miscellany*, Vol. 39 : 229 : 5212.

10. *Page 150, line 2. Genealogy and Life of Asa Gilbert Eddy* by Mary Beecher Longyear.

11. *Page 150, line 11.* Letter recently deposited in the historical files of The Mother Church.

12. *Page 150, line 16.* Letter in the historical files of The Mother Church.

13. *Page 150, line 18.* "My last marriage was with Asa Gilbert Eddy, and was a blessed and spiritual union, solemnized at Lynn, Massachusetts, by the Rev. Samuel Barrett Stewart, in the year 1877. Dr. Eddy was the first student publicly to announce himself a Christian Scientist, and place these symbolic words on his office sign. He forsook all to follow in this line of light. He was the first organizer of a Christian Science Sunday School, which he superintended. He also taught a special Bible-class; and he lectured so ably on Scriptural topics that clergymen of other denominations listened to him with deep interest. He was remarkably successful in Mind-healing, and untiring in his chosen work. In 1882 he passed away, with a smile of peace and love resting on his serene countenance. 'Mark the perfect *man*, and behold the upright: for the end of *that* man *is* peace.' (Psalms xxxvii. 37.)" *Retrospection and Introspection*, 42.

14. *Page 150, line 22.* Professor Traquair's plea in *The Atlantic*, March, 1929, for "equal rights for men" in these days when women have without the asking the position which Mrs. Eddy won long years ago by worth and work, finds no illustration in the career of Asa Gilbert Eddy.

15. *Page 151, line 17.* Original agreement in historical files of The Mother Church.

16. *Page 151, line 28.* "After our dinner was over we assembled in the parlor for a sing in which Mrs. Eddy joined us usually. My son, Warren, was about 5 yrs. old, & every one petted him more or less for he sang nicely and both Dr. and Mrs. Eddy delighted to hear him. This eve Mrs. Eddy grew silent as she often did when impressed by unusual thought arising for her consideration. The singing ceased, & one after another left the room for various reasons. There seemed such good feeling, we spoke of the progress we were making in the cause & felt this was a demonstration of the love she was trying to establish. The boy had climbed into her lap & gave her some caresses. She began to talk to him in something of this fashion, 'Now Warren dear you behaved splendidly today.' 'Well,' he replied, 'I know I did for you didn't look at me any all the time you talked, & now you love me, don't you?' To this Mrs. Eddy tenderly assented, and she told him she had a plan for him to speak on the platform with her. This greatly interested myself of course, as well as the boy. Mrs. Eddy still embraced with loving hugs now & then as their two heads leaned together as if in concurring confidence. Mrs. Eddy continued, 'well, we *must* have a

Sunday School, Warren. You shall be the first scholar.' He fell in with the plans but immediately said, 'how can we have a Sunday School with only *me*.' Mrs. Eddy smilingly told him that was only to begin with, & soon other little boys & girls would come & he would have them to listen to & to play with, but he could not comprehend how so much was to follow, tho if Mrs. Eddy said so & they must come if she told them to. I, the one onlooker, thought it all prattle to amuse the child, & gave no serious thought to either of them nor to what they were saying. I gave special attention tho to Mrs. Eddy's loving tenderness with the child & it found a like response in my own heart's love for her, & at the time she was so beset and distracted by worldly trials & evils on every hand. The boy grew sleepy & was soon abed, while Mrs. Eddy retired to her apartments, to no doubt formulate plans so suddenly started then & there. The following morning Mrs. Eddy asked Warren if he would come upstairs to her parlor awhile to which he readily consented. We never questioned Mrs. Eddy why nor wherefore in those days. So after Warren had an extra touch to his hair & a general looking over of face, hands & clothes, that he might not offend in any way, we kissed & he went to keep his important appointment — to explain the extra care Warren continually reminded us that 'Mrs. Eddy *is fussy* & won't like it so & so.' After quite a stay the boy reappeared full of enthusiasm & fun. We asked him what it meant & he mysteriously replied 'Mrs. Eddy has been rehearsing me.' Further questioning was for a time useless except that some important affair was afoot & the child was alive with its importance. Every little while he would recite in a most dramatic way a line from a song later another line and with each subsequent visit with Mrs. Eddy during the next few days, new words and new lines, were recited in all sorts of ways over & over. Then a message came from Mrs. Eddy, thro him, she would like him to look his best for the coming Sunday, for she was going to open her Sabbath School & he was to speak from the platform at the Hawthorne rooms on Park St., one verse before she began the regular services of the church. We all gladly consented and the boy's best frock a white pique kilt with wide collar & cuffs, a wide blue sash was all carefully attended to for Warren continued to assert 'Mrs. Eddy was terrible fussy,' and she told *him* he was just as important on the platform as she was & must look nice & behave nice & he thought her handsome if she '*was fussy*.' So each day of this very important & busy week was varied with plans & talk over the idea of a Sabbath School. Some praised & others discouraged the project, in the meantime Mrs. Eddy with all her manifold duties of church work, lectures forthcoming & manuscript to be revised, found time to '*rehearse*' the child in the verse he was to recite on Sunday at 3 P.M., Mrs. Eddy was as we all know quite particular in manners. She objected to our saying *thanks* & felt it better manners to say 'thank you' if occasion required.

"So she taught the boy how to walk to the front of the platform, how to bow to the audience, how to scrape his foot or draw it backward and the general fine gestures before his recitation. I don't know which enjoyed most these times, he or Mrs. Eddy. In giving these details his attention & which he practised daily, he caused us endless amusement & many a laugh & scream in which Dr. and Mrs. Eddy joined heartily. But the boy did finely in them all and with watchful coaching of such a woman as Mrs. Eddy, is it any wonder he should meet the excellence she expected. The wonder to me is she could ever find time to attend to these details. It all enforces the fact, however, of her thoroughness in laying foundations. In her mind the idea of the church with a Sabbath School was a truly engrossing affair, so she frequently said, & to this end we must help her. The starting was not easy and numbers, or material to work with were not then plentiful. Most of those interested or attracted to the cause were above the age desirable for such a movement. The younger element being Miss Lilly, Miss Potter, Mr. Orne, Mr. Bancroft, my young sister & myself. I know of only one other *child* besides Warren, the son of Mrs. Rice, about my boy's age, but he was living in Lynn & quite a care, so he did not come to the services regularly with either his mother or his aunt, Miss Rawson, who usually attended. I do not now remember so much of the services on this particular Sunday only we assembled at 3 P.M. as usual, for Mrs. Eddy was very prompt. She had taken greatest pains to look nice as an example to us, who were not as the boy termed '*so fussy.*' She even placed a rose in her hair to the delight of the boy whose beaming face betrayed not the least anxiety, but a consequential air pervaded him which pleased Mrs. Eddy, who so wisely said to us, 'We don't know where this will all end do we,' but we as ever unthinkingly replied 'Well, it won't amount to much anyway,' at least not impressively for the church or for the cause. But Mrs. Eddy made no reply & with undaunted quiet refrained from argument. With her reticule containing some leaves for her sermon she entered the hall from the dressing room in the rear, hand in hand with the boy. They ascended the few steps at the side of the platform. With a graceful bow to an ever respectful audience, she stepped to the front of the platform at the side of the pulpit, and spoke of the Sabbath School in a few words, & as *if it already existed.* She then introduced this little boy, Warren, as one of the representatives of the school, who would recite a short verse. He had followed in her wake & stood deferentially quiet beside her and as she retired, with a face full of smiles he bowed profoundly. In the most assured tones he then recited the following verse Mrs. Eddy had taught him to say & had so often '*rehearsed*' him, that full credit might be done to her & to the school he represented —

'And right is right — since God is God;
And right the day must win;
To doubt would be disloyalty,
To falter would be sin!'

Then another graceful bow and he came down to sit with Dr. Eddy, who seldom was on the platform with Mrs. Eddy, & who enjoyed the company of the boy, relieving me of care, while I sang a solo part, or led the congregational hymns with the quartette.

"The sermon was beautiful, full of the glory of Truth, the healing Truth of Christ. She seemed inspired & it uplifted us all by her positive & explanatory revelations. She referred to 'A little child shall lead them.' The Dr. looked with admiration from her to the boy, who had done so well, for 'a sensitive little chap,' as the Dr. said & by her directing. The singing was fine & the contribution generous. We all felt a new era of the cause was coming. As the audience of less than one hundred parted, more harmony was manifest and a mutual resolution to loyally abide by Mrs. Eddy's leadership. Upon our return at the dinner table the Dr. remarked with so much love, Mary, you have done a great work today, a grand work, & she turning to the boy with a smile said 'It is because I let this little child lead me.' Of course we all looked the adoring love of her we could not speak, and retired to the parlor for our singing with a *God praise* few companies can ever know." Recollections of Mrs. Choate in the reminiscence files of The Mother Church.

Mrs. Choate's many affectionate references, during 1914, to Mrs. Eddy are the more informing because in the eighties Mrs. Eddy more than once lovingly — as was her lifelong habit — reproved her young friend and student in accordance with St. Paul's counsel (II Timothy iv : 2) to his young friend Timothy to "reprove, rebuke, exhort, with all longsuffering"; and also in illustration of her own words in the *Church Manual* (Art. VIII, Sec. 1): "a Christian Scientist reflects the sweet amenities of Love, in rebuking sin, in true brotherliness, charitableness, and forgiveness."

17. *Page 152, line 19.* Mrs. Mary Harris Curtis's recollections in the reminiscence files of The Mother Church.

18. *Page 153, line 11.* Before undertaking to give an impression of Mrs. Eddy's appearance in her Boston pulpit, the author in years past talked with many who then heard her — including the late Miss Frances J. Dyer, then of *The Congregationalist.* He has also read the unpublished recollections now in the possession of The Mother Church of Mrs. Clara E. Choate, Miss Julia S. Bartlett, Miss Mary Alice Dayton, Miss Elsie Lincoln, Miss Mary A. Daggett, Miss Sarah A. Farlow, Mrs. Mary E. Foye, Mrs. Annie R. Hessler, Mr. William B. Reid, and Mr. William Lyman Johnson.

On all, Mrs. Eddy, near threescore years and ten, made the impression of eternal youth, and often imparted the impression to others. Miss Lilian Whiting wrote in the Ohio *Leader,* July 2, 1885, when Mrs. Eddy was sixty-four, that she came away from her first interview with "an utterly unprecedented buoyancy and energy which lasted days."

Mrs. Emma Easton Newman reports in her recollections that when Mrs. Eddy was sixty-seven, Mrs. Newman's father guessed she was about fifty-five. Mrs. Newman's recollections in reminiscence files of The Mother Church.

Mr. Farlow first met Mrs. Eddy when she was sixty-four and observed "she might easily be taken for a lady of forty." Farlow recollections in reminiscence files of The Mother Church.

At fifty-six Mrs. Eddy looked so young that Asa Gilbert Eddy, never once having thought to ask her age, assumed that it was forty when he applied for the marriage license, and it was not till many years after his passing that Mrs. Eddy ever heard of the occurrence. Farlow, 123.

Mrs. Eddy writes in *Science and Health:* "Comeliness and grace are independent of matter. Being possesses its qualities before they are perceived humanly. Beauty is a thing of life, which dwells forever in the eternal Mind and reflects the charms of His goodness in expression, form, outline, and color. It is Love which paints the petal with myriad hues, glances in the warm sunbeam, arches the cloud with the bow of beauty, blazons the night with starry gems, and covers earth with loveliness." *S. & H.* 247.

19. *Page 153, line 28.* Mrs. Eddy wrote an early student: "a Baptist clergyman in Boston (now more of an Adventist) sent for me to supply his pulpit and I did, that gave me the opportunity for six months to keep the 'good tidings' circulating. I healed a large number by my sermons and they owned it at the close of them." Mrs. Eddy's *Letters and Miscellany*, Vol. 17 : 19 : 2050.

20. *Page 154, line 3.* *Church Manual of The First Church of Christ Scientist*, p. 48.

21. *Page 154, line 9.* C. Lulu Blackman's recollections in reminiscence files of The Mother Church.

22. *Page 154, line 33.* Ibid., 3.

23. *Page 155, line 28.* Miss Sarah A. Farlow's recollections in reminiscence files of The Mother Church.

24. *Page 156, line 12.* Miss Mary Alice Dayton's recollections in reminiscence files of The Mother Church.

25. *Page 156, line 15.* *S. & H.*, 465.

26. *Page 157, line 12.* Sarah A. Farlow.

27. *Page 157, line 15.* Mary E. Foye's recollections in reminiscence files, 5.

28. *Page 157, line 27.* *Ira Oscar Knapp and Flavia Stickney Knapp*, by Bliss Knapp, 15.

29. *Page 158, line 2.* *Miscellaneous Writings*, 99.

30. *Page 159, line 10.* *Faith Work, Christian Science, and Other Cures*, 46.

31. *Page 159, line 19.* John ix : 25.

32. *Page 159, line 33.* Bartlett, 7, 8.

33. *Page 160, line 3.* *Ira Oscar Knapp and Flavia Stickney Knapp*, by Bliss Knapp, 6.

34. *Page 160, line 26.* Ibid., 8, 9.

35. *Page 161, line 29.* *The Christian Science Journal*, May, 1892, 68, 71.

36. *Page 162, line 7.* Recollections of Joseph G. Mann in reminiscence files of The Mother Church, 69.

37. *Page 164, line 5.* At first it was called, *The Journal of Christian Science*. Her great happiness in editing the *Journal* is indicated in a letter written January 31, 1884, to Colonel E. J. Smith, to whom she also says "Never was a time when the Cause was in better condition." Mrs. Eddy's *Letters and Miscellany*, Vol. 17 : 51 : 2065.

38. *Page 165, line 17.* *The Christian Science Journal*, September, 1886, 133.

39. *Page 165, line 26.* *The Genealogy and Life of Asa Gilbert Eddy*, by Mary Beecher Longyear.

40. *Page 167, line 6.* The following is an excerpt from one of George W. Glover's letters to his mother, dated January 31, 1895 :

"I have a very valuable mining property which lies next to and adjoining the property of a company that is shipping ore. The company is anxious to get it and have offered seven thousand five hundred dollars, but that is only a pittance.

"If I had two thousand dollars to open it I would realize a good figure as it is now I haven't the money and can't open it out so as to receive what it is worth.

"I do not wish you to feel as if I was asking any thing of you for nothing but if you can assist me at present it would be of great help and I would secure you." Historical files of The Mother Church.

41. *Page 167, line 14.* Mrs. Eddy's Petition.

42. *Page 168, line 5.* Wilbur, 322.

43. *Page 168, line 20.* Letter by Dr. Foster-Eddy February 23, 1920, in historical files of The Mother Church. He passed away November 13, 1930.

44. *Page 170, line 21.* Of this visit she wrote Colonel E. J. Smith June 25, 1884: "I went in May to Chicago at the imperative call of people there and my own sense of the need. This great work had been started but my students needed me to give it a right foundation and impulse in that city of ceaseless enterprise. So I went, and in three weeks taught a class of 25 pupils, lectured . . . to a *full* house, got 20 subscriptions for my Journal, sold about thirty copies of Science and Health, etc. In the class were three M.D.'s and two clergymen—one Methodist, the other Universalist both good thinkers and scholarly." Mrs. Eddy's *Letters and Miscellany* Vol. 17 : 61 : 2069.

45. *Page 170, line 22.* In preparation for the meeting of 1888, Mrs. Eddy long before in March, 1887, had called all her students who could be reached to come to Boston in April, 1887. She was much concerned to have them do so. She wrote Mrs. Annie Macmillan Knott as though the very life of the Cause might depend on this preparatory meeting. (Mrs. Knott's letter of May 16, 1930, to the author.) Mrs. Knott is a member of The Christian Science Board of Directors of The Mother Church, and is the first woman to serve as a member of this Board under the deed of 1892.

Mrs. Eddy never took a chance. "Accidents are unknown to God," she said. *S. & H.,* 424. For every important step in life she made the utmost preparation possible.

46. *Page 170, line 24.* Powell's *Historic Towns of the Western States,* 228.

47. *Page 170, line 32.* *Miscellaneous Writings,* 134.

48. *Page 171, line 24.* Mark Sullivan (*Our Times,* I, 123–131) says that Bryan's historic speech was extemporaneous only in its arrangement. In paragraphs he had made the speech scores of times the two years before up and down the Missouri Valley. Once at least on the floor of Congress he had closed a speech with the phrase : "You shall not press down upon the brow of labor this crown of thorns, you shall not crucify mankind upon a cross of gold."

49. *Page 172, line 7.* *Miscellaneous Writings,* 98–106.

50. *Page 172, line 13.* *The Christian Science Journal,* July, 1888, 209.

51. *Page 172, line 34.* On Mrs. Eddy's visit, four years before, in 1884, to Chicago she was refused a room at the Palmer House, and also three other places in Chicago till someone known to the management became her sponsor. Recollections of Gilbert Carpenter in the reminiscence files of The Mother Church.

52. *Page 173, line 21.* Mrs. Annie Macmillan Knott, who was present in Central Music Hall and later attended the reception in the Palmer House, tells the author that Mrs. Eddy remained at the hotel reception only a few minutes. "She shrank from personal adulation and everything of that sort."

53. *Page 173, line 27.* Wilbur, 311.

54. *Page 173, line 33.* New Thought, too, is a revolt against materialism, and is altogether idealistic. Both in theory and in practice it differs from Christian Science.

55. *Page 175, line 25.* *Miscellaneous Writings,* 359. The following personal

letter, November 28, 1889, addressed to the Church takes us back across the years:

"The Church of Christ (Scientist) in Boston was my patient seven years. When I would think she was well nigh healed a relapse came and a large portion of her flock would forsake the better portion, and betake themselves to the world's various hospitals for the cure of moral maladies. These straying sheep would either set up claims of improvements on Christian Science and oppose the Mother Church, or sink out of sight in religious history. This state of the Church has lasted ten years. It even grew rapidly worse when about three years ago I for lack of time to adjust her continual difficulties and a conscientious purpose to labor in higher fields and broader ways for the advancement of the glorious hope of Christian Science put students in my pulpit.

"As one who is treating patients without success remembers that they are depending on material hygiene, consulting their own organizations and thus leaning on matter instead of Spirit, saith to these relapsing patients, 'now quit your material props and leave all for Christ, spiritual power, and you will recover.' So I admonish this Church after ten years of sad experience in material bonds to cast them off and cast her net on the spiritual side of Christianity. To drop all material rules whereby to regulate Christ, Christianity, and adopt alone the golden rule for unification, progress, and a better example as the Mother Church." Mrs. Eddy's *Letters and Miscellany*, Vol. 1 : 21 : 8.

On December 2, 1889, the Church Board at 9 : 30 P.M. unanimously adopted the following resolutions:

"(1.) That the time has come when this Church should free itself from the thraldom of man-made laws, and rise into spiritual latitudes where the law of love is the only bond of union.

(2.) That the Regulations and By-Laws of this Church be and are hereby declared to be, in all their articles and clauses except that part of Article 1 which fixes its name, null and void.

(3.) That the Corporation be and is declared dissolved and that the present Clerk of the Church be hereby requested to take the steps necessary to give legal effect to this resolution.

(4.) The members of this Church hereby declare that this action is taken in order to realize more perfectly the purposes of its institution as an organization viz. growth in spiritual life and the spread of the 'glad tidings' — and that they will continue as a Voluntary Association of Christians knowing no law but the law of Love, and no Master but Christ in the exercise of all the ministrations and activities heretofore performed by them as a Church of Christ (Scientist).

(5.) That the members of this church hereby make loving recognition of the services and guidance of the founder and late pastor of the church, and also the expression of their grateful thanks to those who in the capacities of assistant pastor or otherwise have fostered its growth." From records of the Church organized in 1879, 265.

56. *Page 175, line 33.* The Christian Science Journal, September, 1890. Also Mrs. Eddy's letter to Miss Julia Bartlett of July 21, 1889:

"Now I repeat that whatever questions in any of the C. S. organizations come up — no reference be made to me, for I hereby state that I *will not* entertain the question nor consider it, and why?

"Because under the counteracting mental influences, if I do this, my counsel is liable to be either carried out too late, or misunderstood, or carried out only in part, and because of all these things the wisdom and necessity of it is not seen nor the good it might do accomplished, and many will say she is a 'hard master.' I have borne this many years and think at this period of my retirement it should be seen that this is why I left the field.   Again my students must learn sooner or later to *guard themselves*, to *watch* and not be misled.

"I appreciate your tasks far more than you can mine and have rewarded you by incessant care for you many years.   It is a *grave mistake* not to do *quickly* all that is worth doing, *delay* gives all away, under our circumstances." Mrs. Eddy's *Letters and Miscellany*, Vol. 55 : 61 : 7695.

57. *Page 176, line 23.* Wilbur, 203.

Chapter VI

1. *Page 177, line 18.* Mrs. Eddy's *Letters and Miscellany*, Vol. 40 : 11 : 5227B.

2. *Page 177, line 29.* To another she wrote: "I cannot and do not receive visits any more from any one but from those who come at my request to help me or who are my students.

"This dear one is the reason, viz. I have so much writing and care as a leader in a cause to which I devote my entire life that I have not time to visit or to be visited.

"Now this is not because I would not enjoy seeing you but because I *cannot* give more than one hour to any one unless it be to work with me in my field of labor." Mrs. Eddy's *Letters and Miscellany*, Vol. 17 : 159 : 2124.

3. *Page 178, line 6.* When Mrs. Eddy first settled, June, 1889, in Concord, she lived at 62 North State Street. In the spring of 1891, she moved to Roslindale, Massachusetts; but within a few weeks she returned to 62 North State Street. In December, 1891, she bought a farm of thirty acres beyond the city limits, and remodeled the farmhouse which she found there into the comfortable home to which, because of its broad and attractive outlook, she gave the name of Pleasant View.

4. *Page 178, line 11.* Mann, 33.

5. *Page 178, line 21.* M. Adelaide Still, 1, 2.

6. *Page 179, line 11.* S. & H., 254.

7. *Page 179, line 16.* Miss Margaret Macdonald.

8. *Page 179, line 18.* Says Miss Abigail Dyer Thompson, 2 : "One day when she asked the gardener to bring a basket of vegetables, carefully packed, to send on the train to one of her students who lived in an ajoining town . . . she sent the gardener to the basement for a generous piece of salt pork. This she had carefully wrapped in paper and tied to the side of the handle so it would be held securely in the basket; she then slipped in a note expressing her pleasure at sending the vegetables from her own garden, and added: 'With the salt pork I think you have all the ingredients necessary for a good meal.'"

9. *Page 180, line 20.* A member of the Chestnut Hill household tells the author that this practice was continued at Chestnut Hill.

10. *Page 180, line 31.   The Meaning of Culture,* 237.

11. *Page 181, line 2.* "The fact is I am allowed no earthly peace and it is this that keeps me from visiting my church oftener, from not one week for vacation, and nothing save servitude. At my age this is all wrong." Mrs. Eddy's *Letters and Miscellany,* Vol. 19 : 187 : 2429.

12. *Page 181, line 23.* Miss Shannon's recollections, confirmed by Mr. Charles H. Welch.

13. *Page 181, line 30.* "The dissolution of the visible organization of the Church is the sequence and complement of that of the College Corporation and Association. The College disappeared, 'that the spirit of Christ might have freer course among its students and all who come into the understanding of Divine Science'; the bonds of organization of the Church were thrown away, so that its members might assemble themselves together and 'provoke one another to good works' in the bond only of Love." *The Christian Science Journal* for February, 1890, 566.

Later, however, with characteristic timeliness, Mrs. Eddy wrote a student: "You recall his (Jesus) . . . turning water into wine for the marriage feast, and even being baptized to meet the necessity of 'suffer it to be so now for thus it becometh us to fulfil all righteousness.' His age or the age in which he lived required what he did and his wisdom caused his concession to its requirements in some instances. Just as this age requires organization to maintain Christian Science." Mrs. Eddy's *Letters and Miscellany,* Vol. 36 : 227 : 4756.

14. *Page 182, line 2.* Mrs. Eddy's *Letters and Miscellany,* Vol. 39 : 231 : 5213.

15. *Page 182, line 16.* Leigh Mitchell Hodges to the author.

16. *Page 182, line 19.* Mann, 48.

17. *Page 183, line 15.* Mrs. Eddy's *Letters and Miscellany,* Vol. 1 : 59 : 21.

18. *Page 183, line 24.* Mrs. Eddy's own story of her relationship with the building of that earlier church is told as follows in her *Message for 1902:*

"During the last seven years I have transferred to The Mother Church, of my personal property and funds, to the value of about one hundred and twenty thousand dollars; and the net profits from the business of The Christian Science Publishing Society (which was a part of this transfer) yield this church a liberal income. I receive no personal benefit therefrom except the privilege of publishing my books in their publishing house, and desire none other.

"The land on which to build The First Church of Christ, Scientist, in Boston, had been negotiated for, and about one half the price paid, when a loss of funds occurred, and I came to the rescue, purchased the mortgage on the lot corner of Falmouth and Caledonia (now Norway) Streets; paying for it the sum of $4,963.50 and interest, through my legal counsel. After the mortgage had expired and the note therewith became due, legal proceedings were instituted by my counsel advertising the property in the Boston newspapers, and giving opportunity for those who had previously negotiated for the property to redeem the land by paying the amount due on the mortgage. But no one offering the price I had paid for it, nor to take the property off my hands, the mortgage was foreclosed, and the land legally conveyed to me, by my counsel. This land, now valued at twenty thousand dollars, I afterwards gave to my church through trustees, who were to be known as 'The Christian Science Board of Directors.'

A copy of this deed is published in our Church Manual. About five thousand dollars had been paid on the land when I redeemed it. The only interest I retain in this property is to save it for my church. I can neither rent, mortgage, nor sell this church edifice nor the land whereon it stands."

19. *Page 184, line 18.* Concord citizens of responsibility never lost an opportunity to express their great regard for Mrs. Eddy; and the author has before him letters of that time from the Mayor, the Concord editors, a United States Senator, and others agreeing with Mr. Josiah E. Fernald's appreciation which is the more impressive because he has never been a Christian Scientist.

20. *Page 184, line 30.* The *Christian Science Sentinel* first had the title of the *Christian Science Weekly,* but received its present name January 26, 1899.

21. *Page 185, line 10.* John Oxenham.

22. *Page 185, line 17.* Mrs. Eddy's *Letters and Miscellany,* Vol. 26 : 71 : 3278.

23. *Page 185, line 22.* Mrs. Eddy's *Message for 1902,* 12, 13.

24. *Page 186, line 25.* Wilbur, 342, 343.

25. *Page 186, line 31.* Reminiscence files of The Mother Church, — Recollections of George Wendell Adams, Judge Septimus J. Hanna, Joseph G. Mann, Mary Stewart, Mary E. Eaton, Emma C. Shipman, Lida S. Stone, Sue Harper Mims; and U. S. Senator George H. Moses.

26. *Page 187, line 3.* Hanna's *Christian Science History,* 11.

27. *Page 187, line 5.* The Class of 98

Adams, George Wendell	Foster, Mrs. Adeline T.
Andrews, Mrs. Effie	Frame, Mrs. Caroline W.
Baker, Mrs. Anna B. White	Hanna, Mrs. Camilla
Baker, Dr. Alfred E.	Hanna, Judge Septimus J.
Betts, Edgar K.	Higman, Mrs. Elizabeth W.
Betts, Mrs. Harriet L.	Higman, Ormond
Blain, Julian	Kent, Mrs. Rose E.
Bond, Mrs. Lulu H.	Kimball, Edward A.
Brown, Miss Alice Seward	Kimball, Mrs. Kate Davidson
Buswell, Ezra M.	King, Mrs. Frances J.
Chamberlain, Miss Jessie C.	Knapp, Miss Daphne S.
Chanfrau, Mrs. Henrietta E.	Lathrop, John Carroll
Clark, Joseph B.	McBean, Mrs. Catherine
Clarkson, Judge Joseph R.	McDonald, Miss Margaret S.
Coates, Lewis B.	McKee, David N.
Cochrane, Mrs. E. Rose	McKenzie, Rev. Wm. P.
Colles, Mrs. Marjorie	Mann, Mrs. Frances Mack
Davis, Mrs. Emma S.	Mann, Joseph
Dole, Rev. Walter	Meehan, Albert
Eaton, Miss Mary E.	Metcalf, Albert
Easton, Miss Emma Gould	Metcalf, Mrs. Mary C.
Fiske, Rev. Henry S.	Miller, Mrs. Frederica L.

Miller, William N.

Mims, Mrs. Sue Harper

Moore, George H.

Neal, James A.

Norton, Carol

Norwood, Edward Everett

Pearson, Charles W.

Robertson, Mrs. Annie Louise

Robertson, Miss Nemi

Shipman, Miss Emma C.

Smith, J. Edward

Smith, Richard

Speakman, Miss Rachel T.

Stewart, John H.

Stewart, Miss Mary

Stocking, Miss Daisette D.

Stone, Mrs. Lida Stocking

Sulcer, Dr. Abraham A.

Thompson, Miss Abigail Dyer

Thompson, Mrs. Emma A.

Tomlinson, Rev. Irving C.

(Representing press)

George H. Moses

Allan H. Robinson

Calvin A. Frye

28. *Page 187, line 9.* Willis J. Abbot's interview with Senator Moses reported in *The Christian Science Monitor* for June 19, 1929.

29. *Page 187, line 15.* Mrs. Lida S. Stone's recollections in the reminiscence files of The Mother Church.

30. *Page 187, line 21.* Miss Mary Stewart's recollections in the reminiscence files of The Mother Church.

31. *Page 187, line 28.* Thompson, 2. 32. *Page 188, line 7.* Ibid., 2.

33. *Page 188, line 13.* Stewart, 6. 34. *Page 188, line 28.* Ibid., 4.

35. *Page 189, line 4.* Mary E. Eaton's recollections in the reminiscence files of The Mother Church.

36. *Page 189, line 15.* Mr. George Wendell Adams' recollections in the reminiscence files of The Mother Church. Mr. Adams was sometime clerk of The Mother Church, and is now a member of The Christian Science Board of Directors.

37. *Page 189, line 17.* Conversations with Eckermann. Bohn's Library Translation, 258, 259.

38. *Page 189, line 24.* Rom. vii: 21. 39. *Page 189, line 27.* Luke x:17-20.

40. *Page 189, line 31.* II Cor. xii:7.

41. *Page 190, line 8.* Powell's *Heavenly Herectics*, 7.

42. *Page 190, line 24.* Shannon, 50, 51.

43. *Page 191, line 30.* Sidney Lanier's *A Ballad of Trees and the Master.*

44. *Page 192, line 6.* Eaton, 3.

45. *Page 192, line 10.* Hanna's *Christian Science History*, 11: Mrs. Eddy to Judge Hanna: I did not refer to mental malpractice,—its members generally had taken the primary course, and this instruction properly comes before that class.

46. *Page 192, line 25.* Mann, 11; also *S. & H.*, 406.

47. *Page 192, line 29.* Mrs. Eddy's *Letters and Miscellany*, Vol. 21:61:2615.

48. *Page 193, line 6.* Charles R. Corning's statement in the historical files of The Mother Church.

49. *Page 193, line 7.* Michael Meehan's recollections in the reminiscence files of The Mother Church.

50. *Page 193, line 10.* General Frank S. Streeter's statement dated October 28, 1906, in historical files of The Mother Church.

51. *Page 193, line 16.* Mrs. Grace A. Greene, 3, 4.

52. *Page 193, line 32.* Matt. v : 44.   53. *Page 194, line 2.*   Mann, 89.

54. *Page 194, line 10.* *Retrospection and Introspection*, 81.

55. *Page 194, line 19.* Mrs. Eddy's *Letters and Miscellany*, Vol. 38 : 103 : 4996.

56. *Page 195, line 29.* Mrs. Eddy's *Letters and Miscellany*, Vol. 39 : 101 : 5140.

57. *Page 196, line 8.* Mrs. Eddy's *Letters and Miscellany*, Vol. 1 : 219 : 90.

58. *Page 196, line 31.* Mrs. Eddy's *Letters and Miscellany*, Vol. 1 : 53 : 19.

59. *Page 197, line 8.* Mrs. Eddy's *Letters and Miscellany*, Vol. 1 : 145 : 53.

60. *Page 197, line 33.* This is the Christian Science equivalent for "carnal mind," found in the Epistles of St. Paul. Tagore is still here, and thus he personalizes "mortal mind":

"Who is this that follows me into the silent dark? I move aside to avoid his presence, but I escape him not. He makes the dust rise from the earth with his swagger; he adds his loud voice to every word that I utter. He is my own little self, my lord, he knows no shame; but I am ashamed to come to thy door in his company."

61. *Page 198, line 7.* S. & H., 226.

62. *Page 199, line 2.* Mrs. Eddy's *Letters and Miscellany*, Vol. 37 : 19 : 4777.

63. *Page 199, line 20.* Shannon, 53, 54.

64. *Page 200, line 17.* Mrs. Eddy's *Letters and Miscellany*, Vol. 3 : 225 : 325.

65. *Page 201, line 14.* *Church Manual of The First Church of Christ, Scientist,* 15, 16.

66. *Page 201, line 24.* Ibid., 97.

67. *Page 201, line 34.* *Christian Science Sentinel*, December 21, 1929.

68. *Page 201, line 39.* *The First Church of Christ, Scientist, and Miscellany*, 130.

69. *Page 201, line 42.* *Retrospection and Introspection*, 79.

70. *Page 202, line 21.* *The Christian Science Monitor*, January 8, 1930.

71. *Page 205, line 6.* *Mary Baker G. Eddy* by Arthur Brisbane.

72. *Page 206, line 2.* Michael Meehan's recollections in the reminiscence files of The Mother Church, 9, 10.

73. *Page 208, line 8.* Michael Meehan's *Mrs. Eddy and the Late Suit in Equity*, 25. Copyrighted and used by permission. In studying the testimony, the author has used Mrs. Eddy's own marked copy. For various reasons the court hearing did not occur till August 13, 1907. On March 6, 1907, Mrs. Eddy had placed her property in trust to Archibald McLellan, Henry M. Baker, and Josiah E. Fernald, — the last two not being Christian Scientists at all.

Among the many outside of Christian Science to whom the author is under greater obligation than can be described for counsel and coöperation are distinctively Mr. Talcott Powell of the *New York Telegram*, and Mr. Josiah E. Fernald of Concord, New Hampshire, who has added to substantial assistance in procuring material for the author, the following authentic personal recollection of Mrs. Eddy:

"After Mrs. Mary Baker Eddy came to Concord to live, she did her banking with the National State Capital Bank, and started her account with the bank on May 16, 1890. Mr. Fernald being Cashier at that time, Mrs. Eddy asked him to look after some business matters for her, and in that way he came to know her. She in turn sent for him to come to her home to consult with him and give such directions as she wished about the business in hand.

" It was a great pleasure to Mr. Fernald to be called upon by Mrs. Eddy to attend to any of her business matters. He always found her a person who knew exactly what she wanted him to do and how it should be carried out. Mrs. Eddy signed her own checks, and ordered such securities as she chose to purchase, having a good knowledge of her business.

" Mr. Fernald remembers Mrs. Eddy in her office or study, which was on the second floor of the house, and was a very bright and sunny southeast corner room facing to the North, with her visitor in a chair at her left in an easy speaking distance. She was always prompt, alert and courteous.

" It was a great pleasure to Mr. Fernald to be chosen one of the three trustees March 6, 1907. He assisted Gen. Henry M. Baker in the settlement of her estate up to the time of Mr. Baker's death, and was then appointed to complete the administration of her estate. After that, with the Board of five Directors of The Mother Church, he was appointed the sixth Trustee under the Will, and has served in that capacity up to the present time. He is very glad to do all in his power to help carry out the terms of the Trust as set forth in the Will.

" Mr. Fernald states that in his relations with his co-trustees, and with the many Christian Science Workers, he has found some of the finest Christian people in the world; and that it is a great joy to be associated with such people, and to be of some assistance in carrying on a work that extends all over the world."
Another valued helper has been Miss Ida Belle Little, Scientist.

74. *Page 208, line 13.* Meehan's *Mrs. Eddy and the Late Suit in Equity,* 27.

75. *Page 209, line 23.* Ibid., 153.

76. *Page 210, line 4.* Ibid., 157–159.

77. *Page 212, line 19.* Recollections of Miss Adelaide Still, Mrs. Minnie A. Scott, and Professor Hermann S. Hering in the reminiscence files of The Mother Church.

78. *Page 213, line 1.* Letter, April 20, 1908, to Hayne Davis in the historical files of The Mother Church.

79. *Page 213, line 5.* Professor Hermann S. Hering's talk with the author.

80. *Page 213, line 9.* Still, 6.

81. *Page 213, line 19.* Mrs. Eddy's *Letters and Miscellany,* Vol. 21 : 101 : 2632. It is interesting that later Mrs. Eddy thought it unnecessary to send this letter.

82. *Page 214, line 6.* Mann, 93.

83. *Page 214, line 27.* Reminiscences of Michael Meehan, 13, as well as *Mrs. Eddy and the Late Suit in Equity.*

84. *Page 215, line 19.* Ibid., 12.

CHAPTER VII

1. *Page 216, line 3.* Farmington (N. H.) *News,* January 31, 1908. In preparation for the writing of this chapter, the author has read many recollections in the reminiscence files of The Mother Church. He has also talked with many of the men and women — still on earth — who were then associated with Mrs. Eddy. Mr. William R. Rathvon has been of special service; but the author has also profited by the words of Mrs. Annie Macmillan Knott, Reverend Irving C. Tomlinson, Professor Hermann S. Hering, William P. McKenzie, Judge Clifford P.

Smith, John C. Lathrop, John G. Salchow, Joseph G. Mann, Miss M. Adelaide Still, Mrs. Emilie B. Hulin, Miss Minnie B. Weygandt, Miss Emma H. McLauthlin, Mrs. Emma Easton Newman, Mrs. Ella W. Hoag, Miss Sarah A. Farlow, Mrs. Lauretta W. Blish, Mrs. Martha W. Wilcox, and Mrs. Minnie A. Scott.

2. *Page 216, line 12.* John G. Salchow served a longer term of unbroken service to Mrs. Eddy than anyone else, except Calvin A. Frye.

3. *Page 217, line 14.* Meehan's *Mrs. Eddy and the Late Suit in Equity*, 156.

4. *Page 217, line 22.* In fact Mrs. Eddy once wrote a student: "I have had no vacation for over 30 years."

5. *Page 217, line 30.* I Cor. xv : 54.

6. *Page 218, line 13.* *The Portsmouth Chronicle* for January 28, 1908, states: "Mrs. Eddy was instrumental in many improvements and charity, and the latter was very little known about for she gave quietly and her gifts were always with the understanding that the name of the giver should not be known."

7. *Page 219, line 23.* *Christian Science Sentinel*, February 15, 1908.

8. *Page 219, line 28.* Letter on this point see Ch. 6, 213.

9. *Page 220, line 2.* Arthur Brisbane thus indicated at the time.

10. *Page 220, line 6.* *Boston Globe*, January 27, 1908.

11. *Page 221, line 5.* John G. Salchow's account of this memorable occasion as told to the author.

12. *Page 221, line 21.* "OPPORTUNITY FOR SERVING THE LEADER. SECT. 11. At the written request of the Pastor Emeritus, Mrs. Eddy, the Board of Directors shall immediately notify a person who has been a member of this Church at least three years to go in ten days to her, and it shall be the duty of the member thus notified to remain with Mrs. Eddy three years consecutively. A member who leaves her in less time without the Directors' consent or who declines to obey this call to duty, upon Mrs. Eddy's complaint thereof shall be excommunicated from The Mother Church. Members thus serving the Leader shall be paid semi-annually at the rate of one thousand dollars yearly in addition to rent and board. Those members whom she teaches the course in Divinity, and who remain with her three consecutive years, receive the degree of the Massachusetts Metaphysical College." Art. XXII of *Church Manual of The First Church of Christ, Scientist*, 67.

13. *Page 221, line 31.* Matthew xix : 29.

14. *Page 222, line 4.* Mark xiii : 33.

15. *Page 222, line 5.* Joseph G. Mann's letter to the author.

16. *Page 222, line 25.* *S. & H.*, 471.

17. *Page 222, line 29.* *American Magazine*, June, 1930, 51.

18. *Page 223, line 10.*

"For Rain

"O God, heavenly Father, who by thy Son Jesus Christ hast promised to all those who seek thy kingdom, and the righteousness thereof, all things necessary to their bodily sustenance; Send us, we beseech thee, in this our necessity, such moderate rain and showers, that we may receive the fruits of the earth to our comfort, and to thy honour; through Jesus Christ our Lord. *Amen*."

"*For Fair Weather*

"Almighty and most merciful Father, we humbly beseech thee, of thy great goodness to restrain those immoderate rains, wherewith, for our sins, thou hast afflicted us. And we pray thee to send us such seasonable weather, that the earth may, in due time, yield her increase for our use and benefit. And give us grace, that we may learn by thy punishments to amend our lives, and for thy clemency to give thee thanks and praise; through Jesus Christ our Lord. *Amen.*"

Other Christians besides Episcopalians still pray for rain. During the summer drought of 1930 all Christians — totalling 625,000 — in Arkansas were called to pray for rain, and notice was sent to all the daily papers.

19. *Page 223, line 19.* Mr. Adam H. Dickey, a valued member of Mrs. Eddy's household and also of The Christian Science Board of Directors from November 21, 1910 to February 8, 1925.

20. *Page 225, line 18.* Through the courtesy of Mr. Rathvon, the author has examined the song book from which Mrs. Ella S. Rathvon many times sang to Mrs. Eddy the songs and hymns which Mrs. Eddy loved.

21. *Page 225, line 20.* Mr. John C. Lathrop was a trusted member of Mrs. Eddy's household and for many years served as a member of The Christian Science Board of Lectureship. At present he is a Christian Science teacher and practitioner.

22. *Page 226, line 6.* Mr. Rathvon's recollections; also 227, line 3; 228, par. 2.

23. *Page 227, line 12.* Salchow.

24. *Page 227, line 30.* Mrs. Eddy's *Letters and Miscellany*, Vol. 52 : 199 : 7344.

25. *Page 228, line 32.* Mrs. Eddy's *Letters and Miscellany*, Vol. 44 : 53 : 5820.

26. *Page 229, line 13.* *Pulpit and Press*, 75.

27. *Page 229, line 15.* Mrs. Eddy's *Message for 1902*, 4.

28. *Page 229, line 22.* Phil. iii : 13, 14. Also Mrs. Eddy's *Message for 1900*, 6.

29. *Page 229, line 33.* Mrs. Eddy's *Letters and Miscellany*, Vol. 36 : 85 : 4667.

30. *Page 230, line 5.* Mann, 93.

31. *Page 230, line 24.* *The First Church of Christ, Scientist, and Miscellany*, 262. Quotations that follow are from Mr. Rathvon's recollections.

32. *Page 231, line 16.* *Poems* by Mary Baker Eddy, 30.

33. *Page 231, line 31.* Presented to The Mother Church by Mr. Merritt.

34. *Page 232, line 4.* *The First Church of Christ, Scientist, and Miscellany*, 191.

35. *Page 232, line 15.* Mann, 99.

36. *Page 233, line 14.* *Miscellaneous Writings*, 7.

37. *Page 233, line 21.* Mrs. Eddy's *Letters and Miscellany*, Vol. 52 : 79 : 7268.

38. *Page 233, line 23.* Mrs. Eddy's secretary wrote November 24, 1908, to Mr. Archibald McLellan: "Our Leader prefers the heavy style of type shown in the title of the paper which I enclose herewith, but insists that the article 'The' properly belongs in the title and wishes it placed there. This will necessitate making another design that can be as easily read as the one enclosed." (Mrs. Eddy's *Letters and Miscellany*, Vol. 51 : 175 : 7178.) This is another indication of Mrs. Eddy's constant oversight of details in the establishment of her Cause.

39. *Page 235, line 31.* Mr. McLellan, a resident of Chicago, had been attorney with R. G. Dun & Co. for eighteen years, when he was called in 1902 by Mrs. Eddy to assume the Editorship of the Christian Science periodicals. When *The Christian Science Monitor* was established, Mr. McLellan became its Editor-in-Chief. Up to the time when Mrs. Eddy desired to make Mr. McLellan a Director, there were but four members of the Board. She caused the By-Law, Article I, Section 5, of the Church Manual to be amended to provide that the Board "shall consist of five members." Then Mr. McLellan was elected the fifth member of the Board.

40. *Page 236, line 10.* Mrs. Eddy's *Letters and Miscellany*, Vol. 25 : 203 : 3191.

41. *Page 236, line 19.* *Christian Science Sentinel*, March 11, 1911, 524.

42. *Page 238, line 2.* Translated from the German.

43. *Page 239, line 12.* Mrs. Minnie Scott, 12.

44. *Page 239, line 15.* Such an instance of reproof which Mrs. Eddy gave one of her beloved students had to do with the student's failure to observe the counsel of Matthew 18 : 15–17 : "Moreover if thy brother shall trespass against thee, go and tell him his fault between thee, and him alone : if he shall hear thee, thou hast gained thy brother. But if he will not hear thee, then take with thee one or two more, that in the mouth of two or three witnesses every word may be established. And if he shall neglect to hear them, tell it unto the church : but if he neglect to hear the church, let him be unto thee as a heathen man and a publican." This Scripture has been a preliminary requirement of discipline since the early history of the Church. Mrs. Eddy wrote : "You are committing an unpardonable sin by talking as you do about the ——s. What you say against them to others you should say *to them*. The Mother Church By-Laws forbid doing otherwise.**** Unpardonable sin means one that we are never pardoned of — but taught through suffering that it is a sin."

45. *Page 241, line 14.* S. & H., 113.

46. *Page 241, line 22.* Mrs. Eddy's *Letters and Miscellany*, Vol. 38 : 223 : 5066.

47. *Page 242, line 15.* Mrs. Eddy's notebook.

48. *Page 242, line 19.* Meehan, 5.

49. *Page 243, line 8.* Mrs. Eddy's *Letters and Miscellany*, Vol. 19 : 11 : 2345.

50. *Page 243, line 15.* Mrs. Eddy's *Letters and Miscellany*, Vol. 3 : 85 : 258.

51. *Page 243, line 21.* Mrs. Eddy's *Letters and Miscellany*, Vol. 36 : 225 : 4755.

52. *Page 243, line 28.* Mrs. Eddy's *Letters and Miscellany*, Vol. 14 : 97 : 1721.

53. *Page 243, line 34.* Mrs. Eddy's *Letters and Miscellany*, Vol. 15 : 99 : 1832.

54. *Page 244, line 17.* Mrs. Eddy's *Letters and Miscellany*, Vol. 32 : 53 : 4095.

55. *Page 244, line 21.* Mrs. Eddy's *Letters and Miscellany*, Vol. 19 : 73 : 2372.

56. *Page 245, line 24.* Wilbur, 66 note.

57. *Page 245, line 35.* Mrs. Eddy's *Letters and Miscellany*, Vol. 55 : 38 : 7682.

58. *Page 246, line 6.* Miss Lydia B. Hall's recollections.

59. *Page 246, line 11.* Sarah A. Farlow, 2.

60. *Page 246, line 22.* *The First Church of Christ, Scientist, and Miscellany*, 138. Perhaps nowhere has Mrs. Eddy indicated more vividly her love and loyalty to Christ Jesus than in her poem :

CHRIST MY REFUGE

O'er waiting harpstrings of the mind
    There sweeps a strain,
Low, sad, and sweet, whose measures bind
    The power of pain,

And wake a white-winged angel throng
    Of thoughts, illumed
By faith, and breathed in raptured song,
    With love perfumed.

Then His unveiled, sweet mercies show
    Life's burdens light.
I kiss the cross, and wake to know
    A world more bright.

And o'er earth's troubled, angry sea
    I see Christ walk,
And come to me, and tenderly,
    Divinely talk.

Thus Truth engrounds me on the rock,
    Upon Life's shore,
'Gainst which the winds and waves can shock,
    Oh, nevermore!

From tired joy and grief afar,
    And nearer Thee, —
Father, where Thine own children are,
    I love to be.

My prayer, some daily good to do
    To Thine, for Thee;
An offering pure of Love, whereto
    God leadeth me.   *Poems*, 12.

61. *Page 247, line 17.* An earlier New England village word for a little restless fusser.

62. *Page 248, line 6.* Mrs. Eddy's *Letters and Miscellany*, Vol. 6 : 227 : 636.

63. *Page 248, line 16.* In the historical files of The Mother Church appears the following statement made by the undertakers in attendance:

To Whom it may Concern:

We were called to the residence of Mrs. Mary Baker Eddy in Chestnut Hill, Mass., at 8-15 A.M., Sunday December 4, 1910, to care for her body. We found it in an excellent state of preservation when first called, and also fifty eight hours after death. No preserving compounds were used until that time. The tissues were remarkedly normal; the skin was well preserved, soft, pliable, smooth and healthy. I do not remember having found the body of a person of such advanced age in so good a physical condition. The walls of the arteries were unusually firm and in as healthy a state as might be expected in the body of a young person. The usual accompaniments of age were lacking, and no outward appearance of any disease, no lesion or other conditions common to one having died at such an advanced age were noticeable.

In the process of embalming we found the body at sixty hours after death, in as good condition of preservation as we always find at twelve to twenty-four hours after death.

This is our voluntary statement made without solicitation or influence of any kind.

64. *Page 248, line 21.* Judge Smith served as First Reader of The Mother Church, was a member of The Christian Science Board of Lectureship, for a period of years was Manager of Committees on Publication, and later was Editor of the Christian Science periodicals. At present he is the Editor of the Bureau of History and Records.

65. *Page 248, line 27.*

> O gentle presence, peace and joy and power;
> O Life divine, that owns each waiting hour,
> Thou Love that guards the nestling's faltering flight!
> Keep Thou my child on upward wing tonight.
>
> Love is our refuge; only with mine eye
> Can I behold the snare, the pit, the fall:
> His habitation high is here, and nigh,
> His arm encircles me, and mine, and all.
>
> O make me glad for every scalding tear,
> For hope deferred, ingratitude, disdain!
> Wait, and love more for every hate, and fear
> No ill, — since God is good, and loss is gain.
>
> Beneath the shadow of His mighty wing;
> In that sweet secret of the narrow way,
> Seeking and finding, with the angels sing:
> " Lo, I am with you alway," — watch and pray.
>
> No snare, no fowler, pestilence or pain;
> No night drops down upon the troubled breast,
> When heaven's aftersmile earth's tear-drops gain,
> And mother finds her home and heav'nly rest.

CHAPTER VIII

1. *Page 252, line 3.* Once in her old age asked by the author how she kept her youthfulness, Ellen Terry answered:

> I pray devoutly,
> I hammer stoutly,
> And always get my way.
> POWELL'S *The Human Touch*, 136.

2. *Page 252, line 27. America Set Free,* 572.

3. *Page 252, line 31.* Reported in *Christian World*, London, England, March 8, 1928.

4. *Page 253, line 15. Time,* June 16, 1930, 21.

Compare the following editorial from *The Christian Science Monitor* of June 18, 1930:

One of the most noteworthy features of many of the recent theories of the physical scientists is the fact that their authors have recognized the necessity of looking right through the fluctuating testimony of the senses in an endeavor to reach basically correct ideas of fundamentals. Of none can this be said more truly than of Prof. Albert Einstein, who just the other day, before the delegates of the World Power Conference in

Berlin, discussed, for the first time in more or less popular fashion, his ideas of space, time and relativity.

His opening sentence was startling in its metaphysical significance. "Conceptions and conceptional systems," he declared, "logically regarded, never originate from sense experiences." It is clear, therefore, that thought must lie behind those things that seem real to human testimony. From this point of view, Professor Einstein proceeded to show how, through the centuries of past investigation, gradually what he designated as "space" has obtained a foundational sense of reality.

One by one the earlier theories had been disproved or corrected until, in his words, "space . . . has swallowed up ether and time and is about to swallow up the field theory and the corpuscular theory as well, so that it will remain as the only theory representing reality."

"Space," however, is not used in an entirely popular sense. It refers more to a structural framework of the universe. This, prior to the theory of relativity, was represented as absolute in itself, "as something the inner substance of which was not capable of being influenced and was in no wise changeable." Later, however, as "the last bit of substance" was removed from ether, "a structure of greater richness of form" for space had to be sought. This was necessary to reconcile the idea with further theories which were found to clash with the primary space hypothesis.

Of course, it is not possible to describe the Einstein theories in a short article. That they constitute a decided advance in the direction of a broadening concept of the unity of power and a clearer realization of the metaphysical nature of the universe is undeniable. It cannot be said that they represent absolute statements of Truth, because at best they aim simply at the explanation of the phenomena of the physical world. Still they are, without any question, aspects of that increase of knowledge welcomed as productive of the human invention that will be succeeded by even more important phases of experience.

There is little doubt that the development of these theories will be far-reaching and will greatly help in relieving mankind of its shackles of limitation. It is important, however, that the theories be seen in their right light, while being recognized as included among the most important contributions to twentieth century material progress.

5. *Page 253, line 20. American Magazine*, June 1930, 138.

6. *Page 254, line 25.* The famous class of 1898 — the last — with its sixty-seven members, was an exception.

7. *Page 255, line 30.* No preacher in Protestantism is more courageous or more understanding of American conditions than Dr. Burris Jenkins of Kansas City. His church is always filled; and yet in his new book, *The World's Debt to Protestantism*, 248, he writes: "Dean Inge has recently said that the golden age of preaching is past. He speaks for England, to be sure; but what happens in England sooner or later is likely to happen in America. The golden age of preaching no doubt recedes into the past in this country as well as in the motherland. The names of commanding preachers in America may be counted on the fingers of one hand. Country people who would listen eagerly for an hour or two hours to a preacher have given place to city people who will not listen with patience for twenty to thirty minutes. It is impossible in the cities to gather evening audiences even for the most powerful men. The 'foolishness of preaching' no longer gathers a gaping crowd on Sunday nights."

8. *Page 256, line 1. The New Case*, 220.

9. *Page 257, line 7. Mary Baker Eddy*, 7, 8.

10. *Page 257, line 13. S. & H.*, 411.

11. *Page 257, line 19.* Ibid., 125.

12. *Page 257, line 22. Powell's Emmanuel Movement*, 154.

13. *Page 257, line 25.* S. & H., 325.

14. *Page 257, line 33.* Bunting's *The Radiant Life*, 174.

15. *Page 258, line 30.* In Mrs. Eddy's earlier days in Boston, Mr. Neal was a bank cashier in a Kansas town. His attention was brought to Christian Science by a friend. He bought a copy of *Science and Health*, and was soon launched on a notable career of Christian Science healing. In 1889 he was under Mrs. Eddy's class instruction in Boston, and from 1892 until he passed on in 1930 he practised healing in Boston and served as a member of the Board of Directors from July 1912 to October 1929, when he resigned.

It was to Mr. Neal that Mrs. Eddy, January 28, 1897, wrote with her own pen the following letter which is unsurpassed in its revelation of her affection for the faithful and of the high value she set on healing.

My beloved Student,

Your letter is my best New Year's gift. I had felt for sometime the fitness you possess for healing I knew it when you were a member of my College class. It looked a waste of your talents to have you in a counting room. Now, thank God, I have at least one student in Boston that promises to be a Healer such I have long waited and hoped to see. Oh may the Love that looks on you and all guide your every thought and act up to the impersonal, spiritual model that is the only ideal — and constitutes the only scientific Healer.

To this glorious end I ask you to still press on, and have no other ambition or aim. A real scientific *Healer* is the highest position attainable in this sphere of being. Its altitude is far above a Teacher or preacher; it includes all that is divinely high and holy. Darling James, leave behind all else and strive for this great achievement. Mother sighs to see how much her students need this attainment and longs to live to see one Christian Scientist attain it. Your aid to reach this goal is *spiritualization*. To achieve this you must have *one God*, one affection, one way, one Mind. Society, flattery, popularity are temptations in your pursuit of growth spiritual. Avoid them as much as in you lies. Pray daily, never miss praying, no matter how often: "Lead me not into temptation," — scientifically rendered, — Lead me not to lose sight of strict purity, clean pure thoughts; let all my thoughts and aims be high, unselfish, charitable, meek, — *spiritually minded*. With this altitude of thought your mind is losing materiality and gaining spirituality and this is the state of mind that *heals* the *sick*. My new book will do you much good. Do not purchase one, Mother wants to give you one. I welcome you into the *sanctum* of my fold. God bless you.

Your loving Teacher

M B Eddy

(Mrs. Eddy's *Letters and Miscellany*, Vol. 28 : 33 : 3524.)

16. *Page 260, line 28.* S. & H., 292.

17. *Page 261, line 20.* Bicknell Young of Chicago, for many years a member of The Christian Science Board of Lectureship.

18. *Page 262, line 6.* Bliss Knapp, member of The Christian Science Board of Lectureship for many years.

19. *Page 263, line 19.* Michael Meehan's recollections in the reminiscence files of The Mother Church, 18. See also in confirmation *S. & H.*, 128.

20. *Page 267, line 19.* *S. & H.*, 468.

21. *Page 268, line 28.* *Miscellaneous Writings*, 287.

22. *Page 269, line 13.* Ibid.

23. *Page 269, line 27.* This letter is in the collection the author has presented to the Board of Directors. The word "friendship" in the last phrase Mrs. Eddy used, like Henry Clay Trumbull in his standard book on *Friendship—The Master Passion*, was thus hyphenated "friendship-love."

24. *Page 271, line 5.* *The First Church of Christ, Scientist, and Miscellany*, 210.

25. *Page 271, line 16.* Miss Mary Burt Messer was an authority on the family before she wrote "The Family in the Making" (1928). At one time connected in New York with the Association for Improving the Condition of the Poor and the Charity Organization Society, for seven years engaged in research for Wisconsin, teacher at Stout Institute, and finally lecturer on the family for the University of California Extension Division, she says (p. 351):

"Breaking through the entire scheme of accepted values, and carrying its methods into all quarters of the world, the movement of Christian Science stands forth as a conception of the Christian religion drawn from woman's insight, quietly advancing women to a position of equality with man in the Christian church, and, conceiving the spiritual or creative principle in feminine as well as in masculine terms. The maternal attribute of the divine is thus advanced in connection with the paternal attribute—not as in the poetic overtones of Virgin worship, but with the living potencies of an operative truth, a conception intimately associated with the restoration to Christianity of its lost power of healing."

26. *Page 271, line 17.* Matthew vii:20.

Twenty Years After

1. *Page 272, line 25.* *The First Church of Christ, Scientist, and Miscellany*, 357.

2. *Page 273, line 5.* *S. & H.*, 126.

3. *Page 273, line 14.* Matt. xxviii:20.

4. *Page 273, line 22.* *S. & H.*, xi. In the *Christian Science Sentinel* March 28, 1931, Judge Clifford P. Smith writes that Mrs. Eddy "has made Christianity more comprehensible to modern thought, less miraculous or mysterious, and more spiritually sensible than original Christianity was known to be before she discovered its Science."

5. *Page 273, line 30.* *The First Church of Christ, Scientist, and Miscellany*, 4.

6. *Page 274, line 9.* *S. & H.*, 146.

7. *Page 274, line 18.* *Miscellaneous Writings*, 184.

8. *Page 274, line 33.* Mrs. Eddy's *Letters and Miscellany*, Vol. 3:225:325.

9. *Page 275, line 15.* Mark Twain quoted in Powell's *Christian Science*, 1917, XV.

10. *Page 276, line 11.* 211.

11. *Page 277, line 15.* Torrance Parker in the *Christian Science Sentinel*, June 7, 1924.

12. *Page 277, line 20.* Matt. vi:34.

NOTE: The following abbreviations have been used in Copyright Acknowledgments.

Science and Health	S. & H.
Miscellaneous Writings	Mis.
The First Church of Christ, Scientist, and Miscellany	My.
Retrospection and Introspection	Ret.
Pulpit and Press	Pul.
Church Manual	Man.
Poems	Po.
Message for 1902	'02.

COPYRIGHT ACKNOWLEDGMENTS

CHAPTER I

Page 29, lines 13–36.
Page 30, lines 4–28; 32–12.
Page 32, lines 1–7;   15–18; 24–31.
Page 33, lines 1–16; 29–15.
Page 34, lines 24–30; 32–35.
Page 35, lines 2–12.
Page 39, lines 7–11; 14–20; 24–26; 30–5.
Page 50, lines 3–22.

CHAPTER II

Page 57, lines 18–20.
Page 63, lines 27–30.

CHAPTER III

Page 80, lines 31–32.
Page 92, lines 3–4; 30–14.
Page 94, lines 31–21.
Page 102, lines 14–15.
Page 104, lines 9–23.
Page 110, lines 4–9.

CHAPTER IV

Page 112, lines 31–2.
Page 113, lines 10–12.
Page 117, lines 18–23.

Page 118, lines 10–13.
Page 120, lines 7–8.
Page 124, lines 33–4.
Page 125, lines 27–34.
Page 127, lines 27–28.
Page 133, lines 16–20.
Page 137, lines 7–26.
Page 143, lines 8–18; 20.
Page 144, lines 12–13.

CHAPTER V

Page 149, lines 10–13.
Page 150, lines 9–11; 12–16.
Page 152, lines 20–27.
Page 154, lines 10–31; 34–23.
Page 155, lines 27–28
Page 156, lines 5–12.
Page 157, lines 3–12; 16–23.
Page 159, lines 29–33.
Page 169, lines 1–20.

CHAPTER VI

Page 178, lines 12–20; 22–5.
Page 181, lines 6–23.
Page 182, lines 22–11.
Page 187, lines 13–15; 16–21.
Page 188, lines 3–7; 9–13; 22–28; 31–4.
Page 189, lines 7–15.
Page 190, lines 25–2.
Page 192, lines 3–6.
Page 193, lines 17–26.
Page 194, lines 1–2.
Page 199, lines 4–20.
Page 205, lines 12–2.
Page 212, lines 17–19.
Page 213, lines 6–9.
Page 214, lines 4–6; 28–33.
Page 215, lines 2–4; 16–19.

Page 163, lines 26–34.
Page 165, lines 9–17 Mis.
Page 170, lines 30–32 Mis.

Chapter VI

Page 177, lines 19–29.
Page 179, lines 11–15 S. & H.
Page 182, lines 3–14.
Page 183, lines 15–17.
Page 185, lines 16–17.
Page 192, lines 27–29.
Page 194, lines 6–10 Ret.; 20–24.
Page 195, lines 29–5.
Page 196, lines 9–27; 32–2.
Page 197, lines 9–17.
Page 198, lines 5–7 S. & H.
Page 199, lines 1–2; 22–26 My.; 30–17.
Page 200, lines 28–14 Man.
Page 201, lines 20–24 Man.; 31–32 My.; 34–35 Ret.
Page 213, lines 20–27.
Page 215, lines 10–12.

Chapter VII

Page 222, lines 24–25.
Page 227, lines 26–30.
Page 228, lines 30–32.
Page 229, lines 12–13 Pul.; 14–15 '02.; 30–33.
Page 230, lines 18–24 My.
Page 231, lines 7–12; 17–18; 20–22 My.; 27–31; 33–4 My.
Page 233, lines 7–14 Mis.; 22–26.
Page 236, lines 8–10; 33–34 My.
Page 241, lines 9–14 S. & H.; 21–22.
Page 242, lines 30–8.
Page 243, lines 11–15; 17–21; 25–28; 31–34.
Page 244, lines 7–17; 19–21.
Page 245, lines 25–35.
Page 246, lines 21–22 My.
Page 248, line 6.

CHAPTER VIII

Page 257, lines 12–14 S. & H.; 19–20 S. & H.; 24–26 S. & H.
Page 260, lines 24–28 S. & H.
Page 267, lines 18–19 S. & H.
Page 268, lines 23–28 Mis.
Page 269, lines 7–13 Mis.; 24–28 S. & H.

TWENTY YEARS AFTER

Page 273, lines 5–8 S. & H.; 17–22 S. & H.; 28–30 My.
Page 274, lines 8–9 S. & H.; 17–18 Mis.; 30–33.

The quotations referred to hereunder have been copyrighted by The Christian Science Publishing Society.

CHAPTER I

Page 31, lines 16–31.
Page 38, lines 27–31.
Page 43, lines 24–26.

CHAPTER II

Page 57, lines 25, 27.
Page 59, lines 15–16.

CHAPTER III

Page 86, lines 18–19.

CHAPTER IV

Page 116, lines 31–33.
Page 127, lines 5–7; 13–14; 29–30.
Page 130, lines 25–35.
Page 132, lines 27; 31–4.

CHAPTER V

Page 161, lines 22–23; 25–29.
Page 172, lines 14–33.
Page 173, lines 26–27.
Page 176, lines 1–19.

CHAPTER VI

Page 185, lines 32–25.
Page 187, lines 1–3 ; 7–9.
Page 191, lines 5–10.
Page 195, lines 10–21.
Page 201, lines 27–29.
Page 202, lines 18–21.
Page 208. lines 1–8 ; 13.
Page 209, lines 21–23 ; 26–28.
Page 210, lines 5–38 n. p.

CHAPTER VII

Page 217, line 14.
Page 219, lines 4–23.
Page 234, lines 26–7.
Page 236, lines 20–28.
Page 241, lines 32–5.

CHAPTER VIII

Page 256, lines 32–7.

TWENTY YEARS AFTER

Page 277, lines 9–15.

CHAPTER VII

Page 223, lines 19–28.
Page 224, lines 6–18 ; 25–5.

NOTES

CHAPTER II

Page 282, Note 2; Note 3.
Page 284, Note 14; Note 17.
Page 285, Note 21.

CHAPTER III

Page 288, Note 1.
Page 289, Note 3; Note 4; Note 12.
Page 291, Note 29.
Page 292, Note 37.
Page 293, Note 45; Note 61.
Page 294, Note 69.

CHAPTER IV

Page 298, Note 45.
Page 299, Note 68.

CHAPTER V

Page 302, Note 3.
Page 303, Note 16.
Page 307, Note 40.
Page 308, Note 55.

CHAPTER VI

Page 310, Note 8.
Page 314, Note 73.

CHAPTER VII

Page 319, Note 63.

The quotations referred to hereunder have been copyrighted in the United States and foreign countries by Edward A. Merritt, William R. Rathvon, Annie M. Knott, George Wendell Adams, Charles E. Heitman and Josiah E. Fernald, The Trustees under the Will of Mary Baker G. Eddy.

CHAPTER II

Page 284, Note 19; Note 20.
Page 285, Note 29.
Page 288, Note 41 My.: Note 42 Po.

CHAPTER III

Page 290, Note 19 ; Note 22.
Page 291, Note 29 S. & H.
Page 294, Note 64 My. ; Note 76 S. & H. ; Note 77 Mis. & My.
Page 295, Note 78 S. & H.

CHAPTER IV

Page 296, Note 21 S. & H.
Page 297, Note 24 Ret.
Page 298, Note 48.
Page 299, Note 63.
Page 301, Note 90.

CHAPTER V

Page 303, Note 13 Ret. ; Note 16 Man.
Page 306, Note 18 S. & H. ; Note 19.
Page 307, Note 37 ; Note 44.
Page 308, Note 45 ; Note 55.
Page 309, Note 56.

CHAPTER VI

Page 310, Note 2 ; Note 11 ; Note 13.
Page 311, Note 18.

CHAPTER VII

Page 316, Note 4 ; Note 12 Man.
Page 317, Note 38.
Page 318, Note 44 ; Note 60 Po.
Page 320, Note 65 Po.

CHAPTER VIII

Page 322, Note 15.

The quotations referred to hereunder have been copyrighted by The Christian Science Publishing Society.

CHAPTER II

Page 282, Note 1.

CHAPTER III

Page 292, Note 30.

Chapter VI

Page 310, Note 13.
Page 313, Note 50.

Chapter VIII

Page 320, Note 4.

INDEX

A

Abbott, Lyman, 164
Abbot, Willis J., interviews Senator Moses, 313
Adams, George Wendell, 17; describes Mrs. Eddy, 187; Class of '98, 312; Clerk and Director of The Mother Church, 313
Adams, John Quincy, 63
Adams, Mrs. Mary M. W., called by Mrs. Eddy to compile rules for teachers, 199
Adams, Rt. Rev. William, published addresses on moral philosophy under caption *Christian Science*, 106
Addison, Joseph, read by Mary Baker, 61, 64
Africa, 49, 282
Agassiz, Louis, 146
Aiken, Mrs. Mary D., 284
Albany, N. Y., 286
Albion, Maine, Mrs. Patterson stopping with Sarah Crosby, 109
Alcott, A. Bronson, calls on Mrs. Eddy and thanks her for Science and Health, 132; visits her at Lynn, 133; at Christian Scientist Association meeting, 133; 146, 300
Alcott Family, the, 218
Alcott, Louisa M., Mr. Alcott speaks of Mrs. Eddy to, 133; meeting with Mrs. Eddy, 163
Aldrich, Judge Edgar, "Next Friends" suit, 208
Aldrich, Thomas Bailey, 146
Alexandria, Va., Lindley Murray's books published in, 60, 64
Allen, George H., 151
Ambrose, Abigail (wife of Mark Baker), birth of Mary Baker, 55; preparation for child, 55; teaches daughter to pray, 56, 57; slavery question

then vital, 63; sends by Mary message to George, 67, 68; letter of counsel to be read on Mary's wedding journey, 76; passes on, 83; Mrs. Glover informs George, 84; Mary at her knee in childhood hears Bible stories of healing, 96; Rev. Richard S. Rust's tribute, 97; her passing on, 97; her understanding, 282; influence on Mary, 283; 285, 289
Ambrose, D. Russell, 287
America, 226, 321
American Federation of Churches, 238
American Magazine, The, July, 1930, Channing Pollock's defense of the times in, 280; 316, 321
Amesbury, 121, 132
Amiel, Henri Frederic, 287
Andrade, *An Hour of Physics*, 279
Andrews, Mrs. Effie, 312
Anglican Church, 31, 35, *see* Episcopal Church
Annie Laurie, 225
Antarctic Expedition, 29
Arens, Edward J., Mrs. Eddy invokes legal protection against, 122, 148; attempts to build personal business, 174; infringement of Mrs. Eddy's copyright, 302
Argentina, lectures in, 49, 282
Armstrong, Joseph, defendant in "Next Friends" suit, 208
Arnold, Edwin, 287
Associated Press, representatives interview Mrs. Eddy, 204
Association, *see* Christian Scientist
Astor, Lady Nancy, 30, 268
Astor, Viscount, 30
Atkinson, N., convert at Methodist revival, 71
Atlanta, Georgia, 186, 250
Atlantic, The, 147

Eastaman, Captain Joseph S., enters Mrs. Eddy's class, wife healed, 161
Eastaman, Mrs. Mary F., healed, 161
Easter, Mrs. Eddy's thought of, 231; sermon to household, 232
Easton, Miss Emma Gould, 312
Eaton, Miss Mary E., 312, 313
Eckermann, 13, 313
Eddington, 13
Eddy, Asa G., success of any project required Mrs. Eddy at head, 112; a true helper, 119; healing while at South Boston, 119; marries Mary Baker Glover, 120, 303; Mrs. Eddy on, 120; she turns to him for help, 129; aid to wife, 148; Miss Bartlett's estimate of, 149; organizer of first Sunday School, 149–151; first uses words Christian Scientist on sign, 149; Mrs. Choate describes activities, etc., 149–150; protects Mrs. Eddy, 150; heals Miss Julia Bartlett, 159; passes away, 165; 295, 300; authority on copyright laws, 302; *Genealogy and Life of,* Longyear, 303; starts first Sunday School, 303; love for Warren Choate, 303; mistaken in wife's age, 306
Eddy, Dr. Ebenezer J. Foster, *see* Foster-Eddy
EDDY, MARY BAKER
    McClure's articles on, 5; Church begins to assemble historical data and letters concerning, 7; why author's request for interview not granted, 8; her attitude toward interviews, 9; time ripe for writing her life story, 9; editorial appreciations at her passing, 10; Christian Science its Founder's creation, 11; letter to Dr. Hamilton Holt, 16; life-size portrait planned, 17; difficulties in having her message understood, 20; author talks with many who knew her, visits home, 22; process for preserving her letters in Church Executive Offices, 23; sources necessary for writing her biography, 25; in her lifetime saw abundant fruitage, 29; Mark Twain's revised judgment of, 40; expectations that cause would

dwindle when she passed on, 40; provides for supervision of Church under Manual, 47; nominates Board of Directors, 47; her deed of Trust creates Trustees of Publishing Society, 48; site of her home used for Pleasant View Home for elderly Christian Scientists, 52; born at Bow, N.H., of New England parentage, 55; dedicated to religious life and heard "voices," 56; healed of fever through prayer, 57; early thought to write a book, 57; predictions as to her future, 57; delicate health, 58; love for her brother Albert and her Lindley Murray books, 59; choice of books, 61; concern for social niceties, 61; interest in preciseness of speech, 62; Bible her Book of Books, 62; patriotic interest and reading newspapers, 63; early pencilings show interest in negroes, 64; takes to verse more readily than prose, 64; a normal girlhood, 65; parting verse to Andrew Gault, 65; early letter writing, 65; removed to Sanbornton Bridge, 65; second letter she ever wrote, 66; letters to her brother George, 67; bridesmaid at a wedding, 68; without funds to join class of village writing master, 68; first visit to Haverhill, 69; letters to Augusta Holmes, 70; books read at 19, 70; interest in Methodist revival and impressions of its effect, 71; values friendship, 72; sympathizes with Augusta on passing of father, 72; visit to Boston and Nahant, 72; writes Augusta town news, 73; on marriage, 74; marries George Washington Glover, 75; their first meeting, 76; going to South Carolina, 76; prayer saves from shipwreck, 76; stand against slavery, 78; frees slaves, 81; husband's death in Wilmington, N. C., 81; Masons care of, 81; again in father's house, 81; son George Washington Glover born, 82; illness, 83; mother's death, 83; father marries again, 84; efforts at self-support, 84; removal to sister

ment of undertakers, 319; regard for James A. Neal, 322; "Friendship," 323

Edinburgh, Mrs. Eddy's congratulations on first church building, 245

Edison, Thomas A., 178

Edmunds, Judge, his daughter and spiritualism, 297

Edwards, Jonathan, 108; his sermon of 1741, 190

Edwards, T. M. (M. C.), Dr. Patterson wishes wife to appeal to, for his release from Libby Prison, 95

Egyptian Book of the Dead, 27

Einstein, 252, 253, 320

Electro-Biology, Grimes, 292

Eliot, President Charles William, 8, 37, 302

Eliot, George, 287

Elizabethan literature, 60

Ellis Family, the, Mrs. Eddy happy with, 121, 297

Elson, Louis, 147

Emerson, Ralph Waldo, starting preaching career in Second Church, 60; 108; Mrs. Eddy's estimate of, 131; minding his mother's cow, 145; lecturing and writing, 146; 218; Mrs. Eddy not influenced by, 284; 287

Emerson, Mrs. Ralph Waldo, wishes to meet Mrs. Eddy, 133

Emmanuel movement, 36, 256

Emmanuel Movement in a New England Town, Powell's, 294, 321

Encyclical letter of late Archbishop of Canterbury, 35

Encyclopædia Britannica, 286

England, 50, 226, 265, 321

English Reader, Lindley Murray's, 59, 61, 62, 63

Episcopal Church, its sacramental system, 5; spiritual healing in, 36, 256; George W. Glover laid to rest in cemetery of St. James' Episcopal Church, Wilmington, N. C., 81; prayers for weather, 223, 317; dignity and decorum of its worship, 274; Mrs. Tilton bequeaths $5000 with restrictions to, 292

Esoteric Christianity, by Warren F. Evans, 293

Essays in Christian Politics, 35

Europe, lectures in, 49

Evans, Reverend Warren F., 96; his books read, 174; more than mesmerist, 292; taught by Quimby to heal, 293; last book *Esoteric Christianity*, 293

Ewing, Judge William G., 38

F

Faerie Queene, Spenser's, 257

Fairbairn, A. M., 108

Faith Work, Christian Science, and Other Cures, 307

Family, Christian Science and the, 268, 269, 270, 271

Family in the Making, The, Messer, 323

Fanny Fern, 138

Faraday, 253

Farlow, Alfred, 3; defendant in "Next Friends" suit, 208; devotion to duty, 279; 289, 290, 295, 296, 297, 298, 299, 306; describes Mrs. Eddy's appearance, 293

Farlow, Miss Sarah A., 299, 306, 307, 316, 318

Farmington (N. H.) News, 315

Farrar, 287

Fernald, Josiah E., appreciation of Mrs. Eddy, 312; Trustee for Mrs. Eddy, 314; Mrs. Eddy consults, 315; Trustee under her Will, 315

Fields, James T., 147

First Church of Christ, Scientist, and Miscellany, The, 199, 288, 291, 294, 296, 302, 314, 317, 318, 323

Fisher, Rt. Hon. H. A. L., on *Monitor*, 42; *Our New Religion*, 117, 293, 295, 297

Fiske, Bishop Charles, *The Living Church*, 279

Fiske, George Walter, 300

Fiske, Rev. Henry S., 312

Fitzgerald, Lady Mildred, visits Mrs. Eddy, 226

Flinn, John J., called from Chicago to advise in starting *Monitor*, 234

Ford, Paul Leicester, Washington's English, 285, 286

Forget-me-not, 70

Fosdick, Harry Emerson, 252